Transformative Digital Technology for Disruptive Teaching and Learning

Generation Z students are avid gamers and are always on social media. Smart like their phones, they must be educated in a smart manner, which involves the use of digital tools. **Transformative Digital Technology for Disruptive Teaching and Learning** provides smart education solutions and details ways in which Gen Z learners can be educated. It covers such digital learning strategies as blended learning, flipped learning, mobile learning, and gamification. It examines creative teaching–learning strategies to encourage modern learners to learn more quickly. The book discusses ways to accelerate the capabilities of teaching and learning transactions. It also covers innovative teaching and learning processes to meet the challenges of digital learners.

Starting with an overview of digital learning resources and processes as well as their advantages and disadvantages, the book then discusses such approaches and strategies as follows:

- Learner-oriented and learner-friendly approaches
- Blended learning
- Active learning
- Experiential learning
- Virtual learning
- Applications of Cloud Computing and Artificial Intelligence
- Gamification
- LMS challenges and techno-pedagogical issues for modern learners

As digital technology is disrupting teaching and learning, especially the skill development of students in the era of Industry 4.0 and 5.0, this is a timely book. It provides methods, approaches, strategies, and techniques for innovative learning and teaching. It discusses how to leverage new technology to enhance educators' and learners' abilities and performance. A comprehensive reference guide for educational researchers and technology developers, the book also helps educators embrace the digital transformation of teaching and learning.

Transformative Digital Technology for Disruptive Teaching and Learning

Edited by
P. Kaliraj
G. Singaravelu
T. Devi

CRC Press
Taylor & Francis Group
Boca Raton London New York

CRC Press is an imprint of the
Taylor & Francis Group, an **informa** business
AN AUERBACH BOOK

First edition published 2024
2385 NW Executive Center Drive, Suite 320, Boca Raton FL 33431

and by CRC Press
4 Park Square, Milton Park, Abingdon, Oxon, OX14 4RN

CRC Press is an imprint of Taylor & Francis Group, LLC

ISBN: 978-1-032-46719-1 (hbk)
ISBN: 978-1-032-67516-9 (pbk)
ISBN: 978-1-032-67517-6 (ebk)

DOI: 10.1201/9781032675176

Typeset in Garamond
by MPS Limited, Dehradun

Transformative Digital Technology for Disruptive Teaching and Learning

Edited by
P. Kaliraj
G. Singaravelu
T. Devi

CRC Press
Taylor & Francis Group
Boca Raton London New York

CRC Press is an imprint of the
Taylor & Francis Group, an **informa** business
AN AUERBACH BOOK

First edition published 2024
2385 NW Executive Center Drive, Suite 320, Boca Raton FL 33431

and by CRC Press
4 Park Square, Milton Park, Abingdon, Oxon, OX14 4RN

CRC Press is an imprint of Taylor & Francis Group, LLC

ISBN: 978-1-032-46719-1 (hbk)
ISBN: 978-1-032-67516-9 (pbk)
ISBN: 978-1-032-67517-6 (ebk)

DOI: 10.1201/9781032675176

Typeset in Garamond
by MPS Limited, Dehradun

Prof. P. Kaliraj *dedicates this book to*
the esteemed Bharathiar University,
his father Mr. M. Perumal,
mother Mrs. P. Rathinammal,
wife Vanaja Kaliraj,
and grandchildren Prithika Karthikeyan,
Kayan Karthikeyan,
Ayaan Prashanth, *and*
Akira Prashanth.

Prof. G. Singaravelu *dedicates this book to*
the Department of Education, Bharathiar University,
his father Mr.R. Govindarajan,
mother Mrs. G. Sankarambal,
wife Mrs. G. Jeevakumari,
son-in-law P. Ramachandran,
daughter S. Yazhini, son Er. S. Sabarirajan,
and grandson R. Jaswickram.

Prof. T. Devi *dedicates this book to*
the Department of Computer Applications, Bharathiar University,
her mother Mrs. Suseela Thirupathi,
mother-in-law Mrs. Singari Doraiswamy,
husband Mr. Ravi Doraiswamy,
son-in-law Mr. Vishnu Prakhash Devaraj,
daughter Mrs. Deepiga Vishnu Prakhash,
son Mr. Surya Ravi, and grandson V. Deera.

Contents

Preface

It is never a new fact that the present generation of students is not the same old genre of students. The Generation Z students are avid gamers and music-goers. As smart as they are, like their phones, they need to be educated in a smart manner, which involves the use of digital tools. This book specifically provides a solution to this issue by detailing the ways in which the future learners of today can be educated. It covers digital learning strategies like blended learning, flipped learning, mobile learning, and gamification. It details the creative teaching-learning strategies for modern learners. Providing knowledge on techno-pedagogy, which encourages modern learners to learn more quickly, the book accelerates the capabilities of teaching and learning transactions. Moreover, the book anticipates to limelight on innovative teaching–learning processes in classroom transactions to alleviate the challenges of modern learners.

The fourth and fifth industrial revolutions are affecting the roles that Indian universities and colleges prepare students for, and educational institutions are committed to helping produce the workforce for this new world and the student experience to match it. Digital transformation technologies are the need of the hour. In order to impart this knowledge across arts and science UG and PG programmes, Bharathiar University has designed guidelines for Curriculum 4.0 and has revamped the syllabi for all subjects intertwining Industry 4.0 and 5.0 tools into various disciplines such as Science, Social Science, Arts, and Education.

Today, the rate at which the transformation is happening is very disruptive in nature, and also exponential changes are being witnessed. We have already witnessed how many conventional business models and technologies have been disrupted in the last few years. Digital transformation technologies such as artificial intelligence and machine learning, augmented reality, virtual reality, and mixed reality are mutating very fast like viruses. No one is able to predict properly the impact of digital transformation technologies on education.

The book explores different methods, approaches, strategies, and techniques in teaching and learning transactions in the classroom by adopting disruptive learning. It explains innovative methods for leveraging new technologies and paves ways that enhance ability and institutional performance.

As educational institutions are innovating education and especially the skill development of students in the era of Industry 4.0 and 5.0, this book comes at the right time to help teachers, scholars, and students. The digital transformation technological tools such as artificial intelligence, mobile computing, cloud computing, and augmented reality are changing the way teaching and learning happen in the modern era. This book is a boon for members of Board of Studies, technocrats, policymakers, pre-service teachers, in-service teachers, scholars, and students.

The revenue forecast of these digital transformation technologies in teaching and learning, in other words in EdTech in 2030, is expected to be around USD 429.5 billion, and the growth rate from 2022 to 2030 in terms of CAGR is expected to be 16.5%, thus creating a good market for the skilled professionals in this area. There is a wider gap in the knowledge resources cutting across digital transformation technologies and the education of arts, science, social science, pharma, and education disciplines. To fill this gap and to prepare the future pillars of our globe to face the Volatile, Uncertain, Complex and Ambiguous (VUCA) world, and to help the academic community, knowledge resource on Transformative Digital Technology for Disruptive Teaching and Learning had been initiated.

This book contains chapters on contextual learning, digital learning, cloud computing in education, gamification, cyber-attacks, artificial intelligence, digital evaluation and blended learning in the classroom, and disruptive teaching and learning strategies.

Starting with 'Digital Learning Resources – An Overview', the basic concepts of digital learning resources, their needs, working procedures, types, uses, advantages, and disadvantages, are discussed in this book. The book proceeds to give an insight into disruptive teaching approaches and strategies such as assistive technology, e-learning, LMS, etc. in 'Disruptive Teaching Approaches and Strategies for the Learners in the New Normal'. 'Disruptive Teaching and Learning Strategies for Modern Learners' exhibits learning platforms such as Google Classroom, Seesaw, Khan Academy, E-Pathashala, Kahoot, etc., which aid in making the teaching process a very successful one. Among the various technologies, Learning Management System (LMS), which is being greatly insisted by the technologist for the effortless management of various organisations, including education, is dealt with in 'Effective Use of Learning Management System for Changing Education Scenario'.

'Blended Approach in Education: An Overview' presents the concept of blended learning, which is an ameliorative method amongst the emerging recent trends in learning and teaching. It aims to enlighten the learners with the conceptual features of blended learning and its paramount significance. It evinces the blended learning principles and its dynamic types that exist. 'Blended Learning – A Novel Approach in Pedagogy' clearly evidences that this is the time using blended learning and its utilisation in all places. In blended learning, both traditional classroom approach and modern advanced e-learning approach complement each other, and with the balanced sense, it outreaches the world with blended learning classrooms everywhere. 'Blended Teaching and Learning Strategies to Cope Education 4.0' describes the need and significance of blended teaching and learning in the contemporary educational system. It is the need of the hour to redefine the modern models of education for the 21st century Industrial Revolution 4.0. The Education 4.0 resource aims to enhance and prepare the talented 2k generation through blended learning in school and higher education transformation.

'Gamification: An Engaging Module for the Future Learners' illuminates in detail the meaning, nature, and characteristics of gamification along with its potentials that take on a progressive and participatory teaching and learning approach. 'Gamification for Teaching Beyond for Creative Learners' highlights the design principles as motivational framework, design mechanics, and elements of games to be integrated in learning along with the rewards for positive impact of gamification. 'Gamification: Future of Innovation in Education' highlights how gamification can help students in optimising learning and improve skills by enhancing student engagement skills. 'Flipped Learning – A Strategy for Focused Group and Personalised Learning' illustrates the concept of flipped learning, how it is an inverse approach and unique, and the four pillars. 'Need-based Mobile Education and Care for the Differently-abled Students' attempts to put forth the need for facilitating flexible learning for the differently-able students, making education and care 'mobile' and bringing education and care to the doorsteps of the learners, inspired by the concept of the bookmobile or mobile library. 'M-learning: A New Definition in Technology-Based Learning' presents a number of opportunities and challenges in mobile-learning, which is one of the practical methods for imparting the educational process in a digital and trendy manner

'Augmented Reality in Education: Modern Technologies and Educational Potentials' gives information about augmented reality and its impact on education, areas of application, and its benefits and challenges in education. 'Educational Augmented Reality: Working Methodology, Opportunities, and Apps' examines and discusses the various capabilities and potential of augmented reality in the education sector. 'Teaching and Learning Mathematics Using Augmented Reality' illustrates how augmented reality technology contributes to the educational field, especially in mathematics, and other fields are also discussed. 'Artificial Intelligence in the Teaching–Learning Process: A Paradigm Shift in the Teacher's Role' discusses the present practices of AI taking place around the world in different aspects of education. It also discusses the practices of AI taking place in the context of fields other than education. 'Cloud Computing Applications in Education' presents an outline of cloud computing and speaks about its applications for collaboration among educational institutions. Finally, 'Mobile Learning in Higher Education' provides an understanding of the importance of mobile learning in education and different types of mobile apps. It also details the advantages, challenges, and impact of mobile learning in education. The chapter ends with an explanation of creating online mobile courses.

The primary audiences for this book are students, scholars, teachers, and teacher educators of higher education institutions who need a reference resource, educationists, and policymakers who would introduce disruptive teaching learning strategies using Industry 4.0 tools in educational institutions. The students, scholars, and teachers can be from arts and science universities and teacher education universities. Practitioners who are interested in introducing disruptive teaching learning strategies using Industry 4.0 and its tools to solve real-world problems can also use this book for reference. It is also meant for the administrative community of universities and colleges who intend to equip their modern learners with the skills of Industry 4.0 and gamification.

Highlights of the Book

The highlights of the book include its learner-oriented and learner-friendly approach for future learners; the blended learning approach and active learning for an effective teaching–learning process; multi-disciplinary learning, experiential learning, and virtual learning for effective classrooms; cloud computing and artificial intelligence in classroom transactions; and gamification, LMS challenges, and techno-pedagogical issues for modern learners.

How to Use the Book

The method and purpose of using this book depend on the role that you play in an educational institution or in an industry or depends on the focus of your interest. We propose six types of roles: student, software developer, teacher, member of a Board of Studies, researcher, and administrator of educational and training institutions.

If you are a student: students can use the book to get a basic understanding of disruptive technologies and their applications in learning. Disruptive approaches and strategies are dealt with in 'Disruptive Teaching Approaches and Strategies for the Learners in the New Normal' and 'Disruptive Teaching and Learning Strategies for Modern Learners'. 'Gamification: An Engaging Module for the Future Learners' and 'Gamification: Future of Innovation in Education' discuss the meaning, nature, and characteristics of gamification along with its potentials, which takes on a progressive and participatory teaching and learning approach, and how gamification can help students in optimising learning and improving student engagement skills. 'M-learning: A New Definition in Technology-Based Learning', which discusses the opportunities and challenges in mobile-learning, helps students to explore the potential of mobile learning.

If you are a software developer: software developers can use the book to get a basic understanding of the use of disruptive technologies in the domain of education.

Chapters like 'Disruptive Teaching and Learning Strategies for Modern Learners' and 'Mobile Learning in Higher Education' will inspire them to develop learning platforms or mobile apps that incorporate disruptive technologies. Chapters like 'Gamification for Teaching Beyond for Creative Learners' and 'Gamification: Future of Innovation in Education' will aid software developers in designing and developing games to supplement educational materials that can help students optimising their learning experience by enhancing student engagement skills.

If you are a teacher: the book is useful as a text for several different university-level and college-level undergraduate and postgraduate courses besides doctoral programs. The chapter on 'Digital Learning Resources – An Overview', provides the basic concepts of digital learning resources, their need, working procedures, types, uses, advantages, and disadvantages. 'Disruptive Teaching Approaches and Strategies for the Learners in the New Normal' and 'Disruptive Teaching and Learning Strategies for Modern Learners' provide insight into disruptive teaching approaches and strategies such as assistive technology, e-learning, LMS, etc., and introduce various teaching platforms useful to teachers. 'Blended Learning – A Novel Approach in Pedagogy' clearly evidences that this is the time to use blended learning and how to use it effectively. The three chapters on gamification provide teachers an insight into how gamification can be integrated into learning. The chapter 'Flipped Learning – A Strategy for Focused Group and Personalised Learning' illustrates the concept of flipped learning, and how its inverse approach can be implemented effectively in classrooms. The chapters on mobile learning present a number of opportunities and challenges in mobile-learning and explain how various mobile learning apps can be utilised in the teaching process.

If you are a member of a Board of Studies: as the world moves fast with Industry 4.0 and Industry 5.0 around, creative people emerge with applications involving disruptive technologies like artificial intelligence, augmented reality, learning analytics, etc. Education imparted to students of this era should be in accordance with these technologies; hence, a curriculum revisit might be essential. The book is useful for a Board of Studies member while framing the syllabus for new courses that discuss these disruptive technologies in the disciplines of art, science, or social science. The chapters in this book that discuss artificial intelligence, augmented reality, mobile learning, and digital learning can be used as a foundation to frame courses on these respective technologies. The chapters on disruptive technologies also will be useful for designing curriculum for new courses based on these new technologies.

If you are a researcher: research is always a vital area where innovation is required and created, or produced. The research work carried out by universities and research institutions should be made available to society so that it benefits the common man. Innovations in the field of disruptive technologies like artificial intelligence and augmented reality can change the way people live. The chapters on disruptive technologies, blended learning, flipped learning, mobile learning, and gamification would help a researcher to comprehend the recent developments in this area and to see where his research is. Hence, this book can serve as a comprehensive reference guide for researchers in the development of tools incorporating these new technologies.

If you are an administrator of an educational and training institution: administrators of educational programmes are constantly striving to combine human and material resources to supervise, plan, strategise, and implement structures to execute an education system. This book will help them with frameworks for designing degree programs, courses, curriculum, and syllabi incorporating the disruptive technologies of artificial intelligence, augmented reality, and mobile learning. Especially the chapters 'Disruptive Teaching Approaches and Strategies for the Learners in the New Normal', 'Blended Teaching and Learning Strategies to Cope Education 4.0', 'Gamification: Future of Innovation in Education', and 'Artificial Intelligence in the Teaching-Learning Process: A Paradigm Shift in the Teacher's Role' discuss the recent trends in the respective areas and would help educators to design their courses with the latest trends in these areas.

Acknowledgements

From Prof. P. Kaliraj
First and foremost, I express my sincere gratitude to Hon'ble Shri. Banwarilal Purohit, former governor of Tamil Nadu, India, who was instrumental in organising the conference on Innovating Education in the era of Industry 4.0 during 19–20 December 2019 in Ooty, which paved the way for further work in the Industry 4.0 knowledge world, and Hon'ble Shri. R.N. Ravi, governor of Tamil Nadu, India, who was instrumental in organising the Conference of Vice-Chancellors of State, Central, and Private Universities in Tamil Nadu at Raj Bhavan, Ooty during 25–26 April 2022, which paved the way to redefine the future course of action, particularly in education and sustainable developments.

My heartfelt thanks go to the Hon'ble chief minister of Tamil Nadu, India, and the Hon'ble minister for Higher Education, Government of Tamil Nadu. I thank the Principal Secretary to Government, Higher Education Department, Government of Tamil Nadu.

I would like to express my thanks to the Secretary to Governor and Deputy Secretary to Governor, Universities Governor's Secretariat, Raj Bhavan, Chennai.

I thank my wife Vanaja Kaliraj, my son-in-law Mr. M. Karthikeyan, daughter Mrs. Ratna Priya Karthikeyan, son K. Siva Prashanth, daughter-in-law Ratna Priya Prashanth, grandchildren Prithika Karthikeyan, Kayan Karthikeyan, Ayaan Prashanth, and Akira Prashanth, and family members for their support and being patient.

From Prof. G. Singaravelu
I submit my sincere gratitude to Prof. P. Kaliraj, Hon'ble former vice-chancellor of Bharathiar University, who endeavoured to solve the problems by using matters and materials of the book named *Transformative Digital Technology for Disruptive Teaching and Learning,* which paves the way to find out the challenges of the teaching–learning process and stretches helping hands for modifying the existing teaching–learning process into innovative techno pedagogical applications in higher education. His herculean task and tireless motivation, often acceleration and encouragement, created the book.

I convey my sincere thanks to the vice-chancellor and registrar for administrative support. I shower my gratitude to the authors of the chapters for their contribution to the chapters, their continuous co-operation in improvising the chapters as and when requested, and for timely communication. I have to thank whole-heartedly all the experts who served as reviewers for making quality and swift reviews.

We wish to thank Mr. John Wyzalek, senior acquisitions editor, Taylor & Francis Group/CRC Press, who believed in the idea of this book and helped us in realising our dream.

I express my sincere and indispensable thanks to Prof. T. Devi, Former professor and head, Department of Computer Applications, School of Computer Science and Engineering, Bharathiar University.

Thanks are due to A. Sivakumar, assistant professor, Department of Education, for his continuous technical effort and academic support in tailoring the book.

From Prof. T. Devi

I record my sincere thanks to Prof. P. Kaliraj, Hon'ble former vice-chancellor of Bharathiar University, who identified the gap in the knowledge world when the professor searched for a book on Industry 4.0 and triggered the process of writing and editing books in the Industry 4.0 series. His continuous motivation during the lockdown period due to COVID-19, sensitisation, and encouragement are unmatchable.

I express my profound thanks to the vice-chancellor and registrar for the administrative support. Heartfelt thanks are due to the authors of the chapters for their contributions, their continuous co-operation in improvising the chapters as and when requested, and their timely communication. I thank all the expert members who served as reviewers for providing a quality and swift review.

We wish to thank Mr. John Wyzalek, Senior acquisitions editor, Taylor & Francis Group/CRC Press, who believed in the idea of this book and helped us in realising our dream.

Special thanks are due to Mr. Glenon Butler, production Editor, Taylor & Francis Group/CRC Press, Florida, for his co-ordination and Ms Tarana Parveen, project manager, MPS Ltd., for her meticulous and swift support.

Thanks are due to Mrs. K. Kowsalya, Assistant registrar; Mr. R. Karthick, assistant section officer; Mr. A. Prasanth and Mr. Vijayakumar of the Office of the Vice-Chancellor; and staff of the Office of the Registrar of Bharathiar University, India.

I thank my husband Mr. D. Ravi, daughter Mrs. R. Deepiga, son Mr. R. Surya, son-in-law Mr. D. Vishnu Prakhash, grandson V. Deera, and family members for their encouragement and support.

Editors Biographies

Prof. P. Kaliraj, Hon'ble former vice-chancellor, Bharathiar University, a visionary and an eminent leader leading big academic teams, has had more than three decades of teaching and research experience. He has held various renowned positions, such as officiating vice-chancellor of Anna University, head of the Centre for Biotechnology of Anna University, dean of faculty at A C College of Technology, and member of the syndicate for two decades at Anna University. Professor Kaliraj had research collaborations with the National Institute of Health in Maryland, USA; Glasgow University in Scotland, UK; and University of Illinois in Rockford, USA. University Grants Commission BSR Faculty Award and the Lifetime Achievement Award from the Biotechnology Research Society of India adorned the professor. About 42 scholars were gifted to receive the highest academic degree under his distinguished guidance. His remarkable patent in the area of filariasis is a boon in healthcare and saving the lives of mankind. He is a great motivator and very good at sensitising the faculty, scholars, and students towards achieving academic excellence and institutional global ranking. Professor Kaliraj is a recipient of the Life Time Achievement Award and Sir J.C. Bose Memorial Award for his outstanding contribution to higher education – research. Professor is the promoter of Industry 4.0 in Bharathiar University (email: vc@buc.edu.in, pkaliraj@gmail.com).

G. Singaravelu is a former professor and head of the Department of Education, director in charge of UGC-HRDC, and senate member of Bharathiar University, Coimbatore, South India. He served as a member-Syndicate, Dean of Education, and Finance Committee member of the Bharathiar University. He has 35 years of teaching experience, and he is the only professor awarded D.Litt, the prestigious highest degree in the university within the southern states of India. He also served as coordinator for B.Ed programmes and CRPF at the same university. He is an editorial committee member in I manager's *Journal on School Educational Technology* and *Journal of English Language Teaching, Research*

Demagogue, etc. The NCERT crowned him its meritorious national award, recognising his innovative gadget in the field of mathematics. He has been honoured with Abdulkalam Award as a Best Teacher, and the Assiyriar Chemmal Award has been conferred to him by Government of Tamil Nadu. He has so far published 25 books besides more than 195 research papers. He has so far guided 6 Ph.D. scholars in Educational Technology and 28 Ph.D. scholars in Education. He participated and presented papers at conferences held at the University of Pennsylvania, Philadelphia, USA, University of Cologne, Germany, Brock University, Canada, University of Malaya, Malaysia, Infrastructure University, Kuala Lumpur, Nanyang University, Singapore, Dubai, and Sharjah. He is a visiting team member of NCTE and NAAC, a selection committee member of Principals and Faculty members, and an Inspection committee member of TNTEU. He has been acting as a member of INFITT, ISFTE, the Research Advisory Board in UGC-HRDC, Bharadhidasan University, Trichy, and Board of studies in various universities. The professor can be contacted at singaravelu.bu@gmail.com.

Prof. T. Devi, PhD (UK), former professor and head, Department of Computer Applications, former Director, Centre for Research and Evaluation, and former Dean of Research, Bharathiar University, focuses on state-of-the-art technology that industries adopt in order to make students ready for the future world. She is a Gold Medallist (1981–1984) from University of Madras and a Commonwealth Scholar (1994–1998) for her PhD from the University of Warwick, UK. She has more than three decades of teaching and research experience from Bharathiar University, Indian Institute of Foreign Trade, New Delhi, and University of Warwick, UK. Professor Devi is good at team building, setting goals, and achieving them. Her research interests include integrated data modelling and framework, meta-modelling, computer-assisted concurrent engineering, and speech processing. Professor Devi has visited the United Kingdom, Tanzania, and Singapore for academic collaborations. She has received various awards including Commonwealth Scholarship and Best Alumni Award from PSGR Krishnammal College for Women (PSGRKCW), Proficiency Award from PSG College of Technology, and awards from Bharathiar University for serving for BU-NIRF, Curriculum 4.0, and Roadmap 2030 and guided 23 Ph.D. scholars. Prof. T. Devi may be contacted at (email: tdevi@buc.edu.in, tdevi5@gmail.com).

Contributors

V. Ambedkar
Department of Education
Annamalai University
Chidambaram, Tamil Nadu, India

R. Amsaveni
PSGR Krishnammal College for Women
Coimbatore, Tamil Nadu, India

M. Balasubramaniam
Department of Education
Bharathiar University
Coimbatore, Tamil Nadu, India

A. Ajumunisha Ali Begam
Department of Education
Centre for Distance Education
Bharathidasan University
Tiruchirappalli, Tamil Nadu, India

Vanitha C
Department of Education
Central University of Kerala
Kasaragod, Kerala, India

Madhurima Chakraborty
Department of Education
Annamalai University
Chidambaram, Tamil Nadu, India

Pranjal Das
Department of Education
L.T.K. College
Lakhimpur, Assam, India

Swapna Sikha Das
Department of Education
Tezpur University (A Central University)
Tezpur, Assam, India

P. Dhanalakshmi
Department of Applied Mathematics
Bharathiar University
Coimbatore, Tamil Nadu, India

Shiba Khatoon
Department of Education
Central University of Kerala
Kasaragod, Kerala, India

Narendra Kumar
Department of Education
Central University of Rajasthan
Ajmer, Rajasthan, India

M. Poorani
Biological Science Education
Bosco College of Teacher Education
Dimapur, Nagaland, India

Sheetal Prajapati
Department of Education
Central University of Rajasthan
Ajmer, Rajasthan, India

M. Punithavalli
Department of Computer Applications
Bharathiar University
Coimbatore, Tamil Nadu, India

Nil Ratan Roy
Department of Education
Tezpur University (A Central University)
Tezpur, Assam, India

T. Sangeetha
Department of Education
Central University of Rajasthan
Ajmer, Rajasthan, India

E. Shrilekha
Department of Applied Mathematics
Bharathiar University
Coimbatore, Tamil Nadu, India

G. Singaravelu
Department of Education
Bharathiar University
Coimbatore, Tamil Nadu, India

A. Sivakumar
Department of Education
Bharathiar University
Coimbatore, Tamil Nadu, India

K. E. Soudha Nalina Kumari
Amirtham College of Education
Kanchipuram, Tamil Nadu, India

P. Subramanian
Department of Educational Planning and Administration
Tamil Nadu Teachers Education University
Chennai, Tamil Nadu, India

E. Suganya
Department of Computer Science
Bharathiar University
Coimbatore, Tamil Nadu, India

Tamisha
Department of Education
Central University of Rajasthan
Ajmer, Rajasthan, India

G. Thirumoorthy
Department of Education
Bharathiar University
Coimbatore, Tamil Nadu, India

A. Tholappan
Department of Education
Centre for Distance Education
Bharathidasan University
Tiruchirappalli, Tamil Nadu, India

K. Vijayarani
Department of Education (SDE)
Bharathiar University
Coimbatore, Tamil Nadu, India

S. Vijayarani
Department of Computer Science
Bharathiar University
Coimbatore, Tamil Nadu, India

Chapter 1

Digital Learning Resources: An Overview

E. Suganya and S. Vijayarani
Department of Computer Science, Bharathiar University, Coimbatore, Tamilnadu, India

Objectives

Nowadays, learning online has become inevitable for all people. Digital learning, also called e-learning, is the confluence of electronic content, technology, and information. If the learning task is being done electronically then there is a need for effective resource platforms. There are lots of digital learning resources available for students and researchers. Based on their preferences and needs the most appropriate learning environment is created by these learning resources. Digital learning resources are not only the key to digital learning but also one of the familiar and significant research topics in the field of education. For researchers, different kinds of digital learning resources are available, especially, for their literature study they need to access online journals, online websites for dissertations, conference papers that are available online, dataset sources, scientific data resources, and so on. This chapter discusses the basic concepts of digital learning resources, their need, working procedures, types, uses, advantages, and disadvantages. In addition, the role of digital learning resources for the researchers' community is discussed. Furthermore, information about the latest technologies of learning techniques will be provided that will be helpful to the researchers to find their resources easily. Various digital learning resources are compared in this chapter, and the researchers will

DOI: 10.1201/9781032675176-1

analyse and find the best resource for their research. The main objective of digital learning in research is:

- To classify the digital learning resources for collecting and analysing the data for research.
- To provide recent technologies for the researchers to utilise them.
- To evaluate the digital learning resources which are helpful to the research.
- To compare various digital learning resources and obtain the most appropriate resources for further learning.

Introduction

In the learning process, the role, needs, and usage of technology are defined as digital learning. In addition, the technology could be virtual, adaptive, augmentative, or personalised. Digital learning enables users to learn from everywhere at any time. It provides many benefits for users for learning. In different research domains, the researchers and experts are often required to conduct a depth search, which includes the effective usage of the internet. This kind of search helps the researchers to get an idea about how the earlier works have been conducted. Normally, internet-based resources are utilised by researchers for a variety of purposes. Some of the significant uses are acquiring knowledge, the status of publications, information about journal databases, alert messages from an e-mail, resource retrieval for assignment completion, and searching information for scientific or academic purposes. Students must be familiar with a web search task to retrieve information from the internet efficiently. At present, there are plenty of e-resources available, which include electronic books, e-journals, journal article indexes and collections, reference works, digital collections, databases, and websites. For conducting research, researchers should know about the existing solutions; hence, the latest research articles are much more important to them.

In the learning environment, the usage of digital media will provide completely innovative collaboration, communication, and networking prospects. Compared to traditional methods of learning, digital learning provides higher adaptability, customisability, and transportability. Training materials are prepared, uploaded, and updated collaboratively on the cloud in the digital world. Learners can assume greater personal accountability at a young age through digital training, which also improves communication and coordination (Education, 2017). The transition from offline learning to online learning has made a tremendous change in people's learning process.

Students can attain strong self-learning capabilities by using online digital learning resources and tools. They can learn to distinguish everything and locate their needs. They learn the way to obtain, find, and use the appropriate internet-related tools, knowledge about understanding the nature of the problem, and the ability to analyse the received responses also possible by them.

This outcome will increase their competitiveness and effectiveness. Analytical skills are very important for learners; digital learning tools will provide this facility to learners. With this knowledge, they can easily develop reasoning skills. Students should learn how to make effective decisions. This is possible by experimenting with the prime challenges with logic and imagination. Apart from this, students who are just remembering and memorising the information given in the textbook are not able to make effective decisions. (Education, 2017).

Digital learning is also termed Technology Enhanced Learning (TEL) and digital education. Normally, this platform offers the innovative and creative usage of digital technology setup for learning as well as the teaching process. Learning digitally encompasses learning that is assisted by technology and supports to offer various activities like the environment where the learning is carried out by the students, the duration of time of learning, and the way they are learning. Now, digital learning concepts and principles change the conventional educational principles and practices. Analysing the use of digital media provides instructors with the potential to establish exciting opportunities (Singh, 2020).

Types of Digital Learning

Digital learning can be divided into different types like virtual classrooms, MOOCs, SPOCs, bootcamps, and social learning. Figure 1.1 illustrates the various types of digital learning.

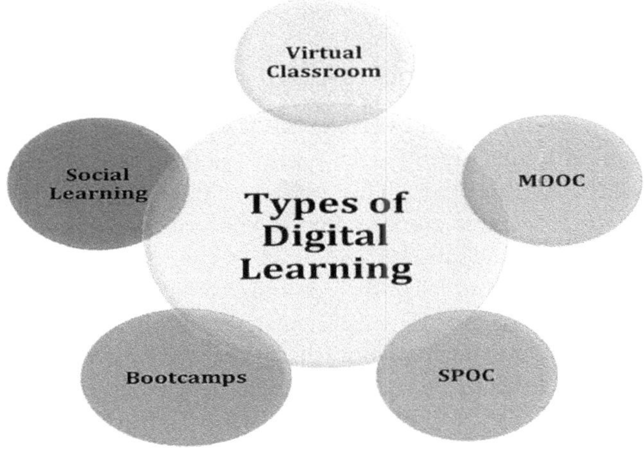

Figure 1.1 Types of digital learning.

Virtual Classroom

Teaching and learning tasks are performed online and called virtual classrooms in which professors and students can share learning material and interact effectively. It is distinguished by the fact that it is conducted in a live, interactive context. Although online education may consist of pre-recorded, asynchronous material, virtual classroom settings require direct interactions between teachers and students. The most commonly used open-source virtual classrooms are EdApp, Deck Toys, Kahoot, eTrain Center, Osmo, Proprofs, Wooclap, Google workspace, Ayotree, Edvance360, Zoom, Blackboard Collaborate, NewRow, Airstack, Panopto, Samba live, Vedamo, Edulastic, Braincert, and so on (Barron, 2020).

MOOCs

In India, one of the best virtual classes is MOOC, and the expansion of MOOC is Massive Open Online Courses. In MOOC, anyone can sign up and attend the classes. MOOC organisations provide a variety of approved courses, and these are delivered through academic institutions. Online courses platform providers like Coursera and edX are examples of MOOCs (Barron, 2020). MOOCs may train and coach for similar purposes from a variety of perspectives, experiences, and regions across the world. However, the majority of MOOC courses are taught free of cost, making them more easily accessible to interested learners. MOOC offers different kinds of certifications, which range from the completion of the minimum number of course levels to the higher levels. Based on the assessment of the examination, the learners who have passed the examination will get these recognised certificates (Kurt, 2021).

SPOC (Small Private Online Course)

This interactive training course, like the MOOC, is meant for a small group of students and is frequently offered by institutions to individual students or employees within organisations. This facilitates interaction with the lecturer and guarantees that learners are monitored. The primary benefits that SPOCs provide are related to the student and teacher connection. Even though the learner has continuous and effective communication with the instructor, as well as other learners in an SPOC, evaluation is more specific and constant. This interaction produces an environment where the students and instructors feel more engaged, resulting in a more trusting and comfortable environment for all involved. SPOCs also assist with classroom learning and virtual classrooms, two styles of learning that integrate face-to-face contact with digital training.

Bootcamps

Another type of virtual classroom is bootcamps. This is for data analytics, web development, and graphic design and provides learners with focused training in a field. Examples of bootcamp organisations are Thinkful, Galvanise, and General Assembly. Bootcamps are intended to help people develop knowledge in a short timeframe to migrate into various occupations or improve their proficiency in a specific field. Many learners are choosing to increase their job prospects and become specialists via rapid, focused training programmes, including bootcamps, instead of registering in an inter-graduate programme. Coding bootcamps, for instance, seek to help students to learn the skills they have to transfer into a digital marketing profession. Bootcamps are typically intended to take a closer look at the objective (Anna, 2020).

Social Learning

Learning is a conceptual model that occurs within a social environment and proceeds primarily through observation or active learning, according to a hypothesis proposed by psychologist Albert Bandura. Consider the social components of people's daily lives. Today, everyone learns by observing, listening, and performing; as well as by combining visual, audible, and learning strategy modalities to grasp creative ideas, retain that learning, and apply it to real-world problems (Powell, 2021). Social learning influences basic values and ideologies, including gender expectations, spirituality, political opinions, and personality. This is accomplished by seeing how individuals around us respond to various perspectives (Jarche, 2021).

Traditional Learning

In most areas around the world, graduates and educators trust that traditional up-close and individual learning methods assist in improving communication skills, such as writing and identity. Undergraduates and professionals are motivated by social skills because they want to know the best way to cope with certain circumstances. Traditional education can provide conversation, motivation, affordability, organisation, and other benefits to students in higher education and others. Interactive allows for efficient connection between students and teachers, helps students boost their interactive educational activity, and helps students quickly clear their questions about a given subject, which is unique among e-learning.

E-learning primarily focuses on providing information, whereas a live trainer can motivate students to overcome specific problems, including the social awkwardness they encounter in e-learning sessions. The e-learning method would not provide aid for helpful activities for less skilled students or slow learners, whereas they can get aid from teachers and students in classroom activities. When evaluating the organisational aspect, it sets a constant timeline for learning a given subject, preventing a student from learning that particular topic at any time (Ponnampalam, 2019). Books and classroom exercises, along with teacher instructions, are far more valuable than online notes and directions when a higher education student or other student needs to pass an exam.

In classroom learning, undergraduates and teachers can understand each other in a better way. This allows teachers to understand their students better, analyse their strengths and weaknesses, act as coaches, lead students, and contribute ideas toward their desired career outcomes. The basic truth is there are no security conflicts in the traditional learning process, as there are in the e-learning process, and there is no process of thinking of security and privacy issues due to face-to-face interaction. This is a fantastic benefit of today's world.

Traditional learning has a negative impression since it is expensive, students depend on teachers, it takes more time, and so on. In traditional learning, students' entire activities are dependent on the teacher's guidance, thus they will never be capable of handling a real issue without depending on others, and any commitment of a bad group in the classroom will spoil the student's future.

Table 1.1 gives the differences between traditional learning and digital learning.

Table 1.1 Traditional Learning vs Digital Learning

S.No.	*Traditional Learning*	*Digital Learning*
1.	It occurs offline	It occurs on the online platform
2.	Motivated to adhere to a timetable and location	Anywhere, at any time
3.	Specified progression	Adaptable schedule
4.	Promotes coordination with teammates	Lack of coordination
5.	Learning from and alongside one another	Promotes a self-directed learning method
6.	The instructor is the major source of information	Online content is the main source of knowledge
7.	Communication between instructors and teammates is significant	There is little interaction

Types of Digital Learning Resources

There are various types of digital learning resources for an efficient learning process. Some of the digital learning tools are given in Figure 1.2.

Adaptive Learning

Adaptive learning is a type of learning technology that uses the newest technology to evaluate and monitor a learner's knowledge of this subject. Its process makes use of the learner's important feedback to identify the learner's abilities and improve content delivery. Learning feedback is frequently used to customise a student's teachings to their understanding and memorisation abilities (Superadmin, 2019). Through providing original content regularly, adaptive learning keeps the learner

Figure 1.2 Types of digital learning resources.

engaged throughout the course. Examples of adaptive learning are Surgent Platform for CPA Exams, Knewton on its Alta platform, Fulcrum, ScootPad, DreamBox, Quizalize, Socrative, Elevate, Splash Math, Matific, and so on (Parmley, 2019).

Advantages

- Many of the advantages of adaptive technology in online classes are equally relevant in traditional classrooms.
- However, because of the world of digital learning, plenty of the issues that adaptive learning can deal with are highly helpful for online classes.
- Since lecturers and students would not communicate in person daily, as is common in online classes, providing technology to assist in making up the difference becomes much more critical.
- The method of adaptive learning is supposed to contribute to improved overall performance in several fields.
- The adaptive architecture provides for a wide range of activities and assessments, as well as numerous opportunities to develop skills and explicit trainer comments.
- The teacher can invest more one-on-one interaction with learners to help them improve certain skills (Bolden, 2016).

Disadvantages

- Incredibly frequent tests, evaluations, and examinations can make things feel very serious and uninteresting.
- Learners may feel isolated on a digitally responsive platform.
- The learner's routes may cause them to skip over critical learning materials and connections to a big deal and particular requirements that might go wrong and miss the correct one.
- Adaptive may not be the best approach to communicating the content of a lesson to students, especially when it comes to the material's applicability to multiple contexts, such as current affairs or life experiences (Kok, 2020).

Badging and Gamification

It is a persuasion procedure that incorporates digital certificates to show learners how much they're appreciated. The certificates serve as a motivator for completing difficult tasks. The obtaining of certifications changes the method of learning into a gamification process that encourages learners to try to 'defeat' new knowledge. Gamification enables learners to become much more active in the learning process by involving themselves in various situations, as opposed to simply paying attention to lectures and studying teaching materials on their own. Gamification provides learners with fascinating and interesting learning environments, as well as a platform for developers' innovation to shine. However, despite the various benefits, gamification may also present some difficulties and challenges. Examples of gamification are Ludic loop, Starbucks, ForestApp, and so on (Stewart, 2021).

Advantages

- Games can transform boring subjects into engaging and fascinating experiences, encourage healthy competition among teammates, and inspire students to feel proud of completing a course after a series of gamified difficulties and activities.
- Students learn and practice problem-solving skills at various levels of play or situations.
- Games provide immediate feedback to help players adjust to new challenges.
- They encourage the application of knowledge to real-world situations and challenges.
- They encourage interaction, collaboration, learner communities, and practice.
- They utilise features such as badges to increase motivation. In gamified learning content, badges can be as basic as digital streamers, stickers, or rewards that students acquire for completing courses or activities within the game.

Disadvantages

- They have high development costs.
- Games can be expensive to design and maintain.
- They cause overstimulation or addiction to video games.
- They are used instead of other types of learning activities, such as hands-on experiments.

Blended Learning

To achieve the best results, blended learning incorporates digital and conventional teaching approaches. Teachers and students interact directly for classes, along with online for immersive discussions and virtual learning. Blended learning will help learners to enhance their independent learning while sustaining a 'team' atmosphere in the classroom (Super admin, 2019). This is more extensible and evaluates the individual's time restrictions.

Blended learning, often known as 'hybrid' learning, is a type of online education that can take many different forms. Although some companies are using blended learning approaches mostly in exceptional cases, others will use them as the major teaching method in their courses. There are several models for promoting blended learning.

The Flipped Classroom Model

Teachers can employ flipped classrooms to assist students in completing academic goals and encourage them as they probably apply topics that were previously studied according to their own. Individual learning can be done at home via online courses and video tutorials, while teaching assistant activities are undertaken in presence in a blended learning environment.

The Enriched Virtual Model

This approach is similar to the flipped classroom. Students generally learn online, although face-to-face interactions with the teacher are essential as well. When compared to typical learning situations, the flipped classroom can be viewed as flipping the initial order of education, whereas the enhanced virtual model begins with remote instruction.

The Individual Rotation Model

Individual rotation models can be used in a variety of academic contexts, incorporating blended learning environments. If necessary, fixed schedules can be substituted with customised learning trips, and various stages can be accomplished online or in person.

Classroom Technologies

Classrooms are efficient with support from social networking, 3D printing, virtual reality, and cloud computing. As the capacities of both teachers and students continue to increase with new technology, expect digital learning and conventional learning to combine. Teachers can see enhanced students' understanding when they utilise technology that helps to involve users in the classroom. Mentimeter and Kahoot are famous examples of classroom technology. Examples of technology in the classroom are as follows:

- **Tablets:** students can have more engagement with the material by using portable devices such as digital textbooks. Students can also save money by buying electronic books rather than printed books.
- **Video conferencing:** high-speed internet can link conference rooms across the world, allowing students from all over the world to attend the same classes. This can also be an efficient approach for learners to interact over long distances.
- **Smartboards:** in most classrooms, interactive, connected display panels can replace whiteboards. This style of the board provides pupils with a more interesting, participating, and proactive learning experience. They deliver

knowledge in a multimedia format by displaying videos and images along with handwritten notes.

- **Cloud servers:** students can use the cloud to access all of the resources they require. This could reduce the use of a traditional computer lab or large libraries.
- **3D printing:** this technology can change the way learners engage with technology by allowing students to simply develop and manufacture models. It is also used to make specific 3D models for science or art purposes (M, 2020).

E-Textbooks

Digital adaptations of textbooks are called e-textbooks, which are less expensive to upgrade than traditional textbooks. At present, most hard copies of books are converted into e-books. E-books are most effective when they are selected to facilitate blended learning.

Advantages

- eBooks can assist in saving money on favourite books. Due to the lack of shipping fees, eBooks are generally 50–60% more affordable than their print counterparts.
- Compared to traditional printed books, eBooks are more adaptable. Individuals who have problems reading the typical book-sized font can increase the text size in eBook readers to effectively make it more enjoyable and easy on the eyes.
- eBooks can incorporate multimedia aspects not accessible in traditional books. To make reading a truly interactive experience, audio and video can be incorporated (Evenden, 2020).

Disadvantages

- Inconvenient to read: sitting in front of a computer or screen for hours merely reading an ebook can lead to obesity, muscular pain, headache, and even higher cholesterol levels.
- Piracy: with ebooks, a file may be transmitted to someone hundreds of kilometres away in seconds. It can even be uploaded to a public server and downloaded by anybody (Lisa, 2021).

Learning Analytics

Learning analytics incorporates data mining into the learning process. The analytics process includes data collection, observation, and evaluation. Learning analytics has traditionally been connected with digital learning environments, where it may be

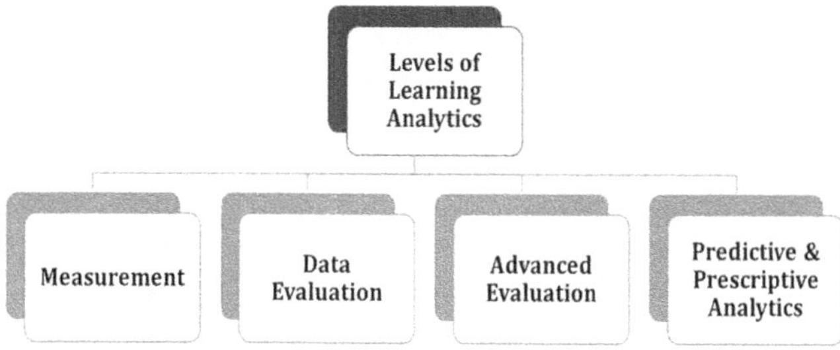

Figure 1.3 Levels of learning analytics.

used to build and implement innovations and designs based on predictive analysis as well as the learning evaluation procedure (Superadmin, 2019).

The Levels of Learning Analytics

These analytics can be classified into four levels: measurement, evaluation, advanced evaluation, and predictive/prescriptive analytics which are depicted in Figure 1.3. Even though each of these stages is appropriately described as 'analytics', the complexity, difficulty, and effectiveness of each level significantly differ from one another.

Measurement: measurement, or the basic principle of observing events and capturing values to inform whatever has happened, is where analytics begins. Measurement does not require mathematical calculations or statistics; however, it does involve data collection. Analytical work is impossible without it.

- **Data evaluation:** once the data has been collected, it is time to begin examining it and determine whether the data indicates either a positive or a negative trend. Applying high-school mathematical calculations like averages, means, modes, and simple statistics, to combine the data and develop benchmarks at this stage.
- **Advanced evaluation:** exciting developments begin to occur in the advanced evaluation and the application of college-level mathematics. Correlations and regression analysis are examples of advanced evaluation. Employing statistical methods to figure out not only what has occurred, but also why it has occurred. Advanced evaluation generates correlation ideas, allowing learners to concentrate on what works well while eliminating unsuccessful information.
- **Predictive and prescriptive analytics:** predictive and prescriptive analytics is the most advanced level of analytics, requiring higher education in mathematics and frequently relying on artificial intelligence (AI) or machine learning supported by large datasets (What Is Learning Analytics?, 2021).

Learning Objects

Learning objectives assist in integrating knowledge, content, and practice evaluations into a user-friendly collection. Typically, the collection target is based on a specific learning purpose. Object terminology in learning objects is quite equivalent to object terminology in computer science. Learning objects enable the development of learning schemes that combine various learning objects to create the desired learning outcome. Multiple learning criteria can be accomplished by providing a repository of learning resources. Creating videos, podcasts, graphics, presentations, timelines, and e-books are the most commonly used learning objects.

Mobile Learning

It is also known as m-learning. It is a word used mostly for learning activities that can be involved over multiple platforms. Mobile learning can also refer to the multi-faceted technique of learning using digital equipment that incorporates both biological and social connections, along with video and digital learning technologies. Mobile learning is useful as it enables students to facilitate the learning process 'on-demand', whenever and wherever learners want.

Advantages

- **Access wherever at any time:** mobile learning is all about learning by a mobile device while connected to the internet; it can be accessed from anywhere worldwide at any time.
- **Covers a large distance:** mobile learning has the advantage of being able to access the same knowledge or tests at different times. Distance is not an issue in mobile learning.
- **Content variety:** there is a lot of content available on the internet. It is quite convenient for anyone to use it because of its vast diversity; also, it can be accessed by a significant number of people from all over the world for various topics or issues.
- **Encourages students:** there is a variety of learning software that employs online quizzes to monitor progress. The research is offered in such a way that it catches learners' attention; as a result, game quizzes are included to motivate students to enhance their past performance.
- **Testsstudents' knowledge:** online tests are created, and students' knowledge is expanded by completing these quizzes, puzzles, or riddles. Apart from learning resources, the internet contains a variety of additional quizzes, puzzles, multiple-choice questions, as well as other games; playing games tests knowledge and even increases IQ level.

Disadvantages

- **Software difficulties:** inability to upgrade to the latest version, a repeated crash that occurs, software conflicts that cause a disruption in the mobile learning experience, and other difficulties restrict the software's operation.
- **Hardware problems:** unlike software, hardware relies on physical devices. The actual gadgets that are used can break down over time. Overuse, pollution, and hard handling, as well as other factors, might cause them to dissolve. These cause phones or other gadgets to stop working properly.
- **Distraction:** there is a lot of distraction when using mobile learning. Many students intend to use their smartphones to discover something, but instead use them to visit social media sites, chat, share images, or play online games. These types of diversions consume time that may be better spent on more important tasks.
- **Misuse:** many students abuse the device for a variety of reasons. Some people abuse it for the sake of entertainment, while others have hidden, malicious purposes that must be stopped.
- Inability to connect to the internet or an insufficient supply (Thomes, 2019).

Personalised Learning

Personalised learning is a learning strategy that is specifically developed to help a single learner. Individuals that would benefit from a customised learning approach are only meant to participate in a personalised learning opportunity. Someone controlling or constructing a customised learning experience for a specific individual and/or learning objective is what personalised learning is all about (super admin, 2019). When a process becomes more generalised or automated, it is classified as adaptive learning.

Online Learning

It allows learners to develop their skills. Even though the sessions are regularly planned and learners can listen to lectures on-demand, online learning is highly popular. Online learning is similar to digital learning in that it includes similar elements. It is compared to digital learning, which refers to publicly accessible, fully prepared classes delivered online to satisfy the expectations of a large number of individuals, such as Massive Open Online Courses (MOOCs).

Open Educational Resources

Resources that can be utilised for educational purposes and are free, openly licensed, and publicly accessible are called OERS. Legal permissions include the capacity to modify, maintain, utilise, reexamine, and transmit the OERS data (super admin, 2019). These are a type of online learning resources that can be utilised to accomplish a specific goal. Course syllabuses, lesson plans, learning units, lab experiments, exercises, course videos, discussion ideas, projects, evaluations, library references, and instructional development frameworks are all examples of open educational resources (OER).

- Many professors currently employ open educational resources in their classes, such as YouTube videos, worksheets made and shared by other professors, and online simulations as learning activities. Course syllabuses, lesson plans, and even whole textbooks for courses can be created and shared by faculty. They can work with academics from their universities as well as faculty from other countries.
- Students can help create OER in several different ways, from basic projects to whole textbooks. To construct a full OER, students at Plymouth State University collaborated to discover government materials, compose subject descriptions, design discussion questions, and produce assignments to go with the materials.
- Instructional designers can collaborate with instructors and learners to incorporate open educational resources into learning and teaching, as well as share and disseminate their course templates as OER. To assist in integrating OER into learning analytics and other course learning platforms, several instructional designers and developers collaborate with libraries and IT companies.
- Librarians are important players in OER efforts, advocating, developing, investigating, and maintaining OER. Librarians can assist in the understanding of copyright and licensing ideas, as well as navigating Creative Commons license alternatives (Examples of OER, 2021).

Virtual Reality

Learners can interact with the real-world learning environment using the Virtual Reality Learning Environment (VRLE). It is a fantastic way to gain experience by utilising a head-mounted display (HMD), desktop computer, and virtual learning glasses. Virtual reality (VR) is a remedy for instances where providing experiences to learners to reach the required learning experience is not reliable or accessible.

Augmented Reality

Augmented reality (AR) provides students with an open platform that augments the actual world's capabilities with computer-generated sensory data. Learners might use their smartphones to discover AR, which provides them with additional information, including interesting content, statistics, and 3D objects. Visual, auditory, acoustic, sensual, and aromatic inputs are used to increase an individual's learning opportunity in AR (Super admin, 2019). In terms of cost and size, AR falls between VR and classroom learning.

Digital Learning Resources for Research

Digital Resources for Data Collection

The process of gathering and analysing data in response to specific needs is known as data collecting, which is the systematic gathering of information to investigate different outcomes in market research. Accuracy and precision are essential for maintaining an experiment's consistency, despite the study's discipline or type (qualitative or quantitative) of data. The data collected is impacted by the panel's accuracy. Higher-quality panels lead to higher data-collecting accuracy.

Even though the aspect of data collecting has expanded in recent years, and with online serving as a saviour for several organisations, the data collection procedure has also evolved. Online data collection has made the whole process incredibly effective and efficient currently (Data Collection, 2021). Online data collection has become more powerful, time-consuming, and effective help of the internet. The internet is often used to study and acquire information via emails, text messages transmitted on smartphones, and further similar techniques.

Online data collection refers to information gathered by sending emails, text messages, and other electronic communications (also during online interviews). The benefit of online data collecting is that survey questions or committee members with plenty of time required to complete the questionnaire for data collection (Data Collection, 2021). Hence, the collected data is quite reliable. Online data collection is an efficient procedure using unique data collection methods. Hence, specific procedures must be followed to obtain reliable data.

General Digital Data Resources

Carnegie Mellon Data and Story Library

The website may appear dated and difficult in terms of technique, but still, it contains a variety of data. The library contains a variety of data sources and stories that assist justify simple statistical techniques and interesting ideas. A website provided by Carnegie Mellon University called the Data and Story Library (DASL) is an excellent source for data and descriptions. DASL offers data from a wide variety of disciplines so that analytics instructors can obtain exciting, real-world examples for their students, including 59,943 cases. An excellent example can be brought to work during a lecture on a specific statistical procedure and make it more relevant. This website is intended to assist teachers in analysing and identifying files to be used in the classroom, as well as to provide a repository for datasets from the statistical literature (All Data Files, n.d.).

Datagov.in

The National Informatics Centre (NIC), a leading ICT enterprise of the Government of India under the supervision of the Ministry of Electronics and Information Technology, developed, implemented, and maintains the Open Government Data Portal. The goal of the Open Government Data Platform India is to make government-owned accessible data. It is widely available and updatable in both human and machine-readable formats. Following various related policies, acts, and rules of the Government of India, thereby promoting accessibility and application of government-owned data and enabling the use of data for national development.

The Open Government Data (OGD) Platform India, also known as data.gov.in, is a platform that supports the Indian government's open data project. This portal provides a level of accessibility to datasets, documents, resources, tools, and technologies released by Indian government ministries, departments, and organisations. It integrates and enhances the greatest aspects of India's India.gov.in with the United States data.gov projects (data.gov.in, 2021). It includes 521,670 resources, 11,438 catalogues, 210 departments, 30.95 M views, 9.06 M downloads, 416 chief data officers, 125,408 APIs, and 2,571 visualisations.

UC Berkeley Data Lab

This massive range of resources is an extension of the Berkeley University of California library system. To obtain information and research on economics, health, politics, business, science, and various disciplines. D-Lab offers multidisciplinary resources for in-depth analysis and guidance, as well as exposure to staff assistance, training, and deployment for software and other requirements. By collaborating with other Berkeley centres, the Centre provides services to researchers from other disciplines and helps to fund Berkeley's graduate programmes and academic research.

D-Lab experts may help with the entire research cycle, including research methodology, survey procedures, sampling procedures, data gathering, statistical analysis, evaluation, and outcome of communication. Consultants are well-versed in technical programmes like R, NVivo, GIS, and Python, as well as reducing data science methodologies like Machine Learning and Natural Language Processing. California Field Polls, Zillow ZTRAX, Census data, and many other resources are available in the repository (D-Lab, 2021).

Internet UPC Database

This is a huge collection of UPCs. Even though the UPC was effectively discontinued, it continues to be usefully related to current data being uploaded. Since its establishment in 2010, it has collected over 1.5 million barcode numbers from all across the world. Users contribute codes to the database. The UPC database includes barcodes from the standard UPC numbering system, the international EAN code number, and the Bookland code number, among others (UPC database, 2021). The product name, price, quantity, and manufacturer are all available in the UPC Database. Additionally, for wishlist applications, a picture of the item, a rating, and a product identifier are provided. It also provides other features, such as an API for developing apps, a check digit calculator, and a QR Code generator. There are currently 313 datasets available in this database.

Amazon Public Data Sets

Discover the vast volumes of data that Amazon focuses on identifying opportunities for improvement. The data are accessible to the public, and all can process it for free. AWS Public Data Sets is a diverse collection of public data sets that may be simply integrated into AWS cloud-based applications. Community data sets are hosted free of charge by AWS, and individuals pay exclusively for the computation and storage they utilise with their applications, as with all AWS services. Large data sets, such as the Human Genome Map and US Census data, usually involve different amounts of time to discover, download, configure, and analyse. Anyone with an Amazon Elastic Compute Cloud (Amazon EC2) instance now has access to these data sets and can start processing them in seconds. Users can also take advantage of the whole AWS environment and interact with other AWS users without difficulty. For example, users can create or use pre-configured server images with tools and apps to examine datasets (Public Data Sets on AWS Now Available, 2008). AWS intends to empower academics across a wide range of disciplines and organisations with tools to enable more innovation, more efficiently, by maintaining this significant and relevant data using cost-effective services like Amazon EC2.

Google Dataset Search

It is an online platform that specialises in discovering data. It's a metadata online platform for data vendors. It means that it analyses a dataset's definitions rather than its content. If a dataset is openly accessible, there is also a reasonable chance this will start showing up in a Google dataset search. Dataset search contained around 25 million multiple data sources from all over the world when it first launched (Toh, 2021). In searching for datasets on this website, Google dataset search uses keyword search and, like standard Google search, provides a simple auto-complete option.

OpenML

OpenML is a data science framework that aims to make machine-learning research more accessible. It offers a significant amount of data from a wide range of fields, including healthcare, education, and climate change. Each dataset with this site has a certain webpage, and data can be obtained in a diversity of formats, including CSV, JSON, and XML. Machine learning is improving human capability to understand nature and design a successful future, but it must be visible and easy to use in research, education, and industry. The Open Machine Learning Project is a collaborative opportunity to produce an open, well-organised, online machine-learning platform that creates open-source tools for finding and sharing publicly available data from any sector, easily imports it into a user's favourite machine-learning environments, develops models alongside thousands of other data scientists, analyses the results against the state of the art, and receives automated suggestions on how to develop appropriate models.

OpenML is easily integrated into current data science platforms. Import datasets, develop algorithms online, upload models at any time download, and share other people's processes, modelling techniques, and analyses with a few code lines or a few clicks (OpenML, 2021). OpenML is immediately integrated into one of the most widely used machine-learning tools but also develops its integrations using the C++ APIs, R, Python, Java, and or use REST APIs to programme against. It has 16,247 data analysis flows, 21,440 datasets, and 260,725 scientific activities.

Github

A collection of high-quality, industry-specific public datasets may be downloaded from GitHub's 'awesome public datasets' repository. According to the Repository, this is a collection of greater premise online data sources. These are gathered from various sources, such as blogs, and user responses. Millions of developers use GitHub, which is the most popular and largest platform all over the world, and organisations to develop, deploy, and manage their software. It is a popular platform for hosting open-source projects. GitHub has more than 200 million repositories, 73 million developers, and 4 million organisations, as of November 2021. With boundless public and private repositories, users can archive it all for free.

World Health Organisation (WHO)

The WHO's database contains everything a person could possibly want to know about global health or world news. WHO is a United Nations agency that integrates states, businesses, and people. It believes in wellness, maintaining world health, and assisting the most vulnerable because anyone, anywhere can enjoy a healthy lifestyle. Global attempts to attain universal health insurance are led by the WHO. They are in charge of leading and organising the international response to emergencies. The Triple Billion Goal is an excellent strategy for the world to attain improved health outcomes including all individuals by adopting scientific strategies and methods (World Health Organization, 2021). The WHO aims to promote everyone's opportunity to appreciate excellent health and well-being by collaborating with 194 Member States throughout 6 regions as well as in the field on more than 150 sites.

UCI Machine Learning Repository

It is a selection of data sources, subject concepts, and data sources employed by the field of machine learning for empirically analysing machine-learning algorithms. Machine-learning data sets are available to students, professors, and researchers around the world through this site. The archive has been mentioned over 1,000 times, indicating its importance. It provides the machine-learning community with 622 datasets as a provider. The searchable interface allows users to view all the datasets (UC Irvine Machine Learning Repository, 2021).

Digital Resources for Data Analysis

Towards Data Science

TDS is Medium's most popular publication, including all aspects of data science. TDS provides a wonderful community in which everyone is allowed to join and share. It is useful for individuals who are trying to attempt to break into data science and obtain their occupation (Pandey, 2020).

PyData (Conference + Videos)

NumFOCUS is a nonprofit organisation that promotes public principles in research, and scientific computing and PyData is an educational programme. They conduct conferences across the world to motivate scholars and practitioners to discuss their research results.

Machine Learning Mastery

For data scientists, especially junior ones, Jason Brownlee's website/blog is a great resource of information. There are numerous tutorials available, extending from traditional statistical modelling methodologies (linear regression, ARIMA) to the most reducing machine/deep online courses (Pandey, 2020).

Kaggle

For beginners, Kaggle has many Kernels/Notebooks that illustrate using machine-learning algorithms in practical applications. The developers of the models and their evaluation metrics frequently include a detailed framework for the study (Pandey, 2020). This Notebook also provides access to the most common ML/DL algorithms that have been applied in Kaggle Kernels on specific datasets (both Python and R).

Recent Learning Technologies for Research

Digital technology has the advantage of being very scalable. This may be applicable in the field of education, where huge classrooms are still a preferred mode of instruction due to their cost-effectiveness all around the world. Various digital learning technologies are depicted in Figure 1.4.

Article-Based Learning

Learners are intended to learn their research topic and related works through article-based e-learning. Nowadays, journal articles, conference proceedings, and dissertations are available in digital format (Bui, 2020). The learner may download the recent article from the official website or search Google.

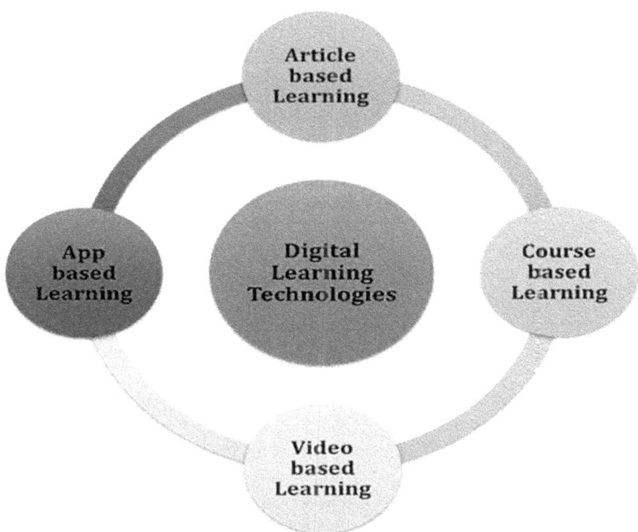

Figure 1.4 Digital learning technologies.

Course-Based Learning

The great advantage of course-based eLearning is the preplanned events. Hence, new learners' who want to know a particular topic can easily register for available open online courses such as MOOC, EDX, Coursera, Datacamp, Udemy, Udacity, Lyda, and so on. These freely available online courses are providing e-certificates to the participants.

Video-Based Learning

As the term suggests, video-based learning is a method of eLearning in which the listener can learn great opportunities to gain knowledge through watching videos. This type of learning is gaining more attention and to transform the typical tedious learning to 'Click Next' eLearning (Video-Based Learning Content, 2019). Learning videos are used by companies in a range of fields, from hiring to refining and reviewing their employees' strengths in different sectors (Bui, 2020). There is a significant need for video-based learning among today's professional learners.

App-Based Learning

Mobile apps can improve the acquisition of information and, as a result, academic success. Learning apps that incorporate gamification can make learning more enjoyable for students. Teachers can develop video projects for their digital learning with the help of mobile learning apps. Students can also use videos to illustrate what learners have learned (Donnelly, 2020). Students can receive short, easy-to-understand lectures about difficult topics rather than long lectures. Mobile learning apps have proved to improve students' learning and graduation levels. Table 1.2 presents the advantages and disadvantages of digital learning resources.

Table 1.2 Advantages and Disadvantages of Digital Learning Resources

S. No.	*Advantages*	*Disadvantages*
1.	Self-Learning	Lack of Attention
2.	Plenty of Information	Technology Issues
3.	Ease of Sharing	Causes Public Isolation
4.	Interesting than Traditional Learning	The Inability to Communicate
5.	Develops Liability for Learners	Difficulty in Online Evaluation

(Continued)

Table 1.2 (Continued) Advantages and Disadvantages of Digital Learning Resources

S. No.	*Advantages*	*Disadvantages*
6.	Increase Learning Opportunity	Lack of Direct Communication
7.	Recorded Lectures	Limited to Specific Regulation
8.	Anytime Resources	Inaccessible to the Computer, Uneducated People
9.	Connected Learning	Shortage of Certification & Quality Assurance
10.	Flexible Options	Needs Strong Self-Motivation and Time Management Skills

Challenges for Digital Learning Resources in Research

Technology continuously changing: technology is rapidly dynamic; hence, the learners/researchers cannot use the same method or tool forever (Basu, 2020). Every software is upgraded frequently with an enhanced version. For technology upgrades, the researchers have a plan and a budget (Lynch, 2018).

- **Limited up-to-date data**: for data collection, the datasets are existent, and new data are updated with delay. Hence, researchers do not obtain the latest data for their analysis. Only a few of the repositories update the recent data on their website.
- **High costs:** various digital resources are quite costly. As a result, researchers may require financial and development support for further research. For instance, grammar check and plagiarism-checking software are more expensive; hence, researchers cannot buy software without funding (Lynch, 2018).
- **Unequal access for individual researchers and institutes:** some of the journals and software require institutional verification. An individual researcher cannot download a paper from a journal without institutional authority.

Conclusion

The term *Digital Learning Resources* includes various types of digital resources that support learning and teaching. These include websites, apps, and software that help students to reach their learning goals. Teachers can use various technological tools to enhance learning. Some of these include electronic grade books, digital portfolios, and learning games. Aside from laptops, digital learning also includes the use of various tools and methods. This chapter discussed a brief introduction to digital learning resources in research. Traditional learning is also described in the chapter. Various types of digital learning resources were discussed. Online data collection websites and digital data analysis tools are clearly explained. Significant recent technologies, advantages, and disadvantages, and research challenges for digital learning resources are given in this chapter.

References

Anna. (2020, October 5). *The Benefits of Attending an Online Bootcamp.* Retrieved from Meratas: https://meratas.com/blog/benefits-online-bootcamptextonline-programs-provide-schedule-flexibilityit-works-better-for-you/

Barron, S. (2020, May 5). *What Is a Virtual Classroom?* Retrieved from OWL Labs: https://resources.owllabs.com/blog/virtual-classroom

Basu, S. (2020, May 23). *8 Problems and Challenges of Digital Education in India.* Retrieved from H2S Media: https://www.how2shout.com/news/problems-and-challenges-of-digital-education-in-india.html

Bolden, H. (2016). *Benefits of Adaptive Learning.* Retrieved from PBworks: http://itecideas.pbworks.com/w/page/113554441/Benefits%20of%20Adaptive%20Learning

Bui, S. (2020, November 19). *Educational Technology Trends In 2020-2021.* Retrieved from eLearning Industry: https://elearningindustry.com/top-educational-technology-trends-2020-2021

Data Collection. (2021). Retrieved from QuotionPro: https://www.questionpro.com/online-data-collection-research-panel.html

data.gov.in. (2021). Retrieved from Wikipedia: https://en.wikipedia.org/wiki/Data.gov.in

D-Lab. (2021). Retrieved from UC Berkeley: https://dlab.berkeley.edu/about/about-us

Donnelly, C. (2020, April 20). *7 Ways Mobile-Based Education Apps Are Changing How Students Learn.* Retrieved from Entrance: https://www.entranceconsulting.com/7-ways-mobile-based-education-apps-are-changing-how-students-learn/

Education, P. (2017, March 23). *Benefits of Digital Learning Over Traditional Education Methods.* Retrieved from Panworld Education: http://www.panworldeducation.com/2017/03/23/benefits-of-digital-learning-over-traditional-education-methods/

Evenden, I. (2020, September 3). *The Pros and Cons of eBooks.* Retrieved from Top Ten Reviews: https://www.toptenreviews.com/the-pros-and-cons-of-ebooks

Examples of OER. (2021). Retrieved from WDE: https://wde.instructure.com/courses/111/pages/examples-of-oer?module_item_id=1728

Jarche, H. (2021, March 10). *Social Learning Theory.* Retrieved from Valamis: https://www.valamis.com/hub/social-learning

Kok, M.-L. (2020). *Strengths and Weaknesses of Adaptive Learning: A Case Study.* Retrieved from eLearning Industry: https://elearningindustry.com/strenghts-weaknesses-adaptive-learning-paths-case-study

Kurt, S. (2021, Feb 28). *What Are Massive Open Online Courses (MOOCs)?* Retrieved from Educational Technology: https://educationaltechnology.net/massive-open-online-courses-moocs-definitions/

Lisa, W. L. (2021). *Advantages and Disadvantages of Electronic Books*. Retrieved from silicon India: https://blogs.siliconindia.com/alice303/Advantages_and_Disadvantages_of_Electronic_Books-bid-XLT89Yeh32634297.html

Lynch, M. (2018, May 12). *How to Overcome 10 Digital Learning Challenges*. Retrieved from The Tech Edvocate: https://www.thetechedvocate.org/how-to-overcome-10-digital-learning-challenges/

M, I. (2020, April 9). *6 Examples of Classroom Tech That Improves Education*. Retrieved from Neo Blog: https://blog.neolms.com/6-examples-of-classroom-tech-that-improves-education/

OpenML. (2021). Retrieved from OpenML: https://www.openml.org/

Pandey, P. (2020, September 17). *Useful Sites for Finding Datasets for Data Analysis Tasks*. Retrieved from Towards Data Science: https://towardsdatascience.com/useful-sites-for-finding-datasets-for-data-analysis-tasks-1edb8f26c34d

Parmley, L. (2019, Feb 22). *10 Adaptive Learning Examples to Model in Your Online Course*. Retrieved from CourseMethod: https://coursemethod.com/adaptive-learning-examples.html

Ponnampalam, P. K. (2019). E-Learning at Home VS Traditional Learning among Higher Education Students: A Survey-Based Analysis., (pp. 213–221). Sri Lanka.

Powell, M. (2021). *What Is Social Learning (and How to Adopt It)*? Retrieved from Docebo: https://www.docebo.com/learning-network/blog/what-is-social-learning-how-to-adopt-it/

Public Data Sets on AWS Now Available. (2008). Retrieved from AWS: https://aws.amazon.com/about-aws/whats-new/2008/12/03/public-data-sets-on-aws-now-available/

Singh, A. (2020). *what Is the Digital Education System and Its Advantages for Students*? Retrieved from The Asian School: https://www.theasianschool.net/blog/what-is-the-digital-education-system-and-its-advantages-for-students/

Stewart, K. (2021, August 27). *What Are the Advantages and Disadvantages of Gamification?* Retrieved from Turing: https://www.turning.com/blog/what-are-the-advantages-and-disadvantages-of-gamification

Super admin. (2019, December 30). *Types of Digital Learning*. Retrieved from Leaderonomics: https://leaderonomics.org/en/resources/article/228-types-of-digital-learning

Thomes, J. (2019, July 17). *Mobile Learning: Advantages and Disadvantages*. Retrieved from eLearning Industry: https://elearningindustry.com/mobile-learning-advantages-disadvantages

Toh, A. (2021, April). *3 Best Sites to Find Datasets for Your Data Science Projects*. Retrieved from KDnuggets: https://www.kdnuggets.com/2020/04/best-sites-datasets-data-science.html

UC Irvine Machine Learning Repository. (2021). Retrieved from UC Irvine Machine Learning Repository: https://archive.ics.uci.edu/ml/index.php

UPC database. (2021). Retrieved from UPC database: https://upcdatabase.org/

Video-Based Learning Content. (2019, November 19). Retrieved from COREAXIS: https://coreaxis.com/insights/blog/video-based-learning-content

What Is Learning Analytics? (2021). Retrieved from watershed: https://www.watershedlrs.com/resources/definition/what-is-learning-analytics/

World Health Organization. (2021). Retrieved from World Health Organization: https://www.who.int/

Chapter 2

Disruptive Teaching Approaches and Strategies for the Learners in the New Normal

T. Sangeetha

Department of Education, Central University of Rajasthan, Ajmer, Rajasthan, India

Introduction

At the onset of COVID-19, all schools, colleges, universities, and educational institutions were closed. Students and teachers were held up in a nationwide lockdown. Still, none of us believed that it would continue for more than a year. Initially, truly speaking there was stagnation in the teaching–learning process. We could say it was a sudden halt in the education system that did not continue for a long time. We could say this halt has paved the way for disruptive education in our country and all over the world. A country like India is a developing nation in all fields, especially in education. Indian schools are still struggling with basic needs such as infrastructure, libraries, and toilets for students. They have to go a long way in academics for availing necessary equipment for students and teachers to facilitate online teaching and learning. Fast internet connections are also another requirement to conduct a successful online class. While basic needs are not fulfilled so far, there is a sudden disruption in the education system due to the pandemic.

 DOI: 10.1201/9781032675176-2

However, there was a lack of training in the use of technology for teaching the teachers, and they were not prepared for developing e-learning activities. Ineffective competence in using educational technologies, and inadequate school and university support, impacted academics' work to a great extent. A sudden need arose for online teaching. Almost 10 years have passed since the World Wide Web (WWW) was developed. So far we have not witnessed educational institutions, teachers, learners, and individuals feeling such a rush for the internet. This rush for the internet was because of the classes being completely online in the new normal. Teachers were pushed to switch over to online teaching–learning.

Objectives

As a part of disruptive teaching approaches and strategies, this chapter will

- Explore assistive technology for mainstream settings and learners with special needs.
- Explain the knowledge of LMS.
- Explore the various LMS used in the field of education.
- Explain a few LMS in detail.
- Provide assistance to disruptive education for diverse learners with technology to have effective learning in the new normal.
- Explore the advantages and barriers due to disruptive teaching approaches and strategies in the new normal.

Current Scenario Leading to Disruptive Education

Disruption in the process of teaching created a kind of anxiety and stress in the teaching community. Teachers were ambitious to teach their students during the pandemic (Christensen, 2006). Initially, they started using their Android mobiles to deliver the content and videos on Whatsapp and Facebook, since they are only accustomed to these social media. Slowly teachers and educators started exploring various online modes of teaching such as Zoom, Google Meet, Swivel, Piazza, etc. Teachers did not even have ample time to get training on all these devices; they explored on their own by watching YouTube demonstrations and being assisted by some of the ICT people. Frankly speaking, most of the teachers did not even know the applications provided in the palate of Google. Necessity is the mother of invention; teachers who were not tech-savvy started to explore technology since their only motive was to cater to the needs of their students. I am one among them. To find out some means to get connected to their students and educate the students at large, the class was set with the proper scheduling, organising, supervising the learners' progress, understanding them, and solving their problems online.

Dewey (1986) posited that 'all genuine education comes through experience', a central element of experiential education in which educators 'engage with learners in direct experience and focused reflection to increase knowledge, develop skills, clarify values, and develop people's capacity to contribute to their communities'. There was a huge transition from traditional teaching to complete tech-based online teaching or e-learning, where disruptive education started to bring in a vast change in education for the new normal.

Disruptive innovation in teaching–learning is an emerging revolution in the system. All learners try to embrace it easily compared to the teachers. Disruptive learning has become innovative and popular since it excels the previous types of methods followed in the basis of teaching and learning with technology. Disruptive technology used for the teaching–learning process was something that overturned a traditional model of teaching in all Indian schools, colleges, and higher education institutions into a tech-based model.

Disruptive Learning Definition

Disruptive teaching–learning in the new normal can be replaced by disruptive technology for the teaching–learning process, where technology has played a major role. Christensen (1997), the founder of descriptive technology, states, 'The situation whereby a new technology or innovation takes over functions of a traditional or established technology has been described by as disruptive technology', later this terminology was amended by Christensen and Raynor (2003) to 'disruptive innovation'. The sudden change in the teaching methods and strategies always ended up in innovative teaching methods. Earlier distance education in India did not achieve its importance, and people were under a myth that face-to-face classes and regular school or college education alone can be an effective mode of teaching and that the achievement would be better than distance education. This pandemic has proved that distance learning, coupled with the benefits of disruptive technology, has led to the concept that one can learn in any kind of environment. Provided that the setting has internet capability, students can excel in the learning process. As a result of this pandemic, disruptive technologies are used to explore the teaching–learning process from primary grades to higher education.

Disruptive innovation in education during the pandemic is a sudden break in the education system itself, which has completely changed the established traditional education system with disruptive technology. Face-to-face classes are practiced all the time, but they were suddenly facing the digital revolution due to COVID-19. Now after a year and a half has passed, the existing systems with a few digital-based platforms are ensured to disseminate knowledge to students in virtual mode. We shall discuss a few digital devices, explored and used by teachers, and being a teacher in higher education, I will also add my personal experience and hands-on experience in this disruptive innovation. I am still striving to learn more and explore the disruptive learning. This chapter will focus on the transformation of a classroom environment into a Virtual Learning Environment (VLE) by the disruptive teaching approaches and strategies for the learners in the new normal.

Disruptive Teaching Approaches and Strategies for Higher Education Learners

Christensen (1997), in his book, *The Innovator's Dilemma*, separates new technology into two categories: sustaining and disruptive. 'Sustaining technology relies on incremental improvements to an already established technology. In contrast, disruptive technology lacks refinement, often has performance problems because it is new, appeals to a limited audience, and may not yet have a proven practical application'). Various kinds of learning can be brought under the umbrella of disruptive innovation in which distance education provides education where the instructor is away from the learner, and may be connected with the learner online or through sending study material to facilitate the student. The student does not have face-to-face contact with the teacher, but all other assistance would be provided to the student. It is also called as D-Learning. On the other hand, distributing the learning process through a general term described as the multi-media method of delivering the content to the learners. A multi-media method is a mixed method consisting of web-based learning through instructional strategies, video lecturing, face-to-face classroom with discussion sessions, television, and radio (KusumYada, 2019).

John Chambers, the CEO of Cisco Systems, stated in 1999 that there will be a period where education will be dependent on the internet. According to his views, the people of information technology and communication specialists will be the next big killer application. It will be so big that it will consume the internet that will make email usage look like a rounding error. There are a large number of technology-based education resulting from disruptive innovation. I have explained a few of them on which I had my personal experience (Adelsberger et al., 2008).

Learning during Face-to-Face Classes

This was the oldest and the only favoured method by all teachers before COVID-19, 'teachers had the greater opportunity to look into the physical and mental processes involved in students' activities, their behavioural patterns, and their habits. Individual learning is within the domain of the individuals that result in a set of experiences; those experiences may be positive, negative, or neutral from the teacher's point of view'. This face-to-face approach was put down by the pandemic, and technology-based teaching was enforced, There is always a contradiction between technologies made available and technologies used in practice. There are numerous disruptive technologies for the teaching–learning process. I herewith acknowledge a few where I had hands-on experience during my teaching. These disruptive technologies were easy to use and free of cost. I hope the readers can also try using a few of the disruptive technologies in their teaching.

E-learning during the Pandemic and the New Normal: online learning is possible only with the facility of the internet, intranet, extranet, Wifi, and Web (Flavin, 2012). Electronic mail is used for the transmission of messages. As a result of disruptive learning, e-mail boxes were overflowing.

mLearning: learning that took place independent of location in this pandemic is mostly by mobile learning (Alexander, 2004). Students from any place were able to attend class through an Android mobile made it possible through the use of mobile devices. Mobile is multipurpose and especially in the hands of students, it is an effective device if they could use it prospectively (Kukulska-Hulme, 2007). I was astonished to see students preparing a complete project using only their mobile device. The PPT presentation was also done effectively. This shows that disruption leads to innovation. Students used various LMS platforms through mobile devices. Various apps were explored and downloaded by students and teachers for the teaching–learning process. mLearning is a device that can be used spontaneously, personally, informally, contextually, portable, and cost-effective.

Google is a hub technology. There is still a debate of whether it is an LMS or not. It consists of Google Classroom. Google Docs is used for document creation. ePals enables global classroom for learning. Emaze is for creating presentations in a collaborative platform. Wikispaces, Genius, ChalkUp, and Google Hangouts, sheets, Slides, Gmail, and Calendar, along with open educational resources, are used for online learning (Singh, 2016). Google Scholar acts as the HEI's academic journal aggregator. Google Classroom has been the most used by almost all teachers during the pandemic, and I felt it comfortable and easily accessible to take classes in Google Meet, as the lectures can be recorded and uploaded for the students as videos for further references. Teachers can assign work for students with a title and deadline for submission. A teacher can also evaluate the students' assignment and send them back with comments. Material for study in pdf can be attached. Google form survey is a very useful tool to collect data. The classroom theme can be set on the wall with colours and the school logo. Effective communication and sharing of knowledge were adorable. It is free for everyone; any individual can benefit.

Massive Open Online Courses (MOOCs), the term came into use in 2008, A MOOC is a course of study made online with the facility of the internet. It can cater to the student community free of cost. It is a learning management system (Flouty, 2016). There are hundreds of MOOC providers. Leeds University and Open University in 2016 facilitated students with credits for the final degree by undertaking a MOOC course. The major MOOC providers today are Coursera, Udacity, edX, Udemy, and FutureLearn. The material prepared is by the top professors and a chance of learning different languages. Higher Education institutions bring awareness of MOOCs, and it is found all over the world entering the education system. The open education system was already an existing system. Now, it has got new opportunities for disruptive innovation in higher education after COVID-19. Though there were various courses available in online mode, now only higher education institutions have started to take up new online learning models and innovative teaching practices.

Moodle is used in teaching–learning as disruptive innovation, and it is a content management system. It is also a free open-source software package for educators with a single robust desire to create an integrated learning system. It can be downloaded on our web server. It has got unique learning strategies such as gamification, competency-based education, accessible grade books, and an interactive online classroom where discussion can be done with the teacher and the peer group (Ambika, 2018). Moodle development includes security by design. A teacher can see the entry and exit times.

Piazza was designed by PoojaNath in 2009 to experience a real class discussion. Her struggles in the classroom inspired her to create Piazza (Piazza. 2009). It aims to give high-quality question-and-answer sessions online for students to learn together. The name Piazza has arrived from an Italian word for 'plaza', which means a city square where people come together to share knowledge and ideas. Thus, this platform tries to recreate a communal atmosphere among students and teachers.

Edmodo is again an educational network that helps connect students in a free learning management system. Student planners and discussion threads are the highlighted resources in Edmodo. Here all students can get answers to their difficult questions. It is easy to create groups, post in the quiz, submit assignments, and get grades. It is safe and reliable software to be used by learners.

Prezzi is used for presentation instead of a normal PowerPoint presentation. **Quizizz** is a free tool. Hundreds of ready-made Quizizz are present on the website, and teachers also can create their quizzes and make teaching–learning interesting. **Kahoot** is a game-based learning platform for learners. Xtranormal, Wordle, Wallwisher, and Delicious are also a few of the interesting teaching–learning platforms (Kahoot. 2012).

Flipped Classroom Approach

The flipped classroom was invented by Jonathan Bergman and Aaron Sams in the year 2007, A flipped classroom is a form of blended classroom wherein the teacher sends a lecture of a pre-recorded video and the content of that subject will be discussed in the classroom (Hamdan & McKnight, 2013). This is typically a reverse format of the traditional classroom. The students are inclined towards self-learning, and the teacher becomes the facilitator. Disruptive technology has been of great support in the blended learning structure of education. In the future, classes will be face to face as well as online learning. It would completely turn into a child-centric education. Blended learning will offer a multitude of real-world skills. Blended learning is student-centred, and it is the bottom-up approach. Blended learning will be an innovative pedagogical approach in the new normal since it can make the learning resources repeatable, reliable, and reproducible.

The Assistance of Disruptive Technology for Diverse Learners with Technology to Attain Effective Learning in the New Normal

Diverse learners are a group of students with different cognitive abilities in a classroom. The traditional classroom may not fulfil the entire needs of the student. Integration of disruptive technology would result in a better understanding and lead to a better learning outcome for diverse learners. Distance learning is a great solution for diverse learners and differently-abled children. Hybrid teaching online and offline for students results in blended learning and creates a special environment for learners. Assistive technologies used in a virtual classroom become an option for students with special needs to explore and progress in education. The use of disruptive technology teaching helps to create an inclusive classroom. Disruptive technology helps students with any type of disability overcome cognitive problems and physical problems. Sophisticated hardware and software are created for individuals with a disability to work and succeed in the mainstream setting.

Assistive technology can plan, organise, and keep track of calendars, schedules, task lists, etc. The student can treat assistive technology as an executive memory where it can store, manage, and retrieve information when needed (Bradford, 2010). Since the learner may have a poor cognitive ability or memory, there is a wide range of assistive technology tools for reading and writing to make the task easier for diverse learners. **Disruptive innovation is very much useful for the five major differently-abled children with disorders like dyslexia, which affects the reading and writing ability of a student** (Holloway & Dawes, 2016). Dyscalculia affects a person's ability to work. Dysgraphia affects students' handwriting, fine motor skills, hand and eye coordination, verbal, and nonverbal disorders.

Electronic math worksheets help students having trouble handling pen and paper. The numbers appear on the screen and are read aloud with a speech synthesiser. Paper-based computer pen records all lectures as the student writes.

Later when the section of the notes is touched by the pen, the recorded voice related to that content will be played, by portable word processors, Talking Calculators, Personal FM listening systems, variable sound recorders, speech synthesisers, alternative keyboards, graphic organisers, proof-reading software, talking spell checkers, and electronic dictionaries. Audiobooks and publications are other disruptive innovations in the inclusive classroom. Certain small applications in our computers can be used for students with learning difficulties such as abbreviation expanders, enlarging the text, numbers, and alphabets for learners to read comfortably, highlighting the colours, and showing videos and pictures related to their subjects. Universal design of learning becomes effective with disruptive innovation.

Disruptive Assistive Technology Used by Special Children and Diverse Learners Globally

Kurzweil 3000 helps students struggling with literacy. It is the leading text to speech assistive tool. Sip and puff systems help students with mobility problems or paralysed students (Stanberry & Raskind, 2009). They just move their face and use the device with the mouth, as a normal person can move the joystick. It is replaced by the keyboard and mouse. Jouse 3 is the best software for Sip and Puff system. Proofreading software like Ginger and Ghotiis used as a spell checker is of great use to dyslexic students having trouble writing the correct spelling of a word. Proloquo2Go, or speech bulbs, is software that helps people with speaking difficulties.

Barriers to Disruptive Innovation

The barriers to disruptive technology may be split into two categories: the student barrier and the teacher barrier (Joseph et al., 2012). In India, there are students from urban and rural backgrounds. At times it is difficult for the student to get connected to the online classroom. They may lack knowledge of using computers, lack access to resources, lack self-confidence, and lack peer relationships. All these factors lead to stress and anxiety in students, whereas on the other end, educators or teachers face numerous problems. For example, many of the educators do not know how to use technology. The administration may not provide ample facilities for online teaching. Lack of vision and leadership, difficulty in taking attendance, no emotional connection with the students, and cheating on exams will become common.

Conclusion

Online learning has significantly reduced the barriers of time and distance for the delivery of education to adult learners and diverse learners. The use of disruptive technologies can be a gatekeeper to acknowledge UGC in its 547th meeting held on 29 May 2020 has discussed the blended mode of teaching. Where 40% of the syllabus of each course other than the SWAYAM can be made online for students. Even after the new normal, all our students will experience 40% of their curriculum in the online mode of education and assessment. The new amendments and decisions by the government are student-centric, and due to this disruptive innovation, are exclusive to the new normal. Policymakers should always consider the welfare of the students and teachers, adopt openness, and make necessary steps to access disruptive education that is affordable for all. Disruptive innovation must create a profitable income for institutions in higher education. Disruptive innovation is a useful lens to view and change teaching methods and to adapt disruptive technology to teach students the new normal (Christensen et al., 2011). This will encourage universities in India to start courses online by setting up open learning platforms, free of cost or with a minimal fee for certification. This facilitation of online learning will be of great boon to the students residing in rural areas, where they need not worry about travelling to the great institutions around the world. They can sit inside the four walls, explore the course, and get their credits. The technology-enhanced learning strategies become effective only when they are put in practice. Students are excited about disruptive technologies since they are the most interesting, as they are the end product of the innovation and creativity of humans to fulfil the need for learning and teaching for diverse learners.

References

Adelsberger, H. H. et al. (2008). *Handbook on Information Technologies for Education and Training* (pp. 577–597). New York, NY: Springer Publishing. doi: 10.1007/978-3-540-74155-8

Alexander, B. (2004). Going Nomadic: Mobile Learning in Higher Education. *EDUCAUSE Review, 39*(5), 28–35. Retrieved from https://er.educause.edu/articles/2004/1/going-nomadic-mobile-learning-in-higher-education

Ambika, K. C. (2018). Study Habits of Students with Reference to Their Electronic Games Playing Hours. *International Journal of Research in Management and Social Science, 6*(1) (VIII) Retrieved from http://empyreal.co.in/downloads/ijrmss-volume6-issue1-viii-january-march-2018.pdf

Bradford, D. (2010). Emerging and Disruptive Technologies for Education: An Analysis of Planning, Implementation, and Diffusion in Florida's Eleven State University System Institutions Electronic Theses and Dissertations, 2004-2019. 4192. https://stars.library.ucf.edu/etd/4192

Christensen, C. (2006). The Ongoing Process of Building a Theory of Disruption. *The Journal of Product Innovation Management, 23*(1), 39–55. Retrieved from https://onlinelibrary.wiley.com/doi/abs/10.1111/j.1540-5885.2005.00180.x

Christensen, C. M. (1997). *The Innovator's Dilemma: When New Technologies Cause Great Firms to Fail.* Boston, MA: Harvard Business School Press: Retrieved from https://www.hbs.edu/faculty/Pages/item.aspx?num=46

Christensen, C. M., & Raynor, M. E. (2003). *The Innovator's Solution: Creating and Sustaining Successful Growth.* Cambridge, MA: Harvard University Press Retrieved from https://www.hbs.edu/faculty/Pages/item.aspx?num=15473

Christensen, C. M., Horn, M. B., & Johnson, C. W. (2011). *Disrupting Class: How Disruptive Innovation Will Change the Way the World Learns.* New York, NY: McGraw-Hill.

Dewey, J. (1986). Experience and Education. The Educational Forum, 50, 241–252. Retrieved from https://www.schoolofeducators.com/wp-content/uploads/

Flavin, M. (2012). Disruptive Technologies in Higher Education. *Research in Learning Technology*, *20*, 102–111. 10.3402/rlt.v20i0.19184

Flavin, M. (2012). Disruptive Technologies in Higher Education. *Research in Learning Technology* Supplement: ALT-C 2012 Conference Proceedings London, UK: Retrieved from https://journal.alt.ac.uk/index.php/rlt/article/download/1352/html?inline=1

Flouty, R. N. (2016). Centralized, Decentralized, Distributed: Disruptive Technology in Distance Education, from Sunrise Semester to Present-Day Moocs. *ERIC Number: ED571902,* City University of New York:NY Retrieved from https://academicworks.cuny.edu/cgi/viewcontent.cgi?article=2301&context=gc_etds

Hamdan, N., & McKnight, P. (2013). A Review of Flipped Learning, Mason University. Retrieved from http://www.flippedlearning.org/domain/46

Holloway, C., & Dawes, H. (2016). Disrupting the World of Disability: The Next Generation of Assistive Technologies and Rehabilitation Practices. *Healthcare Technology Letters* Dec 7, *3*(4), 254–256. doi: 10.1049/htl.2016.0087. PMID: 28008360; PMCID: PMC5168724. http://www.flippedlearning.org/domain/46ISSN: 2455-5746 www.alleducationjournal.com

Joseph, J. et al. (2012). The Barriers of Using Education Technology for Optimizing the Educational Experience of Learners, INTERNATIONAL EDUCATIONAL TECHNOLOGY CONFERENCE, IETC University of Johanensburg, © 2012 Published by Elsevier Ltd doi: 10.1016/j.sbspro.2012.11.051 Retrieved from https://www.sciencedirect.com/science/article/pii/S1877042812050288

KusumYada. (2019). Disruptive Innovative Technologies in Higher Education. *International Journal of Advanced Education and Research*, *4*(49-54) Retrieved from http://www.alleducationjournal.com/archives/2019/vol4/issue1/4-1-22

Kahoot. (2012). Retrieved from https://kahoot.com/what-is-kahoot/Copy right@2022

Kukulska-Hulme, A. (2007). Mobile Usability in an Educational Context: What Have We Learned? *International Review of Research in Open and Distance Learning, 8*(2). Athabasca University, Retrieved from http://www.irrodl.org/index.

Piazza. (2009). Retrieved from https://en.wikipedia.org/wiki/Piazza_(web_service)

Singh, N. (2016). Emerging Disruptive Innovation In Higher Education- A case Study on Online Education Arena. 7th International Conference on Excellence in Research and Education May 5-8, Indore. Retrieved from https://www.researchgate.net/publication/329208902

Stanberry, K., & Raskind, M. H. (2009). Assistive Technology for Kids with Learning Disabilities: An Overview. Reading Rockets Retrieved from https://www.readingrockets.org

Chapter 3

Disruptive Teaching and Learning Strategies for Modern Learners

K. Vijayarani

Department of Education (SDE), Bharathiar University, Coimbatore, Tamilnadu, India

Introduction

The present era is dominated by the digital learning era in which technology plays an inevitable role in knowledge sharing among the masses, across the boundaries of nations. A number of new inventions in the form of technological tools are evolving every day. Changes and innovations have touched all fields, and one such change in our education system that has drastically changed and stepped into a new millennium of learning is online teaching and learning. Among the tonnes of applications in the field of online tools, some are very famous for their accessibility, utility, and user-friendliness. Such software and tools that are very easily utilised are discussed below in this chapter.

Digital Learning

Learning resources are the resources that are prepared and shared in digital formats for access by learners. Access to these resources is made available online on learning

DOI: 10.1201/9781032675176-3

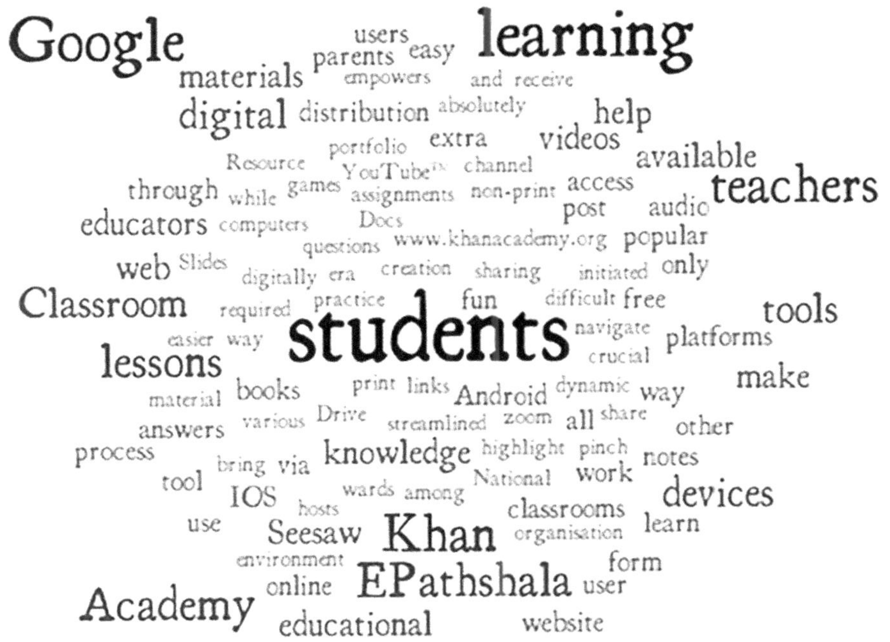

Figure 3.1 Kinds of digital resources (educationworld.in, 2023).

platforms. Digital Library is one in which digital resource collections are made available for learners across geographical boundaries. Databases, books, reports, etc., in electronic form are known as 'digital resources' (Figure 3.1).

Uses of Getting to Know Assets

To involve oneself in learning in a digitally equipped platform, being digitally literate is essential. This includes the calibre to use ICT tools and the media to handle the flood of images, text, and audio-visual content that constantly pours across the globe (Europe's Statistics Society Thematic Portal, 2007).

Advantages of Virtual Sources

- Interactive resources provide immediate feedback to learners.
- Virtual sources provide a variety of learning experiences.
- Digital sources can be used to learn and are available for relearning many times.
- Digital assets are asynchronous: the learner can get entry to them at any time.

- It has by no means been simpler to discover virtual resources on diverse subjects and to percentage them in a path.
- Principles are learned and understood with the help of videos.

E-learning and the Changing Nature of Classrooms

Education at this present time is slowly transforming from a traditional to a modern mode of content delivery through ICT-enabled learning platforms. After working on the slogans such as, 'Education for All', at present, the slogan at the national and international level around the globe is 'Computer and E-Learning for All'.

E-learning has begun to make its way into classrooms in a variety of formats, resulting in a diversification of classroom instruction and activities (learnnovators.com, 2023). The internet/e-learning facilities have now influenced every area of teaching and learning. These can be understood by the following:

- Teachers can prepare the content for teaching from internet sources and books.
- The teacher provides assignments to students where they collect resources and supportive documents online.
- Projects are carried out by the students easily with the help of resources available over the internet.
- The classroom is no longer a default delivery system.
- Due to the knowledge explosion being more accurate, comprehensive, and updated information is available over the internet, which is not available in books.
- Courses are no longer restricted by a strict timetable. Learning time and methods are becoming more flexible as a result of internet availability.
- There will be several online courses available shortly. Although classroom engagement is decreasing, its importance cannot be overstated. Competent teachers will always be needed, and their importance cannot be overstated. Hart (1986) says: 'A load of books does not equal one good teacher'.

Online Digital Learning Resources the Need of the Hour

Digital resources are more useful in sharing updated information and engaging the students in learning. This approach is more student-centric and makes learning interesting. The five digital learning tools that can be used by teachers and students to expand their knowledge and make learning easy and fun are Google Classroom, Seesaw, Khan Academy, E-Pathshala and Kahoot and they are described here (educationworld.in, 2023; education.vic.gov.au, 2023).

Google Classroom

Google Classroom provides access to a variety of online resources to the users of Google free of cost. It helps in accessing a wide range of digital tools in preparing, sharing, and creating content in cloud platforms. It also shares the information in the cloud and makes it readily available anytime for access over the internet. It acts as a bridge between the learner and the teacher in a streamlined way of sharing files. Google Classroom is a platform that combines various tools for teaching and sharing information. Some other important tools that are linked with it are Google Drive, Docs, Sheets, and Slides; Gmail; and Google Calendar (applieddigitalskills.withgoogle.com, 2023).

Seesaw

Seesaw is a knowledge-sharing website that helps college and school goers to use photographs, videos, drawings, text notes, links, and Seesaw, and includes built-in voice recording and drawing capabilities, to enhance their knowledge. Seesaw is available on a variety of platforms, including Chromebooks, desktops, iOS devices, Android devices, and integrated devices, allowing parents access to their children's learning (medium.com, 2023).

Khan Academy

It is a non-profit organisation that was founded to develop integrated line equipment that would assist college students in better understanding various concepts and ideas. The Khan Academy publishes brief built-in integrated shapes of motion pictures on both its YouTube channel and its well-known built-in www.khanacademy.org website. It has built-in supplementary practice sports as well as instructor resources. You may learn for free with Khan Academy. Built-in is available in the form of motion pictures, and built-in. As a result, Khan A can be beneficial to teachers. So teachers can make use of this to replace their built-in and assist students with all or tough content.

E-Pathshala

E-pathshala is a large educational reserve that houses sources for built-in, college students, parents, researchers, and educators. It is available on a variety of platforms, including Android, IOS, and built-in Windows systems. Through ePathshala, students can access all required materials, including textbooks, audio, video, magazines, and a variety of other printable materials, which can be downloaded built-in the person for offline usage with no download limits. E-Pathshala also allows readers to carry as many books as their device will allow. Customers can choose to zoom, highlight, navigate, proportion, and make notes digitally in such books.

Kahoot

Kahoot is one of the important learning platforms, where teachers can upload multiple-choice questions and various types of questions such as choices, fill-ups, and match. Teachers can use this platform to provide game-based activities for the children and engage them in extra questions. This enhances the students to make them more involved in the learning activities and enjoy the fun of learning. This not only complements scholar engagement but also creates a fun-filled instructional surround built integrated.

Multimedia Applications

Many instructional activities benefit greatly from the use of multimedia tools. Students can now create presentations that contain text, graphics, and other media components, rather than just writing essays. Software that extracts photographs directly from sources and inserts them into a composition or essay is easily available.

To create sophisticated video presentations, multimedia software can control and modify sound images from sources such as CD-ROMs and video discs. Multimedia applications are becoming increasingly popular due to their appeal to and usage of a wide range of sights, sounds, and actions that stimulate the senses.

Howard Gardner (2000) and other cognitive psychologists have written about the expanded understanding of the importance of using multiple delivery mechanisms for different learning styles of students. Multimedia learning applications, in particular, are frequently recommended for developing curricula that appeal to diverse learning styles.

The phrase multimedia, often known as 'interactive media' or 'hypermedia', is difficult to describe, which contributes to a lot of misunderstanding. It just implies providing sound to your applications at the most basic level in today's usage of the phrase. At its most complex level, it combines animation, graphics, video, digitally recorded sounds, and text, all of which are managed by a single professional college.

Multimedia applications are interactive, that is through a keyboard, mouse, voice, or external controller such as musical instruments, a digital interface (MIDI) keyboard you interact with the system to control aspects of the presentation. The majority of today's computers rely solely on text displays, sometimes complemented by rudimentary graphics, with stereo sound, animation, and video capabilities introduced later. Multimedia computing provides a richer and more efficient means of communicating information; it allows for the rapid transmission of information in ways that text-only systems cannot.

Multimedia has exploded in popularity in human culture, industry, and education. Multimedia may be applied to almost any type of information we receive,

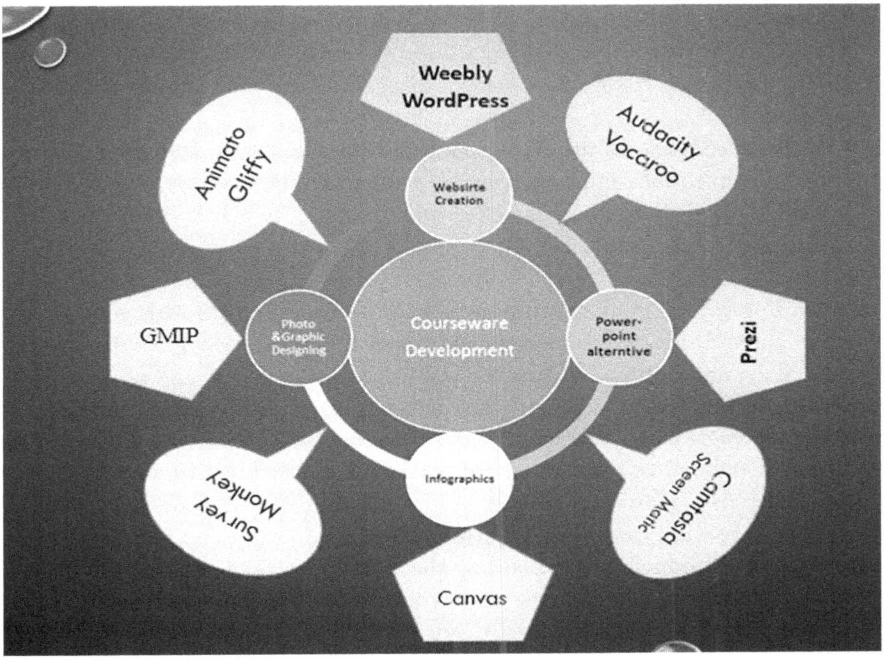

Figure 3.2 Multimedia tools (unicef.org, 2023).

from television to magazines to websites to movies. Multimedia is a powerful tool for both informing and entertaining the audience. Advertising is, without a doubt, one of the most important aspects of any business.

Multimedia in education is incredibly useful in teaching a wide range of subjects to individuals. The human brain learns through a variety of senses, including sight and hearing. Multimedia tools include Wordpress, Animato Gliffy, Audacity Vocaroo, Prezi, Survey Monkey, Canvas, Camtasia (Figure 3.2).

Designing One's Own Multimedia Courseware

When deciding on creating one's own educational material, start by defining the objective, what will be the purpose of it, and also if it will be useful. You may conclude that your target group needs concise, not complex, solutions – in this situation, an OER will not be necessary, but an option could be video material.

Teachers can use videos they have previously downloaded online or record their own videos. Videos effectively utilised in the process of training can be a rich source of information for the educator, facilitating their process of teaching the disabled. Thus, when recording your own lessons, you can achieve two things:

- **Create** personalised digital resources tailored to the needs of your specific group of learners. This material can be shown to learners while a traditional lesson is in the classroom or shared online. Find out how to make a YouTube video.
- **Collect** feedback on the effectiveness of teaching. Learn from your mistakes to then introduce improvements to your teaching style, as well as observe each learner's behaviour to better understand it, which is often impossible during a single lesson. Bill Gates speaks about this practice.

For recording videos, your smartphone should be enough. Although you can also try some audio and video tools with additional functionalities. Examples include Twisted Wave and Loom. The first is a web-based audio editor, and no downloads are required. The second will use your webcam to capture yourself speaking or show the screen of your computer. These are useful tools, especially when you are organising a webinar or need to record material for individual learners.

An interesting solution will also be the creation of whiteboard storytelling, which will have the form of a digital interactive video story and will be an alternative way of introducing or explaining the topic.

When a video is not enough, more complex interactive solutions to choose from can be the use of digital games, instructional mobile apps, or even augmented reality. Any of these can be designed to address the specific disability a learner is facing. When choosing from the already available online solutions, first check yourself if the resource is adequate for your special learner, it may sometimes be a matter of changing the settings to adjust the resource to the abilities of the learner.

Conclusion

This chapter has shed light on a few important tools that are used in the teaching and learning process. The usage of these tools in content creation helps one to provide a better learning experience to the students inside the classroom or through any online teaching platforms. There are numerous online multimedia packages available even though preparing one's own courseware with their understanding and creativity is much more satisfactory and caters to the needs of the learner of that classroom. Even the use of students in the image, videos, and audio of their class makes them more interested and involved in the teaching–learning process.

References

Gardner, H. (2000). *Howard Gardner's Theory of Multiple Intelligences.* https://www.niu.edu/citl/resources/guides/instructional-guide/gardners-theory-of-multiple- intelligences.shtml

Hart. (1986). *A Load of Books Does Not Equal One Good Teacher.* https://www.tribuneindia.com/news/thought-for-the-day/a-load-of-books-does-not-equal-one-good-teacher-%E2%80%94-chinese-proverb-289648

https://learnnovators.com/services/custom-e-learning/?gclid=CjwKCAjw3riIBhAwEiwAzD3TiU2XAzpLwsut4_juDSYVsdrwOOEhsAmT7bksMVwG177lt3GPAXIi2hoCB5AQAvD_BwE Oct 2023

https://www.educationworld.in/top-five-digital-learning-tools-for-students-and-teachers/ Oct 2023

https://www.unicef.org/serbia/en/open-digital-educational-tools-interactive-online-teaching-and-learning, Oct 2023

https://www.education.vic.gov.au/school/teachers/teachingresources/digital/Pages/tools.aspx Oct 2023

https://medium.com/teachers-on-fire/top-ten-learning-tools-for-the-digital-classroom-5b3fefc861b3 Oct 2023

https://applieddigitalskills.withgoogle.com/en/teach Oct 2023

Thematic Portal (2007). *How to Successfully Choose ICT Tools in Early Childhood Education?* https://www.linkedin.com/pulse/how-successfully-choose-ict-tools-early-childhood-michael-hilkemeijer

Chapter 4

Effective Use of Learning Management System for Changing Education Scenario

K.E. Soudha Nalina Kumari
Amirtham College of Education, Kanchipuram, Tamilnadu, India

Introduction

Innovative technologies play an imperative role in the everyday life of people, in this developing world. Modern teaching-learning practices are witnessing continual and significant changes whereby, technology has laid its magnificent base. In addition to this, Davies and Merchant (2009) reported that the understandings and experiences that learners and their teachers have, and need, are rapidly changing as the technology itself changes. As new forms of teaching and learning are emerging, e-learning is considered to be an alternative learning system. On the other hand, there are numerous driving and restricting forces in educating the 21st-century learner who is referred to as the digital native. The use of information and communication technologies (ICT) or digital technology in education is found to be not justifying, and inconsistent with, a focus on the passive delivery of information. Learning is mostly influenced, or stimulated, by external agents, whereby teaching becomes critical (Leamnson, 2000), and thus, embedding digital literacy in education is a challenge for educators and trainers.

DOI: 10.1201/9781032675176-4

Not only higher education but also the school system is not exempted from reacting to this scenario and has implemented ICT into the educational process. Nonetheless, the impact of ICT in education is felt to be relatively trivial. Sarkar (2012) had forecasted that its influence will grow considerably in the upcoming years, and ICT will become a solid representative for change among various educational practices. There are constant efforts being made by educational institutions as well as governing bodies to potentially support the professional development of educators and facilitators in the context of digital literacy and identify its practical implications. For instance, Operation Digital Blackboard launched on 20 February 2019, by the Ministry of Human Resource Development, Government of India, was a massive step to transform nine lakh classrooms belonging to both higher education institutions and schools across the country (Our Bureau, 2019, 20 February). Thus, educators and facilitators can sooner withstand the pressure of new technologies, develop their capacity to address the 'digital challenge', and efficiently switch to various digital learning modes.

As an educator, to excel in handling ICT effectively, one must be a knowledgeable and skilled person to access the internet via computers, phones, and web devices to interact with diverse organisations related to education and training. The robustness of ICT has enabled it to take various forms in educating people across the globe, like open educational resources (OER), learning management systems (LMS), flipped classrooms, blended learning, etc. Globally, there are hundreds of web-based technologies and software products being used by educators and learners to accomplish their learning and training needs. In another sense, when in a new educational setting referred to as e-learning, both educators and learners choose from diverse technologies like television, the internet, computers, software that is appropriate for the online course or programme, and different components like e-books and virtual libraries that belong to virtual universities or learning centres (Snyder, 1998; Rosenberg, 2001). Also, social media is considered to be an integral part of e-learning nowadays (Dalton, 2009; Liu, 2010). Ultimately, among the various technologies, LMS is being greatly insisted on by the technologist for the effortless management of various aspects of education. LMS has proven its versatility in diverse zones like e-commerce, small to large business enterprises, corporate training, and education, too.

Learning Management System Is for Knowledge Management

LMS is a software application or web technology used to plan, design, strategise, implement, and assess a specific learning process. LMS needs to be understood well before becoming its beneficiary. The primary use of a LMS according to

Brush (2019) is knowledge management, i.e., produce, manage, and integrate knowledge. To be specific, LMS is not just a simple application that is used by software experts, but rather, it is a largely essential tool to manage the entire learning process. It ranges from managing training and educational records to distributing online or blended courses. This software-dependent learning environment provides a comprehensive set of tools for educators to manage administrative functions, and learning resources (create and deliver content), and keep track of student progress by assessments (observe, evaluate, and grade student performance). It is a comprehensive, online platform for virtual course delivery with a range of instructional resources and strategies. It supports students, instructors, and administrators with communicative and collaborative tools that result in personalised and fruitful learning experiences.

Even during the COVID-19 pandemic situation, educational institutions were striving to give their best to their students who were currently remote learners. Additionally, many higher education institutions have started using LMS to deliver online courses and augment on-campus courses. Lyashenko and Malinina (2015) have reported that the National Research University, the Higher School of Economics (HSE) Nizhny Novgorod developed a specific LMS-based product in 2010, created as a non-institutional collaborative learning platform for teachers and students. The mission of the Government of India, as mentioned earlier on the makeover of usual blackboards into digital boards, is a sample for advancing towards LMS. This will enhance the quality, ease the access to e-resources for learners, endorse personalised learning, encourage dynamic teachers and intelligent tutors, and explore the latest technologies like machine learning, artificial intelligence, and data analytics. Further, initiatives like e-Pathshala, National Repository of Open Educational Resources (NROER), National Programme on Technology Enhanced Learning (NPTEL), SWAYAM, DIKSHA, etc. providing suitable and quality content, thus facilitating blended and flip class learning (Drishti, 2019, February 21), are examples of LMS implementation in the Indian context.

The education system aims to provide qualitative, systematic, and authentic information support to all its stakeholders, namely students, teachers, administrators, educational institutions, various academic faculties, parents, and society at large. Eventually, LMS focuses on attaining the following:

- Providing an active learning environment.
- Enabling optimal learning of all the participants via both online and offline learning.
- Upsurging students' involvement in all dimensions of the learning process.
- Strengthening the interaction between students and teachers.
- Improving the digital skills of teachers and students.
- Offering an individual approach to the teaching–learning process.

In short, LMS could be represented as a multifaceted boon that has transformed into a mandatory domain of education, especially in the present scenario when lockdown does not surprise us.

Types of Learning Management Systems

Apart from knowing the purpose of LMS in education, it is also essential to understand the types of LMS. To attain the objectives of education, matching our resources and parameters with the possible types of LMS and choosing the suitable one is advisable. There are numerous parameters upon which choosing an LMS relies. According to Alphalearn (2021), there are two types of classifications of LMS based on i) licensing and ii) hosting nature, as given below (Figures 4.1 and 4.2).

i. **LMS based on Licensing**
   Licensing is a vital factor to be considered while selecting an LMS that falls within the requirements and preferences. Based on licensing there are two types of LMSm namely open-source and closed-source.
   a. Open-Source LMS: in this type, all products are free, and they can be customised according to the needs of the organisation. Frequent check-ups of servers are done by field experts. Scalability or limiting the number of users relies on the internal architecture. Compatibility is found for third-party incorporation, and the security issues depend on whether the LMS community is active or not. However, reliable technical support is not provided. If one can code and customise their learning system, then one can opt for this.
   Examples: Android and WordPress Moodle and Chamilo

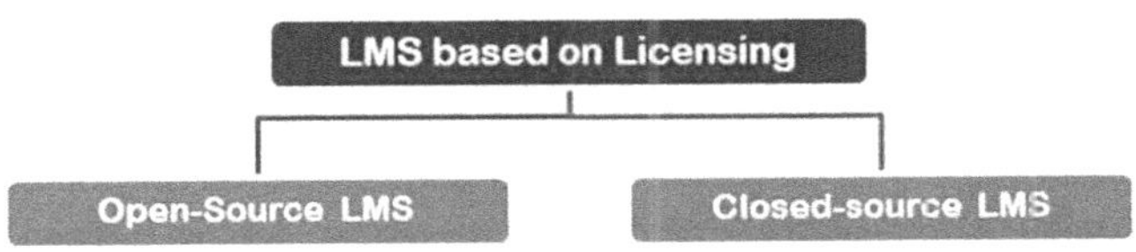

Figure 4.1 Types of LMS based on the nature of the licensing opted.

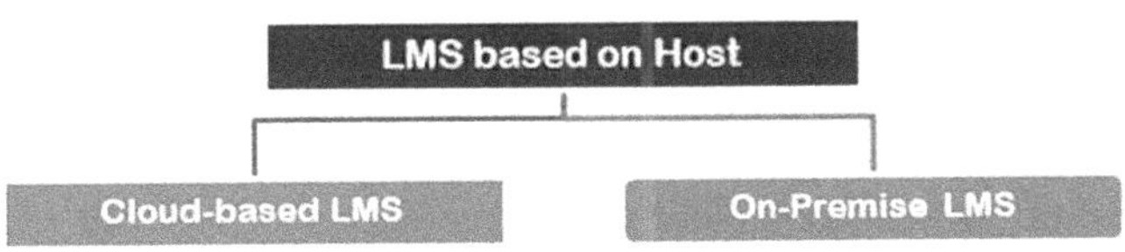

Figure 4.2 Types of LMS based on the nature of the host opted.

b. Closed-Source LMS: in this type, the code is not shared, and all products are payable. This adopts an annual subscription format, and payment is based per user. There are additional payment packages for customisation requirements, third-party integrations, and technical support. It can be hosted on a self-server or even can be hosted on a vendor server by barring additional charges. Hosting on a vendor server guarantees efficient scalability along with the security and stability of data. If someone does not wish to keep bothering with coding, technical support, updates, and data security and also can bear the cost, they can hand it over to closed-source LMS.
   Examples: Sqaurespace and iPhone AlphaLearn and Docebo

ii. **LMS based on hosting nature**
   Another important factor in choosing an LMS is the kind of implementation or the nature of the host. There are two types of hosts, namely cloud-based LMS and on-premise-based LMS. Understanding these along with their merits and demerits is vital.
   a. Cloud-based LMS: this is also referred to as Software-as-a-Service (SaaS) LMS or web-based LMS. This is hosted on an external cloud server. In this type, customisation is limited. The performance is reliable; however, additional payments can avoid occasional slowdowns. Reliable data security options are provided. The cost for this type of LMS is also affordable.
   b. On-Premise LMS: this is also referred to as in-house or self-hosted LMS, whereby the codes are fully purchased. This permits better performance, greater security and control options, and wider customisation features like changing codes and integrations. But this is expensive in terms of the operating system, implementation, maintenance, and other hidden costs.

Basic Features of Learning Management System

Learning management system (LMS) is recognised to be well-associated with the eLearning process. The role of an LMS relies on the objectives of the organisation, the e-Learning course, the requisites of an online training programme, and the expected outcomes. The general use of LMS in education is to organise the learning process, store resources like learning material, conduct the course, and track online learning and training initiatives. Through LMS, the uploaded resource materials are easily accessed by learners who are in remote places. But to understand the worth of investing in LMS, a closer look into the features is essential. This sub-heading intends to explain the characteristics of LMS in relation to the educational process. An effective LMS acts as a vast repository that is capable of multitasking with the following features (Figure 4.3).

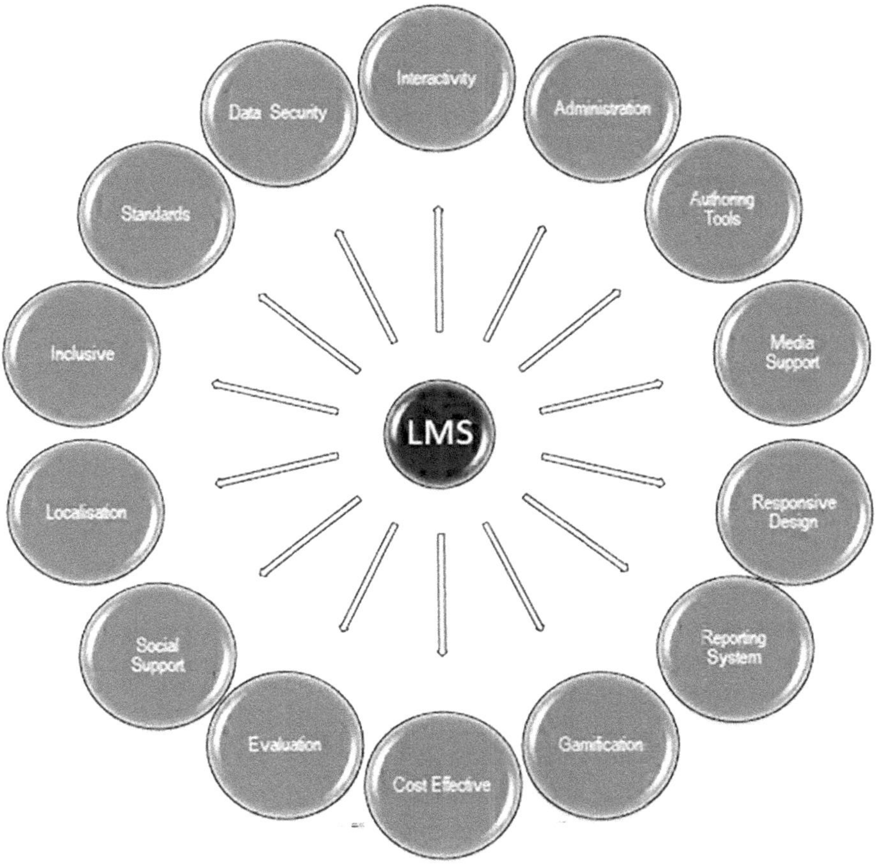

Figure 4.3 Basic features of a learning management system.

1. **Interactive learning environment:** there are numerous synchronous (Whiteboard, Teleconferencing, and Chat Rooms) and asynchronous (Messaging, Bulletin Boards e-mail, and Discussion Forums) methods in LMS to strengthen and maximise the communication between students–teachers and teachers–teachers.
2. **Efficient administration:** LMS manages the learners as well as the staff records, introduces the online courses, allows easy and quick access to resource materials by the learners, enables the instructors to smoothly conduct the course, and tracks and reports learners' progress. In addition, it performs all other essential administrative functions.
3. **Authoring tools:** these tools enable the instructors to develop e-learning courses easily and have provisions for including navigation buttons, pictures, videos, and evaluations. For example, SCORM formats the online

content to be shared across the board. In some cases, the built-in authoring tools allow the development of online materials.

4. **Media support:** an efficient LMS platform supports the learners in overall achievement by adopting numerous file formats like Flash, Shockwave, MP3, MP4, and Rich Text.
5. **Responsive design:** this refers to the multiplatform-friendly online resources that allow all kinds of learners to benefit, irrespective of their device (smartphones, tablets, computers, etc.).
6. **Reporting system:** a robust reporting system exists within the LMS, to determine if the objectives of the online course are attained or need any modifications in the process, determine the percentage of the audience completing the online training or learning course requirements, determine the average time taken to complete it, etc.
7. **Gamification features:** while learning through LMS, online learners could be made to actively engage by allowing them to play games in between the learning process and motivate them through virtual rewards, badges, points, and leaderboards. Also, some of the learning content could be effortlessly learned through gaming. Some of the LMS have built-in gamification features.
8. **Cost effective:** an effective LMS will reduce administrative cost. There are two types of LMS based on the licensing cost of products, which are explained earlier in this chapter.
9. **Evaluation:** this involves the roles of assessment and tracking the progress. LMS like Moodle, Canvas, Google Classroom, ILIAS, etc. allows monitoring and testing online learning on individual and group levels. For example, identify the learners' engagement with the online content, assess learners' performance, and track individual skill and performance gaps. This means various modules like assignments, quizzes, questioning, gaming, chat, survey, and discussion from the extent of participation and performance of students can be assessed.
10. **Social learning support:** integrated social media tools like chat, a news feed, and a discussion forum allow learners to obtain moral support from each other and share their experience with peers.
11. **Localisation:** to provide the same opportunity to all the learners participating in the course, multiple languages are used to teach the learners; hence, the course can be delivered globally.
12. **Inclusive nature:** as mentioned earlier, SCORM-compliant guarantees the interoperability that facilitates the user's access from various devices such as smartphones, tablets, and laptops. The Learning Tools Interoperability (LTI) was introduced by IMS Global Learning Consortium for the applications that are remotely hosted.
13. **Adherence to standards:** LMSs support standards, such as SCORM and AICC.

14. **Data security:** an LMS with better quality ensures data security. For example, Open-Source LMS has limitations in security matters and depends on the activeness of the e-learning team, whereas the vendor server in the closed-source LMS guarantees data security.

Benefits of Using LMS Platforms for Education

The features of LMS speak volumes about the numerous benefits LMS offers to an organisation focusing on education. Here are some of the key benefits of LMS in education.

- LMS effectively handles the administrative functions essential for online learning.
- It delivers course content in an organised manner with a range of delivery methods.
- Effective pedagogical practices enhance the proficiency and performance of the learners.
- The personalisation feature enables users to assign different learning paths to individual learners based on their needs and goals.
- It accommodates learners' diverse interests, learning preferences, learning styles, pace, and skill levels.
- It fosters greater interaction and collaboration between the learners and teachers without geographical limitations.
- It encourages peer-to-peer, learner-centred, and active learning strategies.
- Access to learning materials and tools can be controlled by the learners.
- Learning resources can be utilised before or after the class, i.e., 24/7 accessibility so that students' learning can be enriched.
- The flexible learning environment allows the learners to achieve even if they are not physically available.
- By this, higher education reaches a large group of learners who are globally spread out, in a shorter duration, with reliable content delivery.
- Instructors utilise the class time more effectively by using diverse tools as per the learning situation.
- Communicative and collaborative tools in the LMS lead to better follow-up or feedback along with bringing an overall improvement in the teaching–learning situation.
- LMS stores and organises huge data in a single location and enables it to update and maintain.
- Advanced encryptions enable highly secured data management.
- Constant monitoring of learner engagement and performance assessment is possible.

- It effectively allocates resources by evaluating the goals achieved by the module and updating learning assets to deploy on a global scale.
- It saves travelling time and eliminates allied costs.
- It improves technical skills related to computers and the internet.
- The centralised learning atmosphere guarantees consistency in learning.

Challenges in Experiencing the Benefits of LMS

Undoubtedly, an LMS offers innumerable benefits and is advantageous to all its stakeholders. However, it is evidenced in research that there are certain barriers prevailing in various aspects related to education. Some of the problems related to institutions in LMS implementation are financial constraints, lack of technical and content experts, unavailability of resources, poor internet connectivity, problems in choosing the suitable LMS software, etc. Pratt (2005) stated that as per researchers' view, clear principles regarding implementation have not been formulated so far. On the other end, Lyashenko and Malinina (2015) reported that the challenges that are faced by both educators and learners in using LMS are linked with the tools and technologies. The reluctance of teachers may be listed as their resistance and fear towards the latest technologies, rigidity to change, lack of tech skills, and motivational deficiency. Besides, teachers blame time consumption, failures of the internet and other technical services, and overuse of social media by students. This is only a portion of the problems in implementing LMS for educational purposes.

Media literacy among networked teens is enormously mixed, and they lack training in media literacy (Boyd, 2009). In a study, Livingstone et al. (2011) showed that among students almost 50% were not able to handle privacy settings of profiles on social networks, 37% were not skilled in secured online surfing, 36% did not know how to bookmark a website, and over 50% were unable to block spam. A study on LMS usage by Thiruselvi (2015) reported that students chiefly used Calendars & Announcements and Accessibility features, followed by the use of Learning Materials, Assignments and Quizzes; and they rarely used or avoided most of the advanced features of LMS like Discussion Forums, Chats & e-mail, Instant Messaging, Wikis & Blogs, and Glossaries & Surveys. This shows that the learners are selectively looking for the LMS features related to academic events and timetables, resource material to get good grades, and immediate feedback from the teachers but are not being benefited to the fullest extent. Some other reasons could be poor interest in asynchronous communications of the discussion forum, time consumption, lack of academic communication among peers through LMS, poor communication with the teacher by messages, and habitual usage of private e-mail services.

Conclusion

Though there are various challenges in implementing and using LMS, the facilities provided by the institutions allow the students and teachers to access and benefit from LMS effortlessly. This also makes the human resource management of an organisation very simple and clear. Thus, universities and higher education institutions must encourage using LMS (Ulmer and Leech, 2005). The process of uploading, downloading, and submitting an assignment or other projects is smoothly carried out through LMS. Apart from this, teachers can save time by manually maintaining records of their students' progress. So, educators at all levels must play an active role in LMS integration processes (Doherty and Honey, 2006). The best advantage of LMS is that the progress of students is kept transparent for their parents, and they can also check the important events and payment dates. Certainly, suitable and regular use of all these LMS features may enable students to get better grades and credits.

References

Boyd, D. (2009, May 16). Answers to questions from Twitter on teen practices, Apophenia. Zephoria. https://www.zephoria.org/thoughts/archives/2009/05/16/answers_to_ques.html

Brush, K. (2019, December 30). Learning Management System (LMS). SearchCIO. https://searchcio.techtarget.com/definition/learning-management-system

Dalton, A. (2009). Teaching and learning through social networks, TeachingEnglish, British Council. Retrieved from http://www.teachingenglish.org.uk/articles/teaching-learning-through-social-networks

Davies, J., & Merchant, G. (2009). Web 2.0 for schools. New York-2009 Thomas A. Bailey-"Democrats vs. Republicans"-New York-1968 Manuel Merz-"Wahlkampfim Internet"-2. Auflage-Berlin-2009.

Doherty, I., & Honey, M. (2006). Taking ownership of technology: lecturers as LMS learners. *Proceedings of the 23rd Annual Conference of the Australasian society for computers in learning in tertiary education: Who's learning? Whose technology?* http://www.ascilite.org.au/conferences/sydney06/proceeding/pdf_papers/p35.pdf.

Leamnson, R. (2000). Learning as biological brain change. *Change: The Magazine of Higher Learning, 32*(6), 34–40. 10.1080/00091380009601765

Liu, Y. (2010). Social media tools as a learning resource. *Journal of Educational Technology Development and Exchange, 3*, 101–114.

Livingstone, S., Haddon, L., Görzig, A., & Ólafsson, K. (2011). *Risks and safety on the internet: The perspective of European children. Full Findings*. LSE, London: EU Kids Online.

Lyashenko, M., & Malinina, I. (2015). The use of learning management system projects for teaching a foreign language in the University. *Procedia - Social and Behavioral Sciences, 182*, 81–88. 10.1016/j.sbspro.2015.04.741

Our Bureau. (2019, February 20). HRD ministry launches operation digital board. @ businessline. https://www.thehindubusinessline.com/news/education/hrd-ministry-launches-operation-digital-board/article26319604.ece

Operation digital board. (2019, February 21). Drishti IAS. https://www.drishtiias.com/daily-updates/daily-news-analysis/operation-digital-board

Pratt, J. (2005). The fashionable adoption of on-line learning technologies in Australian universities. *Journal of the Australian and New Zealand Academy of Management, 11*(1), 57.

Rosenberg, M. J. (2001). *E-learning: Strategies for delivering knowledge in the digital age*. New York, NY: McGraw-Hill.

Sarkar, S. (2012). The role of information and communication technology (ICT) in higher education for the 21st century. *The Science Probe, 1*(1), 30–41. Retrieved from http://thesciprobe.com/files/documents/5-The-Role-of-Information-and-Communication-Technology-_ICT_-In-Higher-Education-for-The-21st-Century.pdf

Snyder, I. (Ed.) (1998). *Page to screen: Taking literacy into the electronic era*. New York, NY: Routledge.

Thiruselvi, P. (2015). Usability and Accessibility Features of Learning Management System and its relation to Learning Styles [Doctoral dissertation]. http://hdl.handle.net/10603/233205

Ulmer, J., & Leech, J. (2005). Learning management deployment and integration: policy, requirements, and technical solutions In G. Richards (Ed.), *Proceedings of World Conference on e-learning in Corporate, Government, Healthcare, and Higher education*, pp. 1137–1142, *2005*. http://en.wikipedia.org/wiki/Learning_management_system

What is a Learning Management System (LMS) - Everything You Need to Know. (2021). ALPHALEARN. https://www.alphalearn.com/learning-management-system/

Chapter 5

Blended Learning: A Novel Approach in Pedagogy

A. Tholappan and A. Ajumunisha Ali Begam
Department of Education, Centre for Distance Education, Bharathidasan University, Tiruchirappalli, Tamilnadu, India

Introduction

Education is a prerequisite in all shades of life. Education is the tool to understand the world, to develop as an independent individual, and to address the hardships of life. The educational field has undergone a diverse range of modifications to enhance itself to compete with societal requirements. Educationists supplement the sector with all forms of changes to reinvent the education system. The basic aim of education has deviated from its scratch of providing knowledge to the art of creating erudite minds with all possible skills required to attain global needs. This perspective of education associates with enormous challenges in achieving such aims and visions. Every decade imprinted its variation in education. This modern era has completely revamped the centre of focus from teacher-centred to learner-centred. Parents and learners are looking for the best educational opportunities. To meet these expectations, educationists have taken into consideration future perspectives and thus came out with the contemplated reflection of utilising digital advancements in the teaching–learning process. This brings the concept of blended learning into the picture. This chapter deals with the overview of blended learning and its various dimensions in detail.

DOI: 10.1201/9781032675176-5

Recent Trends in Learning and Teaching

Everywhere, there is a change of trends in almost all sectors. In today's modern world, there are different ways of learning and teaching styles. The COVID-19 calamity is changing the educational topography in unpredictable ways. It's tough to judge what's going to happen in the upcoming educational year. Teaching will likely continue to make use of computerised technology for the foreseeable future. A few of the recent trends in teaching and learning are detailed below.

- **Self-care** – Because of the pandemic the whole events of the world swapped. At the moment, teachers are ahead with assignments to manage the students' stress. Self-care is needed in the present scenario.
- **Blended learning** – It helps the teacher to constantly engage and motivate the students.
- **Personalised learning** – It depends on the student's knowledge. It helps them to show their skills, talent, and interests and also they learn about them, e.g., one-to-one tutoring, online games.
- **Gamification** – Game-based learning, e.g., Likely, quiz, using pictures, bingo cards, dice games, etc.
  e.g., Khan Academy, Duolingo, Quizlet.
- **STEAM curriculum (Science, Technology, Engineering, and Math)** – It's the area that clears students' queries and stimulates the students' critical thinking.
  e.g., Mirror symmetry, bridge building challenge, water cycle in a bag.
- **Experiential learning** – Students learn by doing and by reflecting on their experience. It helps to absorb the real-world situations.
  e.g., Field trips, open-ended questions.
- **Genius hour** – This is a new educational technique. Every day students work on their self-paced and self-chosen project for an hour. It shows students' interest and critical thinking.
  e.g., Creating and researching.
- **Digital citizenship** – Here, students wish to have a healthy relationship to digital technology. Good digital citizenship is needed for today's scenario.
  e.g., The use of the mouse, computer skills.
- **Bite-sized learning** – It's also known as microlearning, breaking down information into small pieces. It gives essential information only.
  e.g., Format of videos, games, and infographics.
- **Social-Emotional Learning (SEL)** – It develops self-control and self-awareness among students. They learn a better understanding of social-emotional skills.
  e.g., Responsible decision-making, self-management.
- **Project-based learning** – Students learn through projects for a while that investigate questions, complex challenges, etc.
  e.g., Designing an app, student's farm.

Blended Learning – Meaning, Definition, Concepts, Features, and Importance

Meaning of Blended Learning

Blended learning is a style of teaching–learning process that involves online educational tools or materials, which provides an immense opportunity for the students in their learning process. In this era of digital education, blended learning is a bridge between the online mode of education and the traditional mode of education, where face-to-face schoolroom activities are amalgamated with technologically mediated activities in the process of syllabus, subject, and delivery. A convenient learning experience and enriched practical experience are ensured by blended learning, which is much needed in this sudden outpouring digital world.

Definition of Blended Learning

Margaret Driscoll (2002) defines blended learning as meaning 'to combine any forms of instructional technology (for e.g., videotape, CD-ROM, Web-based training, film) with face-to-face instructor-led training'.

Procter defined blended learning in 2003 as 'the effective combination of different modes of delivery, models of teaching and styles of learning'.

Launer defines blended learning as 'the combination of technology-supported self or distance study settings and face-to-face settings'.

Concept of Blended Learning

As we are in the trend of student-centred learning, it is that much more important to indulge students in activities that promote deeper learning, reduce stress, and increase students' satisfaction. Blended learning is an instructional strategy that combines eye-to-eye schoolroom activities with computer-mediated activities to deliver the content. It is an amalgamation of synchronous and asynchronous learning tools, thus leading to a creation of a constructive environment for the knowledge-gearing process, thereby increasing the effectiveness of students' learning. In this educational approach, educators and students are meant to be physically in the same space. This blended learning enhances the student–teacher relationship as blended learning frees up time in class. This is because resources like podcasts, video lectures, recordings, and other online components are equipped in the classroom activities to transfer enormous knowledge to the students by the teacher before each class.

Importance of Blended Learning

ICT being the talk of the town, tech-savvy is one of the paramount desires for an individual to survive in this world. As blended learning acquaints computer literacy to the future strength of the world such as greater access to information, enhanced digital fluency, communication, etc. The education system in India is suffering from numerous enigmas like deficit in quality education, failure in providing free and compulsory education, teachers not fully dedicated, and teacher's inefficiency is creating a bad impact on children's education. Blended learning to some extent is serving as a tool to overcome these sufferings in the Indian education system. Blended learning provides a wider area for the educational sector as it paves the way for a variety of learning activities, including information assimilation and making teaching productive. Technology and the scientific domain is the most dynamic area, which requires tech-savvy human sources to work in their field, but the Indian education system is not revised or updated according to recent trends. Blended learning leads Indian education to step ahead towards the techno era, by incorporating knowledge and skills required for the 21st century.

Principles of Blended Learning

A few of the notable principles of blended learning are

Consistency: the focus of blended learning is not on the technology. Instead, it is on the learners. With consistent teaching, the on-site face-to-face interaction is maximised.

Mindset: it is very important to bring the attention of the students before the learning process. The environment provides the preparedness, and for that, a strategic plan and alignment of sessions, access, and equity for all is needed. Mindset or preparedness is not important only for students, but for teachers, also..

Social connection: it is a process of creating a connected learning experience. Learning happens best when people and technology are brought together in innovative ways. Verbally or nonverbally, students can work together without minding of the distance when there is a right blended environment..

Clarity: clarity is the basic trait in all teaching–learning activities. To get success in clarity, use of simply accessible languages can be done. The educating process can start with a 'heading' format continuing with bullet points when possible.

Direction: the educators must ensure that the inquiry moves to resolution. No matter what kind of technology is being used, students always need a teacher with strong classroom management skills and the ability to set up a positive classroom culture.

Variety: in blended learning, multiple types of activities can be included to support learning differences. The main goal is not to focus on making the technology exciting but to make it fit seamlessly into the curriculum.

Assessment: assessment or feedback is the final principle in blended learning. It is to make improvements based on students' input. A purposeful practice when combined with informative assessment is a hallmark of effective teaching in a blended learning framework.

Types of Blended Learning

When formal teaching methods are merged with technology, it is termed blended learning. There are various types of blended learning, all of which determine the percentage to which technology is merged in instruction.

Station Rotation Blended Learning

This model is designed in a way that an instructor introduces the topic or content to the students. Then, the students are segregated into groups and taught through different online learning stations using technology. Finally, formative assessments are done by the tutors.

Lab Rotation Blended Learning

It is the same as the station rotation blended learning, but it is enabled only with school computer labs and teachers deliver the content through computer labs in an innovative way.

Remote Blended Learning

This model is also called enriched virtual blended learning. In this type of learning, students focus on completing the coursework online mode. It would be like flipped learning to learn the content independently, but teachers act as a facilitator and guide to clarify the doubts of the learners.

Flex-Blended Learning

This method of learning takes place on a school campus, but a majority of the content is delivered online. Let's assume a classroom, where all the learners have laptops. The content is delivered online but in a formal class setting.

Flipped-Classroom Blended Learning

Here, students learn the subject matter at residence and the practical activities take place in school. In this model, the teacher assists the students.

Individual Rotation Blended Learning

In this method of learning, personification must develop student learning by enacting the individual schedules or assignments given by the instructor.

Project-Based Blended Learning

Here, students do the project work with the help of online resources.

Self-Directed Blended Learning

Students use both online and face-to-face interaction with the teachers to enhance their personalisation. Students connected with teachers physically and also digitally. The main role of the teachers is to guide the students in the correct path by judging them accordingly with respect to their autonomy and self-criticism.

Outside-in and Inside-out Blended Learning

Projects can be completed by going from outside of the classroom and ending up in the classroom. The contradictory part is true inside out where it starts in the classroom but ends up outside of it.

Supplement Blended Learning

Students explore more by what they learn in a traditional classroom by implementing it online or else what they learn from the online resources they can experience that knowledge in face-to-face learning.

Models of Blended Learning

In 2010, the United States Department of Education researchers said, blended learning classes statistically showed improved results than face-to-face, non-hybrid classrooms. This model is a quickly progressing model that implies flexibility and self-learning experiences and also allows teachers to extend the time they spare for a guided learning process. Schools switch over to blended learning for a diverse cause. There are eight models of blended learning. They are as follows:

Face-to-Face Driver Model

The face-to-face driver model is correlated to an accurate school curriculum. In this model, the preface of the digital manual is predetermined on an individual case basis, meaning only a definite pupil in a grade will play an active role in any form of blended learning model. The face-to-face driver approach permeates learners who are working beyond their standard level to gain knowledge at their own pace using advanced technology in the classroom.

Rotation Model

In this model of blended learning, students pivot between various stations on an allotted schedule – educators work online or with traditional ways of teaching. This model is broadly used in schools. The rotational model of blended learning was persistent to be an adequate mode of raising the success level of a student's ambition. Students used the intelligent adaptive learning software to learn math theories and a usual classroom through this model. Students become more participative in all activities, perform hard, and acquire tangible things that they never applied in their math class environment.

Flex Model

Institutions that are encouraging a non-traditional way of teaching for students often select the flex model of blended learning. In this approach, content is basically presented through online mode. Though teachers are using an online education tool to provide on-site support as needed, the learning process is overall self-guided, as students independently learn the concepts and practice in a digital way of the learning process. Students spend hours in a computer lab learning process in online mode.

Online Lab Model

The online lab model of blended learning is an applicable option for helping students to complete their courses. In this current scenario, students learn entirely in online mode, but students go to the computer lab centre and finish their coursework.

Self-Blend Model

This model of blended learning gives more opportunities to students to take their classes above what is already preferred in their school. When these students attend a traditional classroom, they also prefer to complement their progress through online courses given parallelly. To make this self-blend model of blended learning successful, students must be highly self-motivated and encourage themselves. Self-blend is perfect for the student who wishes to take extra Advanced Placement courses, or who has an interest in the content that is not concealed in the traditional course curriculum.

Online Driver Model

Opposite to face-to-face drivers we have online drivers, in which pupils work from and material is fundamentally expressed via an online platform. Although the face-to-face driver model is arbitrary, students can interact with teachers online if they have queries about their subjects. This model is ideal for students who need more flexibility and sovereignty in their daily timetable schedule. The number of pupils participating in online driver programmes rapidly increases by about 15% each year.

A La Carte Model

This model offers online courses but does not apply to school students to complete that course during their leisure time. This model focuses on improving their self-confidence, creativity, and critical thinking on the subject content, which is allocated to the students.

Enriched Virtual Model

If your students primarily complete their work online and come into school for support on an as-needed basis, then you have an enriched virtual blended learning programme.

Tools of Blended Learning

Blended learning is a fusion of classroom and electronic learning. Electronic tools and technologies are widely used in blended learning for better understanding of the concepts by the students. Blended learning's purpose is to make conventional learning engrossing with e-learning tools, techniques, and technologies as a matter of fact to meet global needs and upcoming challenges. E-learning tools help to overcome geographical barriers for the learners and traditional barriers to communication among student–teacher interaction. Through e-learning, students can better understand and remember the concepts. Electronic learning tools do increase active learners in a zestful way. Electronic tools are easily accessible with the presence of the internet along with gadgets such as computers, laptops, smartphones, etc. Teachers should enrich their knowledge with emerging trends of e-learning tools to gain the learner's attentiveness and performance. Various tools and technologies can be used to establish an efficacious learning platform for blended learning. Some of them are:

Google Classroom: Google Classroom is one of the e-learning tools mainly meant for teachers and students to share academic work. Google Classroom is a free application service that Google has created for educational institutions. It is helpful for teachers to allocate assignments, share course syllabi and study materials, as well as conduct tests through Google.

Jam Board: Jam Board is a bilateral Whiteboard that belongs to the G Suite family. Jam Boards permit visual collaboration among learners. Jam Board is free to use on smartphones, tablets, and browsers. Through Jam Boards visible learning is possible. Teachers can browse the concept using search engines and can use a stylus to write and explain the concept as well as erase by using fingertips.

Popplet: Popplet is an e-learning tool used to create mind mapping, brainstorming diagrams, and animation that pave the way for students to develop skills like organisation, retention of long-term memory, and writing skills. Popplet is a kind of visual learning. The Popplet application is available only on iPad and iPhone.

Ed puzzle: Ed puzzle is an interactive video assessment-centred tool and usage is free of cost. Ed puzzles are convenient for the teachers to grant assignments to pupils via animation video.

Mentimeter: Mentimeter is a real-time feedback collecting tool. It is free to use. It mainly focuses on online collaboration for the academy asking queries to students and making them answer unidentified. Mentimeter is a second-hand tool for brainstorming sessions, polls, conferencing, surveying, and rating for presentation. A personal code is sent to request pupils to access mentimeter.

Edmodo: Edmodo is a pedagogical technology that offers K-12 school and teachers conferences for association, cooperation, and teaching. This application is free to use and a completely teacher-centred one. Teachers can announce assignments or homework and quiz tests via this tool.

Kahoot: Kahoot is a digital play method of learning apps. It is a cost-free application, easy to access in web browsers, and an application. By the way, kids are more curious to learn in this app.

Webinars: Webinars are conducted to enrich the knowledge of students on a specific topic. Electronic platforms are available to accompany the seminar. Instructors have to look into the number of participants that can accommodate the following tools involved in conducting symposiums. Tools used for webinar includes Zoom, Google Meet, Google Hangouts, Go Webinar, Cisco WebEx, and Adobe Connect.

Role of the Teacher and the Students in Blended Learning

In this current scenario, blended learning assumes a fundamental part, and instructors should shape the students incidentally.

Role of Teachers

Blended learning shifts the educator's job from instructor to mentor and tutor. This shift doesn't imply that educators assume an aloof or less significant part in teacher education.

Blended learning provides a pace between online guidance and tutoring, which offers intelligent, tech-based learning, individualised pacing, and security that keep students persistently drawn in and encouraged, and allows the instructor to give guidance, which customises the learning experience and adds the human components of consolation, sympathy, and caring that no one but educators can give.

This new dynamic learning benefits both the learners and teachers. It gives students consent and space to become dynamic students who acquire information straightforwardly, allows them to accept some command over their learning, and assists them with creativity. As more students are working freely, time opens up for educators to give up close and personal help and individualised guidance for students.

Role of Learners

Self-blend students supplement their education with extra online classes in such a way that their whole course might be web-based, requiring the student to utilise their drive to sign in and circle back to the assumptions for the course, without the presence of an in-person instructor.

Blended learning programmes tend to focus on experiential learning, or learning by straightforwardly encountering and investigating a subject. Instructors are bound to go about as facilitators, and students become more responsible for their own schooling.

Blended learning can improve both student commitment and instructor productivity. While it might require more educational consideration, the time can be made up effectively with more clear information, broad guidance, and remarkable instruction openings. At the point, when you put time into making a mixed learning air, the result is profoundly captivating that advances student revenue and learning.

'Carry out your programme and cycle with care, and with eyes open. Be ready to acknowledge and accept change; even an incredible arrangement will not work for each kid. Thus, prepare, and go ahead and disturb the classroom!'

Advantages and Disadvantages of Blended Learning

Though blended learning is the new outlook to pedagogy that amalgamates networked educational items and options for a lively classroom domain, it comprises certain virtues and shortcomings.

Virtues

- It creates a good rapport between student and teacher.
- As blended learning indulges technology in the teaching process, the student's engagement is increased in learning activities.
- It improves students' learning outcomes.
- It is well suited for self and continuous learning.
- Most of the learning styles are covered under blended learning.
- It provides opportunities for experiential learning.
- As blended learning allows personalised learning, students learn through different activities, discussions, courses, games, etc.
- It authorises customised education and substitutes the classic classroom setting.
- The blended environment aids all kinds of learners in unplugging and speaking out their thoughts, as it offers both online and offline modes for sharing ideas.
- Preceptors and tutees have humongous versatility and readiness toward teaching and learning.
- As the blended system tailors conventional as well as e-learning methods, it heavily amplifies the results of mentees.
- It also quenches the essential needs of discrete learners.
- The teacher's involvement in learning is upgraded.

Shortcomings

- It requires longer duration.
- Overdone online reviews may ruin the productivity of the class.
- It inculcates some sort of hesitation and procrastination among learners as technology is easily available.
- Teachers have to spend more time checking the assurance of the proper functioning of technological aids, rather than on preparing for subject content.
- There is uncertainty of internet access.
- Groundwork plays a prime role. So, drafting should be ensured before teaching.

Blended Learning in Higher Education at the Current Scenario

The rapid appearance of technological innovations in the last half-century has made an enormous impact on the possibilities for learning environments, especially for the distant learning environments, which commonly served higher education students. Blended learning is a technique that initiates a more integrated approach to the teaching–learning process. Various learning environments like face-to-face, online, and social networking are blended to provide the most efficient and effective instruction experience. These strategies will generate uses of advanced technology to provide training and development in higher education and within the industry. A progressive range of resources and other emerging technologies include cloud computing, social networking, and so on.

Statistical reports of colleges and universities are transitioning to online or blended learning due to the need to maintain a competitive edge and make classes more attainable to the progressive and diverse student population. Additionally, online teaching offers new, exciting opportunities to broaden the learning environment for divergent student populations. A study states that institutional rationales for blended learning were highly contextualised and specific to each institution. They include the resilience of provision, promoting diversity, reinforcing campus involvement, managing in a global context, and competence.

The concept of blended learning in the enclosure of higher education has initiated an opportunity to improve the teaching and learning process by harmonising the advantages and disadvantages of on-ground and online learning settings. The peculiar techniques of blended learning approaches depend on the impact of starting from low, medium, and high-impact blends.

A possible approach for designing blended learning courses is potentially encouraging indecisive educators to try to integrate learning. According to Silverwood (2006), teachers who could benefit from blended learning may be reluctant to try new procedures because they assume that integrated learning is very complex and highly technical.

It allows teachers to march towards opportunities to experiment with diverse approaches to learning and numerous types of educational technologies without destroying the fulfilled benefits of the traditional course. According to Aycock, Garnham, and Kaleta (2002), learning to exert technology aptly and efficiently can improve with experience.

It also allows teachers the opportunity to get the maximum benefits of blended learning and directs them towards promoting their students' needs. The framework of the course from scratch provides a better venture to rethink and redesign the fulfilled programme with learners' needs in mind. Teachers can consider significant choices for delivering mediums to integrate into their courses, and that will increase the effectiveness of the courses (Carman, 2002).

Educators are not the only ones to benefit from blended learning. Perhaps more importantly, students are given a more global educational experience that can step up retention and plight. Blended learning emboldens self-learning, where students are constrained to look for information online autonomously, rather than just sitting in a classroom setting and relying on an instructor. Blended learning furnishes several linked options for learners; likewise, they interconnect to classroom guidance. In addition, learners will be brought to light up various potential learning resources, which contribute to a richer learning experience. The pupils will actively take part in a discussion; vocalising their thoughts will certainly help to build confidence, success, and communication proficiency transposed favourably with a blended learning course. Blended learning provides a new course of action for educators to engage and connect with students. With declining enrolment of students and the confrontation of the digital landscape putting pressure on systems, faculty, and syllabus, bringing up blended learning could help tap into a new group of students and create a new yield for the course.

Conclusion

This chapter evidences that this is the time of blended learning, and it is in all places. In blended learning, both the traditional classroom approach and modern advanced e-learning approach complement each other, and with the balanced sense, it outreaches the world with blended learning classrooms everywhere. This virtual live learning method is a strong foundation for further pedagogical research work. It is to be noted that educationists cannot rely on blended learning completely, and it is not expected that it will stay forever. Any current trend has its expiration date to be outdated and old-fashioned. It is applicable in the field of education, too. The overarching effort of preceptors and educators will come up with a new innovative method of the teaching–learning process next level to the approach of blended learning without any doubt. Time and perceptions always change. Nothing remains the same. It is only the rational motive of a pedagogue, to create the change that possibly facilitates the students with the betterment they always deserve, that stays forever.

References

Aycock, A., Garnham, C., & Kaleta, R. (2002). Lessons learned from the hybrid course project. *Teaching with Technology Today*, 8(6), 9–21.

Carman, J. M. (2002). Blended learning design: Five key ingredients. http://www.agilantlearning.com/pdf/BlendedLearning Design.pdf

Driscoll, M. (2002). *Blended learning: Let's get beyond the hype. E-Learning and Digital Media*. https://www.researchgate.net/publication/286029739

Silverwood, T. (2006). Blended Learning Made Easy. http://www chs.nihon-u.ac.jp/institute/human/kiyou/74/10.pdf.

Chapter 6

Blended Approach in Education: An Overview

A. Sivakumar

Department of Education, Bharathiar University, Coimbatore, Tamilnadu, India

Introduction

The modern world has become a technopark; everything in the world is now simplified and has become user-friendly for our convenience. Similarly, innovation in education, as well as the teaching and learning process, has become most needed. It upgrades the traditional mode of learning. To create interest among learners, we use various teaching aids for students. The classroom consists of a composite of average learners, below-average learners, and gifted learners. The task of the teacher is a complex one – to teach all the students in the stipulated time. Employing the same methodology for all students seems absurd. So, we use different teaching–learning materials for teaching. Teaching–learning resources like text materials, flashcards, charts, portraits, teaching models, video records, audio-visual aids, and PowerPoint presentations are used in modern-day classrooms. Blended learning is the upcoming concept of learning. Blended learning is the combination of a regular classroom system with digitalised learning material (Partridge, Ponting, & McCay, 2011). Blended learning creates interest in learning. It also helps them to retain their knowledge lifelong.

 DOI: 10.1201/9781032675176-6

Blended Learning in Education

Blended learning is the kind of teaching–learning method that is the combination of face-to-face traditional classroom teaching methods with ICT tools (Lim, Wang, & Graham, 2019). A formal education programme can be learned by the student in part through online learning. In a blended learning environment, the teacher acts as the guide or a coach, not a knowledge provider as in the traditional method of teaching and learning (Huang, Ma, & Zhang, 2008). The blended learning environment includes face-to-face classes and online classes. It is the teaching–learning technique where ICT tools are used in the traditional classroom. It helps to learn the concept or content visually through a blended classroom environment. Learners can also use online resources to get more knowledge about the topic.

Blended learning is a mixture of regular classroom learning and online learning. A discrete method in blended learning is a combination of classroom instruction, blending simulations, and blending managerial coaching. The learning experience is different for each student in the aspects of interest, aptitudes, achievements, abilities, innovation, motivation, creativity, and problem solving. These learning experiences allow the learners to recall information so that they remember and merge it with other experiences to develop new knowledge.

Aims and Objectives of Blended Learning

Blended learning allows the students to increase their learning skills, provides rich access to information, improves learning ability, and provides opportunities to learn and to teach others. Blended learning helps

- to improve the learners' skills
- to enhance interest among students
- to ensure students' participation
- to understand the content or concept clearly
- to score high marks
- to retain knowledge for a long time
- to discuss with peer groups
- to learn without any distraction.

Need and Significance of Blended Learning

Blended learning is useful to both the teacher and the learner. Students can be involved in the classroom and it provides a detailed explanation of the content with pictures, audio, video, presentation, etc. The significance of teaching and learning through blended learning is to:

- Increase student commitment to learning.
- Improve interaction between teacher and student.
- Help students understand their responsibility for learning.
- Enhance time management and flexibility among the teacher and learners.
- Improve student learning outcomes.
- Provide flexibility in teaching and learning environments.
- Encourage self and continuous learning.
- Provide more room for experimental learning.

Teacher's Role in Blended Learning Classroom

In a blended learning classroom, teachers must not only be knowledge providers. They have to act as a guide or a coach for their students (Huang, Ma, & Zhang, 2008). All the teachers must be updated in the field of digital learning with more subject knowledge. They have to create innovative techniques for their students (University of Central Florida, 2013).Interaction in the blended learning classroom improves the learner's involvement. Thus, it could help them to get more knowledge and retain it throughout their life.

Learner's Role in Blended Learning Classroom

Learners in a blended learning classroom must be active while learning. They should have basic knowledge about innovations in the field of education. Learners should be updated on the new technologies in the market. The classroom doesn't need the teacher to be present every time; students can learn by themselves. Learners should follow every step taken by the teacher so that they can achieve as follows:

Increases Student Interest

By integrating blended learning in the teaching and learning process, learners' interest in learning new things, and focusing on their listening skills and knowledge about the subjects they are studying, are greatly increased.

Student's Focus Improves

The use of ICT to gather information and data and the right use of resources (internet) to conduct research motivates the students to focus for maximum periods, and this commitment also helps to develop their learning skills. It also helps them to complete their research study.

Provides Autonomy

The freedom to use electronic learning materials of their choice will increase a learner's strength to set the right learning objective and also understand their achievement level.

Promotes Ownership to the Students

Blended learning gives students ownership over learning, which makes them reliable and responsible for their learning.

Provides Instant Diagnosis of Information and Feedback from Students

Blended learning helps to check, evaluate, and give feedback on students' performance and also helps the teacher to modify their teaching methods to improve their efficiency.

Enables Students to Learn Anywhere

The use of internet resources in blended learning allows students to learn from anywhere and at any time.

Aims for the Student's Future

Blended learning offers a variety of real-world skills like the following:

- Research skills.
- Self-educated.
- Self-identification.
- Development of a 'self-driving force'.
- Decision-making skills.
- Responsibility.
- E-learning and knowledge.

Development of ICT in India

E-learning helps to improve the literacy rate in any country. The use of e-learning in the education field (schools, affiliated colleges, universities) paves the way to achieve learners' goals and also motivates the students. The Government of India considered e-learning a mode of education, especially during the pandemic. The first online education activity programme, Net Varsity, was done by the National Institute of Information Technology (NIIT limited) in 1996. However, the National

Association of Software and Services Companies (NASSCOM) Market Intelligence Service report states that e-learning is in its beginning stage. The Bachelor of Information Technology (BIT) and Advanced Diploma in Information Technology (ADIT) are in collaboration with Edexcel, UK, and the Ministry of Information Technology, Government of India. The Yashwantrao Chavan Maharashtra Open University (YCMOU) used e-learning for its Electronics Engineering Diploma Programme (EEDP) in 2002. In the year 2000, Tamil Virtual University was started to offer e-resources for the Tamil Communities living across the globe and to those who are interested in learning Tamil. Indian Institute of Management, Bangalore (IIM-B) used the e-learning method to facilitate face-to-face teaching and learning. The University Grants Commission (UGC) organised a dialogue on 'Enhancing Higher Education through E-learning' in collaboration with the Common Wealth of Learning (COL) Vancouver from 17–19 November 2003 in New Delhi.

Components of Blended Learning Classroom

As we discussed, a blended learning classroom is a combination of traditional and online learning. It has several features in both the online and offline modes. Teachers coach the students to manage themselves in any learning situation. The teacher offers blended activities that are suitable to the subject content, and the teachers need to concentrate on the curriculum requirements while developing learning materials (Cleveland-Innes & Wilton, 2018). Some examples of blended learning are as follows:

Face-to-Face Blended Class

This model is the same as the traditional classroom environment, wherein the normal classroom time, eight hours, has been replaced by online activities. The online activities used include readings, quizzes, or other assessments that can be done outside the school or college. This formatting model allows both teacher and learner to share their experiences through interactions and discussions.

Online Blended Class

In blended online classes, all the activities are mostly conducted through online platforms, and at times it requires personnel and guided labs based on the content for better understanding.

Flipped Classroom

The flipped classroom reverses the face-to-face classroom. Students in flipped classes learn their subject through lecture videos online and then discuss the contents in the classroom among peers and teachers.

The Rotation Model

In this model, the students of a course rotate between different modalities like station rotation, lab rotation, and individual rotation. For example, in the station model students rotate between stations in the classroom. In the lab rotation model, students rotate among locations on campus, and in the individual rotation model, a student rotates through learning modalities on an adapted schedule.

The Self-Blend Model

Self-blending is a programme-level model where learners, after enroling in colleges or universities, take online courses along with their normal degree courses. They can select their own choice of courses as additional online courses from any major they prefer.

The Blended MOOC

Massive Open Online Course (MOOC) is an online education system that provides a variety of online courses, which aims at large-scale interactive participation. It includes different features like videos, e-content, quizzes, and exams in their curriculum without any time and location constraints, making it more professional than real-time education. MOOCs also provide a discussion session for the user, which helps to build a strong rapport between the teacher and learner.

In the blended MOOC programme, students choose an online course and use MOOC materials provided in the forum, and then they discuss it in the classroom.

SWAYAM

SWAYAM, initiated by the Government of India, is designed to achieve the three fundamental principles of education policy, namely access, equity, and quality. The main aim of this programme is to provide the best teaching–learning resources to all students around the country.

ICT Tools for Collaboration

Learner-centred education has always helped learners to achieve the curriculum objectives and also helps to improve their skills in the learning process. Collaboration at the individual level encourages the teachers in preparing the study materials, active student participation, and increased academic achievement of students. It helps motivate the learner. Blended learning may not be teacher-centred. The learners engage in innovative and productive activities by using several ICT tools, such as the following.

Blogging

A blog is usually designed by the teacher, and the teacher adds the learners into the blog. Some information/queries may be posted in the blog along with learners' views, ideas, opinions, examples, strategies, etc. Blogging is usually given as an activity, and the teacher guides the students in the posting process.

Sticky Notes

Sticky note tools can be used for online brainstorming (Idea Flip, Jam board, Lino. it, etc.) Brainstorming can be done as a synchronous or asynchronous activity.

Shared Documents

Different tools such as Google Docs, Google Slides, Ether Pad, Scatter Spoke, idea boards, etc. are introduced to students to share their documents or to view documents. Most of these tools are free to use and can be used at any time depending on their internet facility.

Concept-Mapping, Mind Mapping, and Infograph Tools

Concept-mapping and mind-mapping ICT tools like Concept-board, Miro, Google Drawing, Bubble, etc. help learners in their online programme and make them understand the concept of the topic/content easily. We can also edit the content by adding images, sketches, links, etc. for better understanding.

Comprehensive Activity Tools

Comprehensive activity tools, which include Padlet, Miro, Whimsical, etc., create effective workspaces. Main features like wireframes allow the learners to develop project management and teamwork abilities.

Apart from the above ICT tools and platforms, many different tools can be designed by teachers and students. The use of these free tools must encourage students to create innovative tools and also use them appropriately. Well-structured computer labs on the campus help learners in their online activities.

Technology Infrastructure for Implementation

Approaches used in implementing blended learning are:

- Recorded videos of the entire course are shared with the students in Pen Drive/CD or e-text.

- Internet-Based Learning (IBL) (search & learn), which includes assignments and projects, helps to encourage self-learning.
- Project-based learning can be used for completing group projects, and it also helps learners to generate innovative ideas.
- Satellite-based TV Channel – Kalvi TV (/mass learning/adult education/ farmer education), introduced by the government, helps to convey the subject to students in villages where internet facilities are very poor.
- Online Assessments – weekly quizzes, assignments, tests, and homework at regular intervals help to assess their learning outcome.

Characteristics of Online Mode of Learning

Online mode of teaching and learning involves different learning activities such as:

- Accessing uploaded e-resources on the internet by the teacher.
- Accessing URLs and digital libraries suggested by the instructor.
- Studying MOOCs/ SMOCs, etc.
- Attending the online classes of the instructor.
- Being involved in self or peer activities using any ICT tools like Google Meet, Zoom Meet, Skype, etc.
- Attending workshops/webinars related to the curriculum.
- Uploading the completed assignments in the ICT platform.
- Participating in online tests/quizzes.
- Exploring virtual labs, simulations, museums, etc.
- Attending e-conferences, online short-term training programmes, etc.
- Participating in internships/projects conducted online.
- Being involved in any activity involving or similar to the course curriculum through online learning.

Characteristics of the Offline Mode of Learning

Face-to-face (F2F) Mode refers to offline classroom teaching or the traditional mode of teaching and learning. Several activities performed in the offline mode are as follows:

- Attending the instructor's short-duration lecture for understanding complex concepts.
- Clearing doubts that arise while self-learning or group learning.
- Discussing the information obtained from online resources with peers in the classroom.

- Using collaborative learning and creativity of new knowledge.
- Making full use of the library.
- Making field visits, internship visits, etc., that help the learner to gain practical knowledge.
- Using face-to-face interaction, physical training, apprenticeships, internships, etc.
- Participating in any instructional activity physically on the campus or outside of the campus by students and teachers.

Virtual Labs

There are many online sources for the blended learning classroom. A few of them are listed in Table 6.1.

Table 6.1 List of Virtual Labs

Title	*Country*	*URL*
MERLOT	USA	< www.virtuallabs.merlot.org/>
NASA Biolab	USA	<www.nasa.gov/offices/education/centers/kennedy/technology/Virtual_Lab.html>
Phet Labs	USA	<www.phet.colorado.edu/en/accessibilit>
Macmillan Learning	United Kingdom	<www.macmillanlearning.co.uk>
Siemens	USA	<www.siemens.com/global/en.html>

Benefits of Blended Learning

The UNSW (2022) has mentioned the following benefits of Blended Learning:

- Every student has their own pace in the learning process.
- It offers flexibility in learning at any time and anywhere without any distractions and deviation of time and location.
- Enhanced interaction: blended learning offers easy interaction among students and also between students and teachers.
- Students engage themselves actively in an online community. ICT skills are very much needed to be a persistent learner, and blended learning guides students in using various online technologies.

Online Learning Platforms

Proper learning management systems are crucial if one wants to make the most of the eLearning initiatives. From corporate training to online education, the best learning management systems can help to meet the goals. The online LMS tools are listed in Table 6.2.

Pedagogies for Blended Learning

Learner-centred educational activities develop learners' overall personalities. A blended learning classroom provides for energetic learners and lethargic ones. The availability of online resources helps students to attend class anywhere and at any time at their convenience. A few learning processes for the blended classroom follow.

Idea Generation

Students in higher education are mature learners and have experience. The blended learning method provides an opportunity for learners to share their knowledge, ideas, and views on the subject, either in the classroom or on an online platform to a great extent. Teachers upload the external links and materials on online platform systems before the classroom sessions. These resources are very useful to the listener to get previous knowledge of the subject before the class, and students can understand the class easily. This makes effective utilisation of classroom time for further discussions and to clarify students' doubts.

Brainstorming

Brainstorming constantly helps students to think instinctively and get new ideas and concepts. It enhances self-learning and self-thinking. These activities make the learner active in learning.

Concept/Mind-Map

Creating a cognitive schema of the content helps students to understand the topic from all aspects. Relative pictures, sticky notes, and drawings make the process meaningful learning.

Creativity

Education enhances the creativity of a student. Story-creation tools help learners to understand their subject knowledge more precisely, thus improving their expression skills.

Table 6.2 Tools for Blended Learning

Title	*Country*	*Licensed*	*Free Source*	*URL*
Moodle-2002	Australia		✓	<www.moodle.org>
Google Class Room-2014	USA	✓		<www.classroom.google.com>
NEO-2014	India		✓	<www.neolms.com/india>
Pro Profs *Training Maker-2010*	USA		✓	<www.proprofs.com >
Instructure-2008	Australia	✓		<www.instructure.com>
D2L-1999	North America	✓		<www.d2l.com>
Black Board	Brazil	✓		<www.blackboard.com>
Totara Learn-2017	New Zealand, United Kingdom & USA	✓		<www.totaralearning.com>
Claned	Finland	✓		<www.claned.com>
Matrix LMS	San Francisco, USUSA	✓		<www.matrixlms.com/india>
Calf-2006	USA	✓		<www.nuvedalearning.com/calf>
Adobe Captivate Prime-2015	USA	✓		<www.adobe.com>
Spot-2017	France	✓		<www.spotlms.us>

Real-World Exposure

Exposure to the real world while doing higher education will assist the students to face the real world. Field visits provide them with a better understanding of the process, as well as pros and cons in their field, and also help them to gain practical knowledge in their subject.

Case Study

Teachers use case studies to bring real-world experiences to those learners who cannot afford them. A case study enhances the learners' understanding of the topic. By assessing their case studies, the instructor comes to know the understanding level of the learners in their research topic.

Cooperative Learning

Cooperative learning strategies like Team-Pair-Share, Jigsaw, Team-Pair-Solo, One-stray, Fishbowl, PQP, etc. are successful when using face-to-face modes. This method will help in increasing the learner's responsibility for learning. The teacher can make sure all learners are participating in the significant learning process. Some of the ICT tools can also be used in CLS in online mode.

Digitalised Trends in Evaluation and Assessment

Though the teacher is using blended learning in the classroom, they should think about the innovative method in evaluating summative as well as formative evaluation. The University Grants Commission's 2021 document on Blended Mode of Teaching and Learning highlights several inventive assessment strategies.

Summative Evaluation Strategies

Open Book Examination

Open book examination provides a forward outlook from the usual approach of examination, where there is more rote learning than understanding. There are no restrictions for a teacher in selecting the questions, and it also facilitates students to present their answers more critically, thus improving their thinking skills and creativity.

Group Examinations Conventional Theory Papers

Group examinations were originally used only in projects and laboratory assessments and not for theory papers. The group examinations involve sharing of knowledge, which in turn helps in better understanding and cooperation among students. It also reduces rote learning.

Oral Examinations

The oral or spoken examination is usually used for differently-abled learners. It will improve their result and make the examination easier and faster. This is possible only with the aid of new innovative technologies.

Formative Evaluation Strategies

E-Portfolio

An e-portfolio is an inclusive tool for self-evaluation. It is a collection of the best assignments of a learner and the reflection of individuals about their assignments and the challenges faced during the teaching and learning process.

Creative Products

ICT tools enhance the learners to come up with different innovative ideas as a result of solo or group learning activities. Effective feedback from the learner helps to improve new technologies and also provides room for the innovation of more new technologies. It gives learners the chance to modify and improve their ideas.

Classroom/Online Quizzes

The teacher can use some innovative ICT tools for quizzes and games based on the curriculum for the students. It will create interest among the students, and it is quite effective compared to the usual written tests. The repetition of questions and answers may be discouraged for formative evaluation.

Use of AI Tools

Artificial intelligence (AI) technology can be used for many evaluations. During the pandemic time, most of the exams were conducted via online mode. A variety of AI tools should be used for evaluation. AI may reduce expenses during formal examinations, and travel time can also be saved by the online mode of assessments.

Feedback for Blended Learning

Feedback helps to know the effectiveness of any programme. Feedback for blended learning is obtained either in face-to-face mode or online mode. The teacher can use any audio-visual format or written format to give feedback. Feedback states the mistakes done by the students and also helps them to improve their learning level. Positive feedback motivates them to do even better and also helps them gain a better understanding of the subject.

Conclusion

This chapter provided a detailed version of the guidelines for blended learning in schools, colleges, and universities. Universities and affiliated colleges should make sure all the essential requirements to implement blended learning are met, and they should monitor the process regularly for successful implementation. Blended learning helps learners to improve their skills in the learning process. It should be carefully implemented and must be used as an additional learning experience. It should not be used as a substitute or replacement for actual classroom learning. Every educational institute should try implementing blended learning in higher education throughout our country to innovate new technologies that can be incorporated into our education system.

References

Cleveland-Innes, M., & Wilton, D. (2018). *Guide to Blended Learning* [E-book]. Commonwealth of Learning, Canada. Retrieved November 2018, from <https://oer4nosp.col.org/id/eprint/35/1/Cleveland-Innes-Wilton_Guide-to-Blended-Learning.pdf>

Huang, R., Ma, D., & Zhang, H. (2008). Towards a Design Theory of Blended Learning Curriculum. In: Fong, J., Kwan, R., & Wang, F. L. (eds.), Hybrid Learning and Education. ICHL 2008. Lecture Notes in Computer Science, vol 5169. Springer, Berlin, Heidelberg. <10.1007/978-3-540-85170-7_6>

Lim, C. P., Wang, T., & Graham, C. (2019). Driving, sustaining and scaling up blended learning practices in higher education institutions: A proposed framework. *Innov Educ, 1*(1). <10.1186/s42862-019-0002-0>

Partridge, H., Ponting, D., & McCay, M. (2011). *Good Practice Report: Blended Learning.* Australian Learning and Teaching Council. Available at: <https://eprints.qut.edu.au/216216/>

Teaching.unsw.edu.au. (2022). *Planning and Designing a Blended or Online Course | UNSW Teaching Staff Gateway.* [online] Available at: <https://teaching.unsw.edu.au/planning-and-designing-blended-or-online-course> [Accessed 18 March 2020].

University Grants Commission. (2021). *Blended Mode of Teaching and Learning: Concept Note.* [online] Available at: <https://www.ugc.ac.in/pdfnews/6100340_Concept-Note-Blended-Mode-of-Teaching-and-Learning.pdf> [Accessed 18 March 2021].

University of Central Florida, & American Association of State Colleges and Universities. (n.d.). *Blend Kit Course: DIY Project Tasks.* Blended Learning Toolkit. Retrieved June 27, 2013, from <https://blended.online.ucf.edu/blendkit-course-diy-project-tasks/>

Chapter 7

Blended Teaching and Learning Strategies to Cope Education 4.0

G. Thirumoorthy and A. Sivakumar

Department of Education, Bharathiar University, Coimbatore, Tamil Nadu, India

Introduction

Innovations in the field of education, socio-economic change, scientific innovations, etc., are interrelated. Especially the modern educational system and information and communication technology (ICT) are having reciprocal impacts. During the last three decades, huge software and hardware technologies were invented and adopted for teaching and learning processes. Many customised ICT devices and software applications were introduced to explore and excel in education. As a result, the students of these technology natives are fond of digital learning and ignore conventional teaching and learning. Any new technology cannot replace a teacher. Hence, it is the need of the hour to blend traditional and ICT-based teaching and learning methodologies to rejuvenate humanistic and holistic education.

 DOI: 10.1201/9781032675176-7

Contemporary Definitions for Blended Approaches in Teaching and Learning

The innovative initiatives of blended education and learning refer to an educational approach that combines online teaching and learning that are transferred through online interaction to students along with traditional classroom approaches. It adopts many approaches to teaching and learning methods that can be adapted to address students of many learning styles and strategies according to their needs. It takes place where about 50% of the learning occurs within the digital environment and online instructions with a focus on learning through multimedia content, such as animation, video, and audio. Blended learning is a combination or mix of Web-based virtual online and offline technology to achieve a learning objective. It also combines a variety of pedagogical strategies to get the best learning results, with or without the use of instructional technology, and combines any kind of educational technology combined with in-person instruction (Driscoll, 2002).

Later, Panopto (2020) defined 'blended education' (also known as 'hybrid learning') as an approach to teaching and learning that integrates modern ICT utility and digital approaches with conventionally facilitated activities in the classroom that are guided by the instructor and provide students more freedom to tailor their learning exercises and involvements.

From the human resources point of view, Caroline (2021) defined 'blended learning' as a style of training that provides learning opportunities using the internet and electronic media, as well as conventional face-to-face training.

Learning with blended approaches in education is a method of instruction that mixes classroom instruction with online instruction in physical classroom training and online learning activities (Kokoulina, 2021). Blended learning is a type of instruction that combines several resources, particularly a combination of in-person lessons and online or offline digital learning resources (Macmillan Dictionary, 2021).

During COVID-19, the University Grants Commission (UGC, 2020) provided a formal guideline for 'blended teaching' in higher education in colleges and universities. Henceforth, higher education institutions in India might be promoted to deliver up to 40% of any course online.

Further, in blended teaching and learning, some lessons are taught to students face-to-face in a physical classroom, and some reciprocal instruction in a self-directed or student-directed study occurs over the internet. The blended teaching and learning approach is a combination of offline and online teaching and learning in a way that one complements the other, and it is a subjective method that combines in-person instruction and learning and remote or internet-based learning. Blended teaching and learning may be renamed hybrid or flipped teaching and learning.

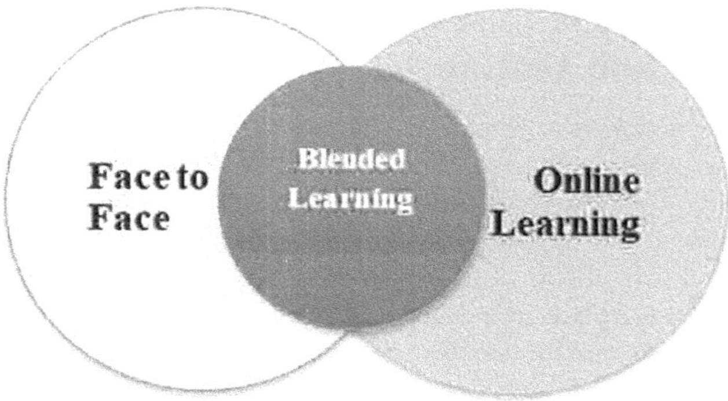

Figure 7.1 Blended learning.

Blended, hybrid, or flipped teaching and learning is the process of moving from face-to-face classes to incorporating online teaching and learning. This allows for more interactive forms of learning to take place during the teaching and learning process. Teaching often involves students exploring the lecture materials in digital form as homework or during teaching and learning time (Figure 7.1).

A Brief History of Blended Teaching and Learning

A blended approach to learning, or hybrid learning or flipped learning, has a long history, and it has a long journey. While introducing printing technology, the onset of blended learning started to flourish. Later, along with the development of 21st-century digital technologies, blended learning has also attained its javelin stage (Table 7.1).

Table 7.1 Brief Route Map of Blended Teaching and Learning

Years	*Invention*
1297	Wang Chen Invented a Revolving Table of Type to Increase Printing Speed
1450s	Printing Machines were Invented and Ready to Use Commercially
1830s	Invention of the Computer
1840s	Introduction of the First Distance Courseware

(Continued)

Table 7.1 (Continued) Brief Route Map of Blended Teaching and Learning

Years	*Invention*
1960s & 1970s	Introduction of Computer Training and Applications
1970s to 1980s	TV-Based Technology to Support Live Training
1980s & 1990s	Memory Storage (CD-ROM) and the Rise of Learning Management Systems (LMS)
1998	The Onset of the First Generation of Web-Based Teaching and Learning
Contemporary Technology 4.0	Javelin Stage of Blended Learning Integration or Hybrid Learning or Flipped Teaching and Learning

Digital technology, hybrid connectivity, and cheap availability of electronic and ICT devices provide a holistic environment to move towards learning in a hybrid manner. The introduction of smartphones, desktops, palmtops, laptops, and 4 G networks at affordable costs acted as an opportunity to experiment with the blended teaching and learning during the COVID-19 obstacles.

Blended Approaches to Cope with Education 4.0 Teaching and Learning

Until the last few decades, the learning and teaching communities were able to manage their teaching and learning process without adopting modern technology. In the modern era, it is inevitable to adopt ICT to blend conventional teaching as well as learning. The elderly learner and teacher may be technology immigrants, and they may struggle in the adaptation of ICT. They may suffer due to a lack of skills, competency, and phobia of ICT. It is very fortunate to have teachers and students who are technology natives and who are interested in engaging in a digital environment. The teacher and learner who were born during 2k possess innate traits, aptitudes, and positive attitudes towards digital teaching and learning. But, unfortunately, the teacher and learner belonging to technology natives are polarised towards ICT or digital teaching and learning. Due to the catastrophic shift of ICT-based intrusion, so many holistic pedagogies were fossilised. It is the need of the hour to bring out and rejuvenate the ancient and Vedic methods and models of teaching and learning to blend with modern ICT-based teaching and learning.

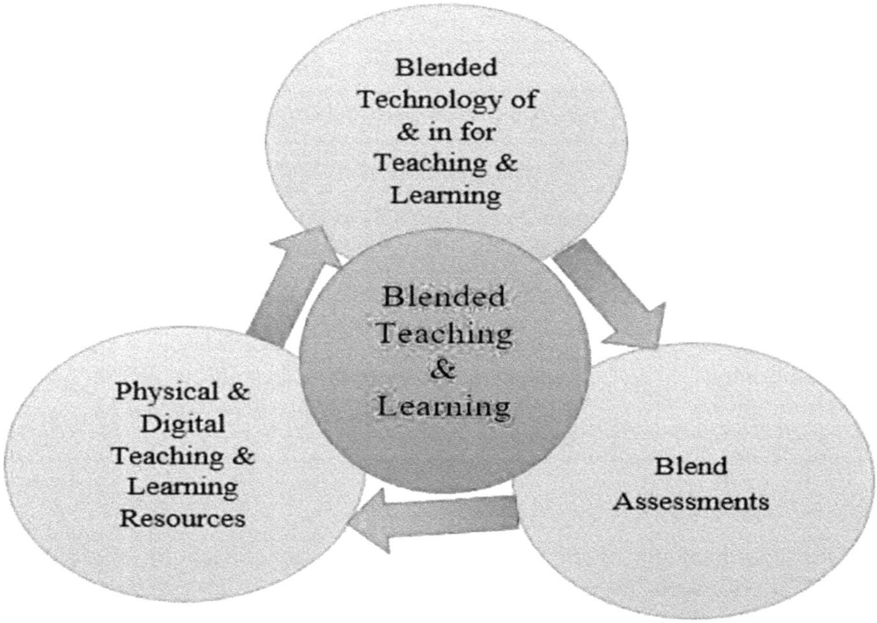

Figure 7.2 Triangulation strategies to instigate blended teaching and learning.

Triangulation Strategies to Instigate Blended Teaching and Learning

For holistic blended modern teaching and learning, we need to blend conventional and modern technology in the following three areas of the teaching and learning process. The blended approach should be implemented by using physical and digital teaching and learning materials as well as technology in and technology of teaching. Learning and blended assessments also need to be incorporated (Figure 7.2).

Physical and Digital Teaching and Learning Resources for Blended Teaching and Learning

Both the physical and digital forms of teaching and learning materials need to be made available for holistic blended teaching and learning. The teacher and student communities should have to train to acquire the competency related to ICT to excel in blended teaching and learning flexibility. With blended learning, the teacher's responsibilities are changed from knowledge source to mentor, facilitator to guide to create thirst among the learner towards learning without limit. There are very advanced technologies available for the reproduction of hard copies of teaching and learning materials. In the modern world, there are huge ICT-based teaching and learning materials such as digital books, audiobooks, modules, animated materials, storytelling applications, etc., which are available in both online and offline modes. Further, the teachers can draw from a comprehensive toolbox of traditional or conventional and digital or ICT-enhanced strategies to best meet the needs of the students (Best, 2021).

Educational Technology for Blended Teaching and Learning

Technology in education means the applications of modern sophisticated machines, ICT gadgets, or tools to raise educational standards and opportunities. It includes hardware such as broadcast/telecommunication media, projected media, audio media, visual media, audio and visual media, E-storage, software technologies, etc.

The boomed ICT inventions, low cost, and easily available hardware and software technologies are providing a holy opportunity for teaching and learning communities to make use of these technologies for teaching and learning. Hardware technologies such as modern desktop and laptop computers, smartphones, huge memory storage hard disk, I Touch, iPad, writing pad, Kindle, MP3 player, projector, microphone, printer/scanner, etc., provide the greatest opportunities to enrich teaching and learning activities. Along with these hardware technologies, software applications such as online and offline mobile applications, Google Tools, Microsoft tools, Flash, QuickTime, Windows Media Player, Real Player, editing software, recording software, math/engineering software, graphics editing software, etc. are all very useful for the preparation of teaching and learning materials to attain outcome-based teaching and learning (Figure 7.3).

Technology of Education for Blended Teaching and Learning

The use of psychological theories, methodologies, laws, and norms in the field of education and related disciplines is referred to as educational technology. This is done to enhance, promote, and maintain the quality of education. The techniques of curriculum planning, classroom transactions, assessment, and evaluation also come under the technology of education. UNESCO (1974) stated that using a combination of human and technical resources, educational technology is a systematic technique to plan, carry out, and evaluate the educational process in terms of general and specialised objectives. This results in more effective instruction.

Figure 7.3 Software and hardware technology in education.

Source: Open sources of Google Image.

The Association for Educational Communications and Technology (AECT, 2008) states that educational technology is creating, utilising, and managing relevant contemporary ICT technological procedures and resources to facilitate learning and enhance learner performance, which is known as educational technology. The use of technology in education is derived from psychology, sociology, philosophy, teaching methodology, etc.

Blended Assessments

Blended assessment in learning is an assessment method that blends both physical face-to-face and digital or virtual assessment. Flexible or blended examination systems became inevitable during the COVID-19 period. Many educational systems were forced to conduct examinations online as well as offline in a blended mode. There is a variety of tools that came into existence in present times, and artificial intelligence is helping to excel in effective blended assessment. Beyond that, the National Mission on Education through Information and Communication Technology (NMEICT), National Programme on Technology

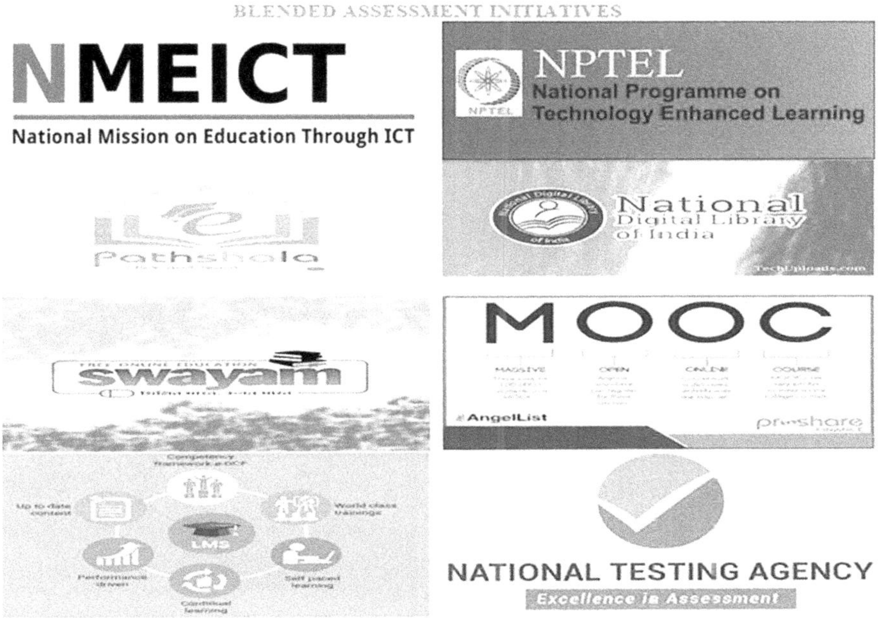

Figure 7.4 Blended assessment initiatives.

Source: Official website.

Enhanced Learning (NPTEL), e-PG Pathshala (ePG), National Digital Library (NDL), Study Webs of Active-learning for Young Aspiring Minds (Swayam), Massive Open Online Course (MOOCs), learning management system (LMS), National Testing Agency (NTA), other modern ICT Tools, etc., provide great opportunities and initiatives to execute and excel blended assessments (Figure 7.4).

Virtual Lab to Cope with Blended Teaching and Learning

The onset of virtual laboratories was started in 1977 for physiology. Later the focus was expanded from physiology to the life sciences in general. In India, the Virtual Labs project was initiated by the Ministry of Human Resource Development (MHRD), Government of India, under the guidance of the National Mission on Education through Information and Communication Technology (NMEICT). India's first Virtual Science Lab for Children was initiated by the Council of Scientific and Industrial Research (CSIR) Jigyasa (Curiosity) Programme in 2021 in collaboration with Kendriya Vidyalaya Sangathan (KVS) (Arora, 2021). The virtual lab will be an interesting platform in which the students can read, have fun, and carry out those experiments (Figure 7.5).

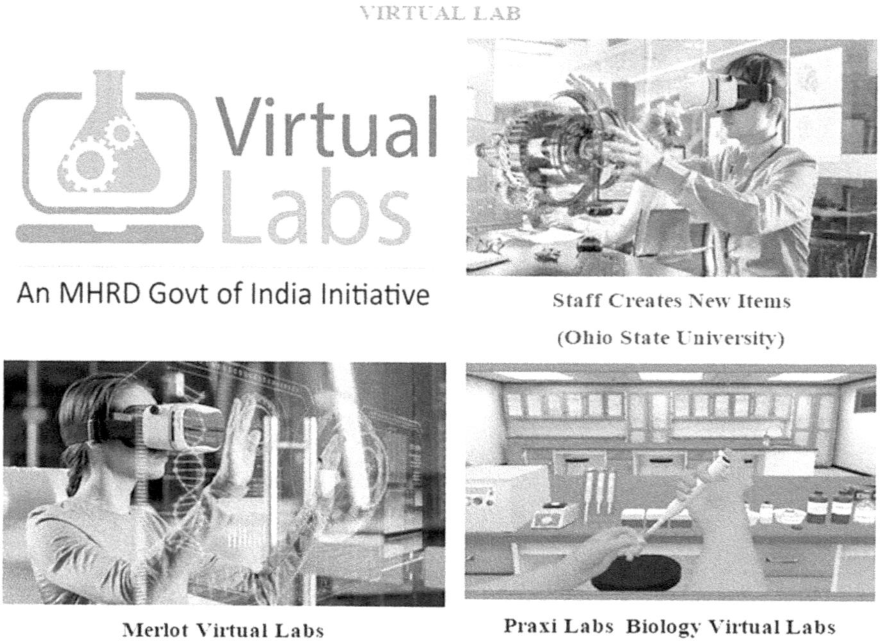

Figure 7.5 Virtual lab.

Source: Official website & Open sources of Google Image.

Types of Blended Teaching and Learning

According to the needs, the ideal blended approaches in teaching and learning methods could be chosen by the teacher and the learner. In the modern technology-integrated world, many blended teaching and learning methodologies can be initiated, such as blended learning in station rotation, individual rotation, lab experience rotation, remote blended learning, flex classroom approaches, and a flipped classroom learning environment (Figure 7.6). Blended learning was experienced while doing Project, Self-Direction while Learning, Inside-Out and Outside-In approaches while Learning, Supplementary Blended Learning, Brain or Mastery approaches in Learning, etc. This 21st-century standard for teaching and learning enables a new approach without being blended with conventional and modern technology. The digital resources, tutorials, podcasts, online educational games, and illustrated reference material will also enlighten the students to more than a stack of drab hand-outs and engage the learner as edutainment. The blended methodology connects a digital environment in which students live and present as cognitively engaging, dynamic, and cloud-based learning that cannot be achieved in physical class alone.

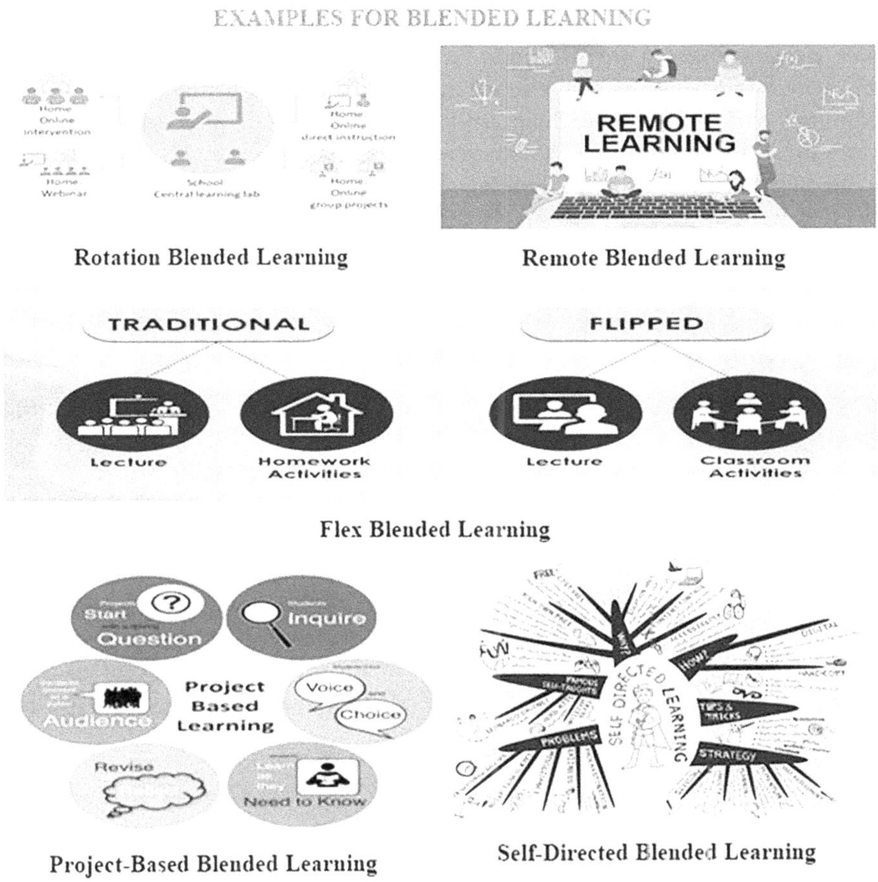

Figure 7.6 Examples of blended learning.

Source: Open sources of Google Image.

Merits of Blended Teaching and Learning

The incorporation of information and communication technology (ICT) is inevitable in all fields. Especially pertaining to education, the students are polarised towards ICT-based learning. The blended approach blends modern technology with conventional teaching and learning methods. Web conferencing, eBooks, simulations, movies, and games are some of the contemporary digital learning resources, artificial intelligence, clouds, etc., that effectively blend learning.

The blended teaching and learning methodology provides a great opportunity to blend and renovate fossilised pedagogy with modern technology. It offers freedom in selecting the teaching and learning materials and blended learning methodology, which may keep the student interested in the learning process and track learning engagement and improvement. Blended learning can provide edutainment for the learner and teacher by providing video games, television programmes, hard and soft teaching, and learning material, intended to be both educational and enjoyable. The student-centred and peer involvement is more in the blended teaching and learning, which leads to huge knowledge **retention.** Blended learning can be customised and can choose suitable methods for small groups as well as for large groups.

Challenges in Blended Teaching and Learning

Even though the blended approaches in education provide various opportunities for teachers and learners, there are many challenges, such as a lack of flexible environment for blended teaching and learning, lack of constructive peer interaction, lack of accountability in accessing the knowledge gain, non-affordable advanced technologies, insufficient methodology to assess the learner outcomes, and lack of guidance and policy to initiate blended teaching and learning. The competency of technology has become a great challenge for both learners and teachers. Preparation of the lesson plan and instructional design is a practical challenge. Blended learning is an innovative methodology. While execution is not an easy task, creating the content and blended teaching, learning, delivery, and engaging, etc., is challenging for several reasons.

Summary

A must-have modern strategy, hybrid or blended learning blends in-person and online teaching and learning possibilities to give students a memorable and meaningful learning experience. There are many practical difficulties and challenges while initiating blended teaching and learning. The material, methodology, and evaluation are needed to customise blend teaching–learning. The teacher, learner, and educational management are needed to accommodate blended learning because technology is an inseparable element among the technology-native 2k generation students. Hence, traditional teaching and learning strategies need to be blended with modern technology as edutainment.

References

AECT. (2008). Competencies and Indicators - AECT Standards, 2012 Version. In *Educational Technology: A Definition with Commentary* (2nd ed.). Hillsdale, NJ: Lawrence Erlbaum Associates. https://cehs.usu.edu

Arora, S. (2021, November 25). *Jitendra Singh launched India's 1st Virtual Science Lab for Children*. Adda247.

Best, J. (2021, April 6). *How to Use Blended Teaching in Your Classroom*. 3P Learning. Retrieved November 2, 2021, from https://www.3plearning.com/blog/what-is-blended-teaching/

Caroline. (2021, September 14). *What Is Blended Learning?* https://www.easy-lms.com/. https://www.easy-lms.com/knowledge-center/lms-knowledge-center/blended-learning-definition-and-meaning/item10385#benefits-blended-learning

Driscoll, M. (2002). Blended learning: Let's get beyond the hype. *E-learning*, 1(4), 1–4.

Kokoulina, O. (2021, January 18). *Blended Learning: Definition, Models, and Tools*. Explore the eLearning world with us. https://www.ispringsolutions.com/blog/blended-learning-a-primer

Macmillan Dictionary. (2021). Blended Learning (Noun) Definition and Synonyms.Macmillan Dictionary | Free English Dictionary and Thesaurus. https://www.macmillandictionary.com/dictionary/British/blended-learning

Panopto. (2020, November 5). *What Is Blended Learning?* Panopto Video Platform. https://www.panopto.com/blog/what-is-blended-learning/

UGC. (2020). *Blended Mode of Teaching and Learning: Concept Note*. University Grants Commission New Delhi. https://www.ugc.gov.in/pdfnews/6100340_Concept-Note-Blended-Mode-of-Teaching-and-Learning.pdf

UNESCO. (1974). *Revision of the 1974 Recommendation Concerning Education for International Understanding, Co-Operation and Peace and Education Relating to Human Rights and Fundamental Freedoms*. https://www.unesco.org/en/education/1974recommendation

Chapter 8

Gamification: An Engaging Module for the Future Learners

Madhurima Chakraborty and V. Ambedkar

Department of Education, Annamalai University, Chidambaram, Tamilnadu, India

Introduction

Learning is the process of acquiring new skills, understanding, knowledge, values, attitudes, behaviour, and so on. Learning occurs when an individual's zone of proximal development (Vygotsky, 1978) moves to an upper level. This zone of proximal development is the most immediate psychological, cognitive, and vocational development of the learners with the help of more knowledgeable others. In a classroom situation where the teachers and the students are stakeholders, the teacher is the 'more knowledgeable other', with the help of whom the students are going to develop their potential in the different behavioural domains.

To facilitate the total development of the personality of the learners, a learner-centred curriculum is required. According to Prensky (2001), a lot of what has been included in the school curriculum is not motivating, and the prerequisite of learning is motivation. As motivation initiates and guides goal-oriented behaviour, it leads toward maximum learning outcomes. The Interactive Games and Entertainment Association came up with a study that showcased that 92% of parents believe that video games can serve as an effective educational tool. The reason behind games' appeal to students is the four freedoms of play (Klopfer

DOI: 10.1201/9781032675176-8

et al., 2009), namely to try out different identities, to fail, to experiment, and to put forth effort.

- *Freedom of experiment:* students are allowed to apply different methods and strategies to solve any problem.
- *Freedom to fail:* students are allowed to do and re-do until they acquire the right set of skills to solve any problem.
- *Freedom to try out different identities:* students are not subjected to a pre-determined set of solutions to any problem. There is nothing right and wrong, and all approaches are welcomed.
- *Freedom of effort:* students are always motivated to put in the effort and solve problems at their own pace.

Nowadays games seem to drive learners towards engagement. The youth of today stays loyal to the game, and therefore, the educationists of the present day came up with 'gamification', which is the application of the mechanics and dynamics of gaming in a non-game context. Bedwell et al. (2012) taxonomy suggests that gamification differs from serious games in its approach, i.e., serious games include a combination of all elements of the game, whereas gamification includes recognition, extortion, and incorporation of game elements individually and also a worthy combination of the ones serving the purpose. Incentivising in education is not new, and the use of technology to teach is also not novel in the present scenario. It is the approach and methodology to serve the purpose of learning that makes gamification the buzzing trend.

Gamification alludes to the 'use of game design elements within non-game contexts' (Deterding et al., 2011). The term emerged in the early 2000s, gaining popularity around 2010. According to Merriam-Webster, the word 'gamification' was added to the English lexicon in the 21st century, describing it as the incorporation of game elements, like point and reward systems, and incentivising tasks for people to participate. Gamification makes games potentially tedious and therefore effective because it evokes people's natural desires to overcome challenges and achievement.

Gamification is the logical transfer of elements of play into pedagogical practices. This transposition includes some basic principles and rules, primarily a point system, linear accumulation of points, tokens, visualisation of the progress, levels, ranking of players, feedback, and rewards. Pedagogical acts are described as 'impositions' (Reichenbach, 2000) on adults or youth to facilitate lifelong learning and education. Fink described education as a basic phenomenon for human co-existence, and to facilitate education, the orchestral overlap of the temporal and spatial quality of games is vital. This overlap resembles pedagogical practices, and that is the reason game logic works in classroom settings.

Gamification depends on four components: (1) elements, (2) design, (3) game, and (4) non-game contexts.

- *Elements* distinguish gamification from serious games (Deterding et al., 2011).
- *The design* juxtaposes game design elements with game-based technologies. Game-based technologies include aspects such as game remotes, controllers, or engines, whereas gamification refers to a deliberate approach, design, or methodology.
- *Game* is defined by Salen and Zimmerman (2004) as 'a system in which players engage in an artificial conflict, defined by rules, that results in a quantifiable outcome'. It depends on the rules of play (Groh, 2012).
- *Non-game contexts* do not specify the possible arenas in which gamification could be applied, but the contexts have to be someplace outside the game itself.

Werbach and Hunter (2012) identified 15 important components of gamification. They emphasised the 'PBL triad', i.e., the system of points, badges, and leaderboards interplaying, which they consider characteristic features of gamified applications. Among those 15 components, the major ones are points, badges, leaderboards, performance graphs, meaningful stories, avatars, and teammates.

Systematic Mapping of Gamification in Education

In gamification of education (Huang and Soman, 2013), gamification is outlined as a five-step process.

- To understand the target audience and the context.
- To define the learning objectives.
- To study the experience.
- To identify the resources.
- To apply gamification elements.

Steps to Gamify a Classroom

- **Determination of learners' characteristics:** the teachers should know the students to implement new strategies, tools, and techniques to teach so that the students can benefit from them.
- **Definition of learning objectives:** the teacher should specifically and clearly define the learning objectives at the beginning of the learning process so that the learners stay motivated as they will know the purpose of the lesson.
- **Creation of educational content:** the educational content or activities to be created for gamification should provide scope for multiple performances or

multiple attempts, feasible, with increasing difficulty levels and multiple solutions.

- **Addition of game elements and mechanisms:** the key element of gamification is to add the tasks that learners have to perform. All the dynamics and mechanics of gaming should be included while planning the task.

Psychological Foundation of Gamification and Theory

The symbiosis between learning and games is evident, witnessing the continuous and progressive development of practices, to design games and gamification courses. The psychological foundation of including game elements in education is to provide social links, promote knowledge-seeking behaviour, develop creativity, improve mental health, and reduce isolation.

The different types of gamification strategies employed in learning are challenges, immersion, and social-based gamification. The challenge-based strategy calls to overcome challenges. The immersion-based strategy uses a story and is characterised by audio-visual richness, and the social strategy promotes competition and collaboration. Gamified activities have also proven themselves to amplify students' motivation: intrinsic and extrinsic. On par with this, the self-determination theory steps up to lay down the three basic psychological needs: *relatedness, autonomy, and competence* (Richter et al., 2015). Deterding chooses these three separate categories to divide the idea of gamification. Kim also emphasises these three as being the key goals to a well-structured gamified system and explains these as,

- To achieve *relatedness* means understanding the users, their drives, and usage of game mechanics to invoke positive emotions in them. Relating the system to them in some personal manner is vital.
- To achieve *mastery* or competence, the user has to accomplish interesting and challenging tasks that suit the level of the learners, followed by positive feedback that encourages users, lending them a sense of attainment.
- To achieve *autonomy* the users must feel the urge to achieve the goal. Being forced to often leads to boredom. Gamification lights up the way and makes learning fun.

Gamification must serve at least one of the needs. The other two theories that relate to gamification are flow theory and the goal-setting theory. The goal-setting theory states that students' performance comprises four factors: the complexity of the task, the situational reign or constraints, the commitment of the students towards the goal, and the received feedback (Locke and Latham, 2002, 2006; Landers, 2015). This theory says that gamification requires challenges, feedback, collaboration, rewards, competition, and motivation to make the learners progress in learning. The flow theory optimises the physical as well as the psychological state of learners, maximising enjoyment and engagement. Here, gamification demands acute and comprehensible goals, indicators of achievement, immediate feedback, and balance between the challenges, the skills of the students, and the realised importance of the activity.

Dynamics and Mechanics of Gaming

A few instances of game mechanics used in gamification are as follows:

- Finishing off a task and getting rewarded with points or badges or stars, referred to as **Goals.**
- The position or rank of learners, referred to as **Status.** The Status of learning is indicated with the help of Leaderboards that show the winner and also inspire users to work harder and compete, to maintain their status on the Leaderboard.
- **A Community** of Learners involves a group of learners who engage themselves in tasks, act to solve them, complete the activities prescribed, and achieve the objective or goal.
- **Feedback** serves as the most crucial part of gamification, where tricks, tips, and quizzes are made at the disposal of the user throughout the process.
- **Prize or Reward** fuels the user's engagement and motivation in the learning process.

A few of the dynamics of 'gamification' are as follows: (Table 8.1)

- **Constraints** are the challenges to which the learners are posed.

Table 8.1 The Gamification Module for Every Class

Dynamics	*Constraints*	*Emotions*	*Progression*
Mechanics	**Challenge**	**Reward** **Competition** **Co-operation** **Resources** **Acquisition** **Feedback**	**Reward** **Resource** **Acquisition** **Feedback**
Elements	**Earn points & avoid elimination**	**Badges, Competition, Collaboration, Collection of points or stars & Leaderboard**	**Tokens, Points collected & Position on leaderboard**

- The **Emotional** component comprises collaboration, competition, motivation, and all aspects of the affective domain of learning.
- **Progression** of the learners is shown as the end result or the result the learning experience created, how far the learners were able to comply and achieve.

Benefits of Gamification

- **Gamification makes learning interactive and fun:** the mechanics and dynamics of games when applied in the learning environment intrinsically motivate the learners as they can gauge their progress. Dickey (2005) explained that progression is a cardinal element of a game as it levels up the engagement and motivation of the player. Its primary objective is to inform the player on how much progress he or she has made in a particular level.
- **Creates an addiction towards learning:** the learners, when receiving rewards for each progression made, get into the habit of performing better. This habit formation leads to addiction to learning.
- **Opportunity to face real-world application:** gamification promotes learning by doing. Hence, the learners have to face tasks similar to real-world difficulties, analyse the problem, and apply their knowledge and skills to solve it, as they are expected to do the same when a real-life problem pops up.
- **Gamification enhances the learning experience:** as gamification involves the learners and enhances their participation, it makes the learners solve their tasks themselves, promotes self-paced learning under the observation of the teacher, and assertively enhances the learner's experience.

References

Bedwell, W. L., Pavlas, D., Heyne, K., Lazzara, E. H., & Salas, E. (2012). Toward a taxonomy linking game attributes to learning: An empirical study. *Simulation & Gaming: An Interdisciplinary Journal*, 43, 729–760.

Deterding, S., Sicart, M., Nacke, L., O'Hara, K., & Dixon, D. (2011). *Gamification using game design elements in non-gaming contexts*. In Proceedings of CHI Extended Abstracts, 2425–2428.

Dickey, M.D. (2005). Engaging by design: How engagement strategies in popular computer and video games can inform instructional design. *Education Training Research and Development*, 53(2), 67–83. DOI: https://doi.org/10.1007/978-3-319-10208-5_2

Groh, F. (2012). Gamification: State of the art definition and utilization. *Institute of Media Informatics Ulm University*, 39, 31.

Huang, W.H.Y. & Soman, D. (2013). *Gamification of Education. Research Report Series: Behavioural Economics in Action.* Rotman School of Management, University of Toronto.

Klopfer, E., Osterweil, S., & Salen, K. (2009). *Moving Learning Games Forward.* Cambridge, MA: The Education Arcade.

Landers, R.N. (2015). Developing a theory of gamified learning. *Simulation & Gaming.* DOI: 10.1177/1046878114563660

Locke, E.A. & Latham, G.P. (2002). Building a practically useful theory of goal setting and task motivation: A 35-year odyssey. *American Psychologist,* 57(9), 705.

Locke, E.A. & Latham, G.P. (2006). New directions in goal-setting theory. *Current Directions in Psychological Science,* 15(5), 265–268.

Prensky, M. (2001). *Digital Game-Based Learning.* New York: McGraw Hill.

Reichenbach, Roland. (2000). *Die Zumutung des Erziehens und die Scham der Erziehenden.* In Anton Bucher, Rosemarie Donnenberg and Rudolf Seitz (Eds.).

Richter, G., Raban, D.R. & Rafaeli, S. (2015). Studying gamification: The effect of rewards and incentives on motivation. In T. Reiners & L.C. Wood (Eds.), *Gamification in Education and Business* (pp. 21–45). Berlin: Springer International Publishing.

Salen, K. & Zimmerman, E. (2004). *Rules of Play: Game Design Fundamentals.* Library of Congress Cataloguing. ISBN: 0-262-24045-9.

Vygotsky, L.S. (1978). *Mind in Society: The Development of Higher Psychological Processes.* Cambridge, MA: Harvard University Press.

Werbach, K. & Hunter, D. (2012). *For the Win: How Game Thinking Can Revolutionize Your Business.* Wharton.

Chapter 9

Gamification for Teaching Beyond for Creative Learners

A. Sivakumar

Department of Education, Bharathiar University, Coimbatore, Tamilnadu, India

Introduction

Undoubtedly, the incorporation of technology in education has enriched the learning standards of students and has enabled educators to deliver their finest skills. The understandings and experiences that learners and their teachers have, and need, are rapidly changing as the technology itself changes (Davies and Merchant, 2009). However, the pace of adaptation to digital technologies is pointedly higher among students than among teachers. In other words, more students try to learn new things by interacting digitally with content, people, and public groups. As a consequence, Heick (2018) stated that the increased digital interaction of learners led to the increased use of the term 'digital citizenship'. The students of the present day are rightly referred to as digital natives, who were born in a digital world. They have diverse learning styles and connect every learning process of theirs with technology. It is their attitude towards the learning process and higher expectations from teachers that threaten the teachers. They do not expect teachers and a routine classroom. Instead, they look up to a facilitator in a digital environment.

DOI: 10.1201/9781032675176-9

Fulfilling the expectations of the learners about the infrastructure and the teachers has become challenging. Understanding and implementing a novel technology in the learning process is a tough task. Each time it is encountered, it takes some time for the users to adapt to it. Apart from the difficulties in infrastructural aspects, the challenges faced about defining the role of a teacher or facilitator are crucial. The modification of the learning process toward students' needs, preferences, and requirements is becoming a widely unsolved yet important challenge. In connection with this, a significant gap between the existing learning process and the learners' abilities has been observed. Teachers are forced to equip not only their subject knowledge but also their technical skills to be capable facilitators in the digital learning environment. Recently, the rise of the concept called 'multimodality' (Kress, 2003; Walsh, 2009) refers to the versatility of digital competence that holds various tools, modes of communication, and strategies. These could be effectively used in the teaching–learning process to enable learners to be motivated and engage actively. Among the various novel inclusions of technology in the learning process, one is gamification, which is increasing.

Concept of Gamification

Gamification is a strategy recently gaining importance in the educational field and being incorporated into learning. It was originally a process of adding game mechanics into nongame environments. As stated by Kapp (2014), gamification is gaining momentum in everything from marketing to website development and even learning environments. However, this is rooted in motivational theories. This is an approach that technically and psychologically instigates innumerable elements and features of gaming. According to Marczewski (2013), it is the use of symbols, elements, and ideas of games in a context unlike that of the games, to increase motivation and commitment, and influence the behaviour of users. Nowadays it is widely used in commercial websites, online platforms dedicated to community interaction, intranet setups serving business enterprises, and learning management systems (LMS) of educational institutions to surge participation. Therefore, the main focus of gamification is consistent in terms of participation but varies in its functions based on the nature of the work in which the participants are engaged. For example, if business collaboration increases in websites, consumer-engagement increases, the employees' efficiency increases, or it stimulates the learners to score higher.

In the past and today, games are a part of our culture, enabling us to learn sportsmanship and exchange experience. Each one of us would have played some kind of game and would have experienced the fun and enthusiasm. On the other hand, most of us would have experienced this modified version called gamification while surfing online, knowingly or unknowingly. Simply, gamification takes some or all elements of games and adds them into a new environment to attain the expected goals, which may pertain to training, business, skills, learning, task completion, etc. The common elements of games like story narration, rewards, reinforcements, and solving mysteries are included in gamification to hold the participants' focus, interest, and thoughts. This integration offers chances for abundant fun, more engagement, and better motivation. It makes the participants not just existing, but performers.

Gamification is often confused with other closely related concepts, namely (Kapp, 2014) games and simulations. Since they share more traits in common, they are considered to be synonyms of each other. Thus, before understanding the concept of gamification, it is vital to understand the difference between these three. Urh et al. (2015) undoubtedly, the terms 'game' and 'gamification' must be distinguished from each other. Generally, a game refers to an activity in which players engage just for amusement or fun, where there may be set rules or may not. In reality, gamification is a learning environment that includes some of the game aspects but not entirely the game itself as a tool (Škuta and Kostolányová, 2016) and expects the learners to attain certain educational objectives. On the other side, simulation is used to practice certain skills and Kapp (2014) referred to 'simulation' to be a virtually controlled situation where learners can practice specific behaviours and experience the impacts of their behaviours. Some examples are learning car or flight driving, testing the functioning of equipment and software, practicing the movements in gymnastics, modifying interpersonal skills, and practicing surgical operations, etc. in an online simulator. A mere understanding of the differences among these three does not ensure the effective implication of gamification. Thus, this chapter further attempts to explore gamification in learning and instruction, elements of gamification, and the theory behind gamification that will enable us to familiarise ourselves with the process of gamification and apply its' principles in an instructional design.

Place of Gamification in Education

According to Kiryakova et al. (2014), the key problems in education are lack of engagement and motivation of students to learn, and teachers use new techniques and approaches to overcome this. Presently, there is evidence for successful attempts at the inclusion of ICT in education. In addition, rewarding the efforts of the learners is an effective means to enhance their active engagement. One such major attempt to make learning enthusiastic and enjoyable is termed 'gamification'. This is rapidly gaining status as omnipresence in learning and instruction. The concept of game thinking and gamification is being increasingly adopted in the learning process, especially in relation to skill development. Hurix (2020) reports that it is estimated to reach a global market value of $11.94 billion by 2021. To engage people more, promote learning, and solve problems in learning, the incorporation of game-based mechanics, aesthetics, and game thinking was termed 'gamification' by Kapp (2014).

The use of games in education is common, and also evolutionary psychologist Gray (2013) supports this and says that it is self-directed, intrinsically motivated, and imaginative. The concept of a game is relatively familiar to any learner, as most of us have been acquainted with at least one game and hence, experienced real-life games. Similar principles are utilised in most of the online formats of gamification to enable the learner to achieve certain skills or master the necessary content. Giang (2013) reported that Gabe Zichermann, founder and chief executive at Dopamine Inc., said that activity or work that feels like a fun game improves the ability to learn new skills by 40%, and there are three main components essential for gamification to succeed, namely feedback, friends, and fun. While this mainly refers to the outcomes of companies, it also applies to education. The recent enormous use of e-learning platforms is encouraging gamification and providing a favourable environment for its implementation (Kiryakova et al., 2014). Thus, gamification could be successfully used in the classroom for the active engagement of learners.

Gamification in learning will lead to commitment and motivation of learners towards the activities they are involved in and make their achievement of objectives easier. By comparing the process of game and education, Kiryakova et al. (2014) stated that in games, the player is expected to overcome the obstacles and achieve a specific task; and likewise, in education, the learner is expected to achieve the objectives by interacting with the content. Since the tracking of players is a vital element of a game, the collaboration of game elements in education makes tracking of the learners' progress easier and an inevitable part of learning. Also, gamification makes tracking learners' progress in achieving the learning objectives automated, and Glover (2013) reported that students' learning path is determined by the achieved levels of knowledge and skills. In addition, gamification for learning and training establishes a better competitive spirit among the learners. Evidentially, gamification affected users in distinct ways based on their personality traits, indicating that its effect depends on the specific characteristics of users (Smiderle et al., 2020).

Generally, educational institutions have stated preferring the implementation and use of a Learning Management System (LMS) due to its efficiency in managing human resources, tracking the progress of a student, and serving even remote learners. With the help of LMS, educational institutions offer a range of e-learning courses incorporated with learning resources and activities. Among the various activities, LMS could also provide gamification features (e.g., Docebo) to the learners that can motivate and engage the learners as well as automatically track their progress. Play Posit is an LMS recognised by the National Science Foundation for bringing positively significant student learning outcomes and knowledge attainment.

Steps Involved in Designing Gamification

Another important aspect of gamification is that it could be used both in regular classrooms and e-learning environments. The elements and techniques of games can be aptly used in the classroom without the aid of any advanced technologies or software. For example, paper-based games to find numbers and words, quizzes, etc. can bring gamification into the physical classroom. On the other hand, the inclusion of gamification in an e-learning environment is quite simple. Based on the expected learning outcomes, the technology and instructional design are chosen and implemented. Various elements of games can be used both online as well as in a regular classroom. To develop an effective gamification in e-learning, the following steps were provided by Kiryakova et al. (2014).

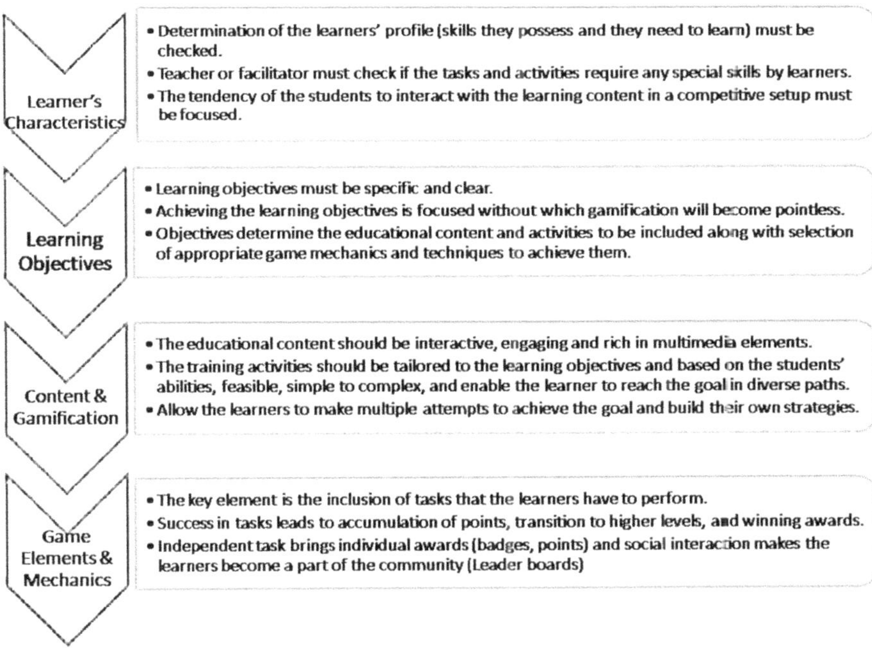

Chart 9.1 Steps in Designing Gamification.

Design of Gamification

As mentioned above, the main focus while designing gamification for educational purposes must be the learning outcomes and the abilities possessed by the learners. Since the base idea of gamification is motivation, the self-determination theory gains more importance in game designs. Thus, the design must include the three basic elements of this theory, as given: it has features of autonomy where the user can voluntarily participate and can control their learning experience; it provides a feel of connectedness or relatedness to the learner; and it must have a competent design with icons to guide the learners quickly and comfortably instead of having confusing and overwhelming features. Apart from this, it is essential to understand that both intrinsic and extrinsic motivations play their roles in encouraging the learner. The common errors that must be kept in mind while designing a gamification model are manipulations and tricks used to force the learners to participate, too much focus on the game aspects, failure to achieve the actual objectives, and lack of standards. Here is an example of a model that is best suited for the learner-centred gamification design.

Types of Gamification

Based on the purpose that gamification is intended to serve, Kapp (2014) refers to two types used in education, as given below:

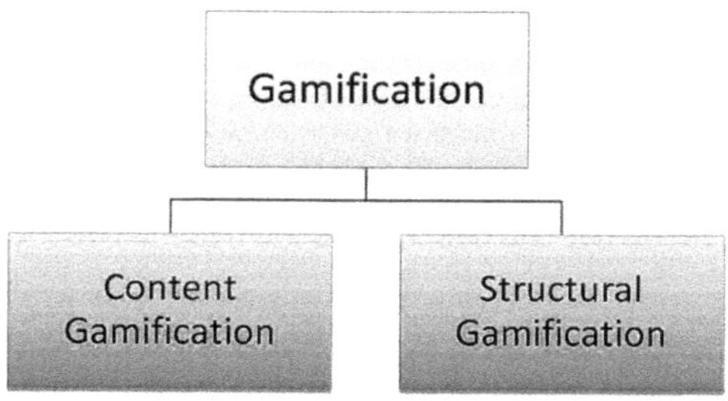

Chart 9.2 Types of Gamification.

- **Content gamification:** the chief focus of content gamification is to alter the entire learning content in order to make it like a game by applying the elements and mechanics of the game. In another sense, the information or content is presented to the learner in an interactive game mode. The elements of a game-like story narration, mystery, adventure, task to reach the next level or information, problem-solving, etc. are used to convert the learning material. For example, adding a story to illustrate the importance of the environment and making the learner play a game to make the soil fertile and green.
- **Structural gamification:** the application of game elements just to boost or stimulate the learner to go through and finish the content is structural gamification. Game-like alterations are limited to the structure or outline of the instructional material and not to the original content. For example, adding some features to the lessons like promotions by leaderboards and badges,

levels to reach to find the answer to the quests, rewards for watching a video, quizzes to enter the next content, virtual points, etc. During the process, the learning material is not altered or disturbed. Only the strategy in presenting it is modified.

Principles and Mechanics of Gamification

Design principles of gamification are the aspects that define the features of the learning environment (Škuta and Kostolányová, 2016). Visible status, social engagement, freedom of choice, rapid feedback, freedom to fail, goals and challenges, storyline, and the principles are listed based on their frequent occurrence by Dicheva et al. (2015). Some of the minor principles still in use are Unlocking Content, Personalisation, Onboarding, and Time Restriction. Using the mechanics of gamification allows people to engage, get motivated for the right actions, endorse learning, and solve problems. Game mechanics are the rules and rewards that appear in a game. Kiryakova et al. (2014) indicated that these are familiar to players as most of them have played or continue to play different games. Game mechanics refers to how anything operates and includes rewards, virtual points, levels, adventures, badges, and leader boards that keep the participants engaged with gamification. The game elements have been divided into 'design principles' and 'game mechanics' (Škuta and Kostolányová, 2016), and game mechanics are tools that help realise those design principles (Ollson et al., 2015). Users also experience the game dynamics (emotions, behaviours, and desires) while moving to the next step or getting feedback on success. Thus, both game mechanics and game dynamics work hand in hand and require a powerful LMS. Though there are varying lists on the game mechanics, here are the seven chief gamification mechanics given by Mehrotra (2019), which are recognised globally and used often. They are discussed in Table 9.1.

Table 9.1 Game Mechanics and Their Purpose

S.No.	*Mechanics*	*Purpose*
1	Points	Earning points in gamification motivates the learner to unlock and move to the next level or task in learning. These points enable the learner to progress in the course and also to buy game items and rewards.
2	Badges or Achievements	When the learner achieves something, badges are given. Badges are represented wherever the learner's name is displayed

(Continued)

Table 9.1 (Continued) Game Mechanics and Their Purpose

S.No.	Mechanics	Purpose
		(e.g., leader board) in the LMS. This boosts the learner to compete well.
3	Levels	A learner is allowed to move to the next level, on completion of a task or gaining some points, solving a mystery, etc. Each time the level goes up, the game becomes tough, and new skills or learning modules are introduced.
4	Progress Bars	During gamification, the learner can visually see the progress in the course and how much is yet to be completed. These progress bars are often represented by ranging colours and animations.
5	Leaderboards	More and more achievements enable the learner to get a place on the leader board, which is considered to be very important in gamification.
6	Rewards	Based on the progress in the gamified learning environment by the response to tasks or evaluations, rewards like points, badges, levels, place on leader boards, and progression in the status bar are given.
7	Learner Interactions	Recently, interaction among learners is also gaining importance in gamification. This can be a good motivator and allows the learners to guide, compete, discuss skills, play cooperatively, and share their achievements.

Elements of Gamification to Be Integrated into Learning

Gamification was described by Kapp (2014) to be the process of applying game elements, game mechanics, and game thinking to nongame situations to bind all the enthusiasm, joy, and determination people exhibit while playing a game. These are the foundations behind the use of gamification while marketing a product and teaching a new skill or concept. Huang and Soman (2013) stated that students' motivation to participate in training depends on the context of the learning process and what follows from their achievements. For example, the apps that we might have used for fitness, language learning, or for online shopping would have given visual feedback, rewards like points, and aspects of fun. To understand the concept of gamification, it is essential to relate it to the traditional games that we have already experienced and to break down such games into smaller units to finally compare it with the former. Apart from this, as an educator or facilitator, it is vital to identify and integrate the necessary instructional strategies with the game. Thus, any game offers the players some elements to get motivated and play consistently, as below:

- **Goals and objectives:** these decide whether the gamification is efficient or not and the quality of interactions. Establishing clear goals, purpose, and learning outcomes is a crucial part of it. Goals must be clear in terms of incentives, rewards, feedback, and progress indicators.
- **Rules:** rules are nothing but instructions to attain the educational objectives and allow the learners to follow the directions, play a fair game, and achieve.
- **Interactions:** any learning environment that uses gamification includes different modes of interaction among the players like conflict, competition, cooperation, etc. These can be used alone or in combination. However, in a learning environment, it is wiser to avoid conflict and encourage competition and cooperation to motivate the learners healthily.
- **Feedback:** irrespective of the traditional games or a gamified e-learning environment, feedback plays a key role. This can be positive or negative but directs the learners to play a fair game.
- **Achievements:** it contributes to increasing the motivation and engagement of the learners. These achievements must be shown as progress bars or rewarded time and then should not become the main focus of the learners.
- **Rewards:** based on the nature of achievement, it is given in the form of points, badges, and leaderboards. These rewards are the ones truly helping to motivate and engage learners. Rewards must be effectively used for each correct answer or solved mysteries or tasks completed. Placement in leaderboards gives a sense of social status to the learners and encourages social interactions.
- **Levels:** the challenges in consequent levels must move from easy to difficult in any gamified learning environment. That is, it should be progressing from simple to complex for the learner.
- **Story narration:** narrating a story always develops curiosity among learners and creates a special interest in them. This provides ample interactivity and enables the learners to become more creative and attentive.
- **Failure and chance:** failing to progress in a task must not demotivate the learners from achieving the objectives. Hence, there must be maximum scope for them to replay, and undo the steps, and a sufficient chance to reattempt the same level or task.

- **Scoring:** this is the only means through which the learners understand their progress and also represent it to others in the community of learners. Transparency and clarity in scoring are essential.

Challenges in Implementing Gamification in Education

Any novelty is always associated with its own pros and cons. Likewise, gamification has some challenges in its successful implementation in the learning process. Using gamification techniques in learning requires careful planning, restructuring the prevailing teaching methods by educators, and most importantly a holistic curriculum. Simultaneously, it is questionable whether the educators and the educational institutions are well aware, equipped, and mentally prepared to welcome gamification into their zone. Unfortunately, game-based learning strategies are mostly in print and still used parsimoniously in the education system, whether related to school or higher education. While gamification in education is still in the process of development, the analytical review of Dichev and Dicheva (2017) reveals that there is insufficient evidence to support the long-term benefits of gamification in the field of education; the practice of gamifying learning has outpaced researchers' understanding of its mechanisms and methods; the knowledge of how to gamify learning or activity in harmony with the specifics of the educational context is still limited. However, numerous ongoing types of research prove it to become more than just a buzzword.

Conclusion

Undoubtedly, games possess elements that make them influential tools to make learning enthusiastic. Additionally, the influence of gamification in elevating the standards of the learning process is indisputable. Apart from being a dynamic tool to achieve educational objectives, gamification offers the scope to customise learning according to the learners (learner-centred) and also connect with remote learners. To successfully implement gamification in education, it is important to understand and adhere to the mechanics and elements of games. Incorporating these elements and mechanics strategically into the learning material or module needs expertise both in the subject as well as technology. Logically, execution of gamification can lead to a classroom that can transform learners to be actively engaged, highly skilled, and well-trained, and also achieve their long-term goals.

References

Davies, J., & Merchant, G. (2009). *Web 2.0 for schools: Learning and social participation.* Peter Lang, New York.

Dichev, C., & Dicheva, D. (2017). Gamifying education: What is known, what is believed and what remains uncertain: A critical review. *International Journal of Educational Technology in Higher Education, 14*(9). 10.1186/s41239-017-0042-5

Dicheva,, D., Dichev, C., Agre, G., & Angelova. G. (2015). Gamification in education: A systematic mapping study. *Educational Technology & Society, 18*(3), 75–88.

Giang, V. (2013, September 19). *'Gamification' techniques increase your employees' ability to learn by 40%.* Business Insider. https://www.businessinsider.in/gamification-techniques-increase-your-employees-ability-to-learn-by-40/articleshow/22730218.cms

Glover, I. (2013). *Play as you learn: gamification as a technique for motivating learners* [Paper presentation]. World Conference on Educational Multimedia, Hypermedia and Telecommunications 2013, In: HERRINGTON, Jan, COUROS, Alec and IRVINE, Valerie, (eds.). http://shura.shu.ac.uk/7172/1/glover_-_play_as_you_learn_-_proceeding_112246.pdf

Gray, P. (2013). Play as preparation for learning and life (an interview with Peter Gray). *American Journal of Play, 5*(3), 271–292. https://www.journalofplay.org/sites/www.journalofplay.org/files/pdf-articles/5-3-interview-play-as-preparation.pdf

Heick, T. (2018, December). *The definition of digital citizenship.* TeachThought. https://www.teachthought.com/the-future-of-learning/the-definition-of-digital-citzenship/

Huang, W. H., & Soman, D. (2013). *A practitioner's guide to gamification of education.* Rotman School of Management, University of Toronto. https://mybrainware.com/wp-content/uploads/2017/11/Gamification-in-Education-Huang.pdf

Hurix Digital, Gamification: 5 effective ways to Gamify learning in higher education. (2020, June 15). https://www.hurix.com/gamification-gamify-learning-higher-education/

Kapp, K. (2014, October 9). *Tutorial video welcome - Gamification of learning | LinkedIn learning, dahulunya Lynda.com.* LinkedIn. https://www.linkedin.com/learning/gamification-of-learning

Kiryakova, G., Angelova, N., & Yordanova, L. (2014). *Gamification in Education* [Paper presentation]. Proceedings of 9th International Balkan Education and Science Conference. https://www.researchgate.net/publication/320234774_GAMIFICATION_IN_EDUCATION

Kress, G. (2003). *Literacy in the new media age.* Routledge, New York.

Marczewski, A. (2013, March 11). *What's the difference between gamification and serious games?* Game Developer. https://www.gamedeveloper.com/business/what-s-the-difference-between-gamification-and-serious-games-

Mehrotra, M. (2019, May 16). *Gamification mechanics – What are they and why are they important?* eLearning. https://elearning.adobe.com/2019/05/gamification-mechanics-important/

Ollson, M. , Mozelius, P., & Collin, J. (2015). Visualisation and gamification of e-Learning and programming education. *The Electronic Journal of e-Learning, 13*(6), 441–454. https://files.eric.ed.gov/fulltext/EJ1087309.pdf

Smiderle, R., Rigo, S. J., Marques, L. B., Peçanha de Miranda Coelho, J. A., & Jaques, P. A. (2020). The impact of gamification on students' learning, engagement and behavior based on their personality traits. *Smart Learning Environments, 7*(3). 10.1186/s40561-019-0098-x

Škuta, P., & Kostolányová, K. (2016, May). *The Inclusion of Gamification Elements in the Educational Process* [Paper presentation]. DIVAI 2016, 11th International Scientific Conference on Distance Learning in Applied Informatics, Štúrovo, Slovakia. https://elibrary.kubg.edu.ua/id/eprint/15832/1/N_Morze_Mkonf_05_2016_GI.pdf

Urh, M., Vukovic, G., Jereb, E., & Pintar, R. (2015). The model for introduction of gamification into E-learning in higher education. *Procedia – Social and Behavioral Sciences*, *197*, 388–397. 10.1016/j.sbspro.2015.07.154

Walsh, M. (2009). Pedagogic potentials of multimodal literacy. In *Handbook of research on new media literacy at the K-12 level: Issues and challenges* (pp. 32–47). Information Science Reference. https://acuresearchbank.acu.edu.au/item/85926/pedagogic-potentials-of-multimodal-literacy

Chapter 10

Gamification: Future of Innovations in Education

Narendra Kumar, Tamisha, and Sheetal Prajapati

Department of Education, Central University of Rajasthan, Ajmer, Rajasthan, India

Introduction

Gamification is described as an educational platform that aspires to give feedback and incentives, to internalise student external motives. It is defined as a new trend aimed at enhancing learners' interest, involvement, motivation, and loyalty. The design of the game has the basic purpose of increasing the motivation of students and providing them with a goal so that they can be encouraged to solve problems, enhancing communication skills, and providing them with reinforcement to gain facts, information, and skills acquired by a person through the experience. Elements of the game provide opportunities to engage players in activities. In many games, you also have competition and even cooperation among players. In an instruction context, gamification is using game-based mechanics, aesthetics, and thinking to engage people in action learning and solve problems in a non-game context. It helps in gaining momentum. Gamification has many elements. It is self-contained. It is built structurally. It helps in teaching and reinforcing various skills.

Gamification, when it is concerned with education, is still a new subject. The term 'gamification' was first coined by Nick Pelling in 2002. Ryan Schaaf, Assistant Professor of Technology at Notre Dame of Maryland, was the first

DOI: 10.1201/9781032675176-10

person to associate gamification with the context of education. In 2008, Brett Terrill used the term 'chemical equation' in his blog, and he defined it as 'taking game mechanics and applying them to other web properties to increase engagement.' Gamification is a multi-disciplinary concept. It brings about all domains and puts them together to enhance knowledge engagement, motivation, and behavioural changes in the learner. As we all know, student learn best through experiences, and gamification brings the learner's imagination into real life so they can relate more to the context with the help of gamification compared to their normal daily classroom and theoretical studies. For 21st century learners, gamification has been one of the most innovative technologies when it comes to education. It has a lot of future potential. As we all know, traditional classroom settings are not sufficient for students, and new learning processes have been taking place for a long time in education. Also, it is a given that students should learn on their own, and the teacher should only act as a facilitator. This new technology can offer students a great experience with education and learning and give students an interactive environment. Integrating technology and education can bring a lot of improvement in the field of education in any new approach to learning, and teaching can emerge that can help in building a great future in education. As we all know, the most difficult task today is to bring out the motivation in the learner. It helps the learner to internalise their motivation and create loyalty to the subject. Students are more interested in playing games than studying as the game provides them rewards, reinforcement, and enjoyment. When we combine both education and gamification, it provides feedback and rewards, offers motivation to learners, and increases their interest in this subject as it also helps in improving communication problem solving, and many other skills. With gamification in education, students can enjoy learning like they enjoy playing games. It can also help to bring out learning achievements in students and bring out psychological and behavioural changes in students.

Gamification and Game-based Learning

We have all played games as part of our childhood, and these games may or may not have had particular rules or objectives. Most games are competitive, and there is a tendency to win or lose the game. The enjoyment part of the game comes first, and the rewards mostly come second to give the player motivation to play. Games are very engaging, and they have been used in education for a long time. In our classroom also, the teacher used to provide us with games, and there used to be some activities and rewards for the games that were used to reinforce skills. Game-based learning uses learning to achieve a specific outcome. Students learn by playing games that promote critical thinking and problem-solving in children.

The main aim of game-based learning is to get a good outcome from the student. The game has a specific objective in most cases.

Gamification, on the other hand, is the gaming component of our courses. It integrates game mechanics in a setting that is not for a game. The engagement of the learner provides extrinsic rewards, such as badges and achievements, and game-based learning mostly provides intrinsic rewards. Gamification is flexible when it comes to the environment or the pace at which the learner wants to learn. In gamification, assessment is not within the game. In game-based learning, the content of the lesson is adjusted in the game. The gamification process is the opposite of game-like as gaming aspects are adjusted to fit the content of the lesson. Some examples of gamification are Duolingo, class dojo, Quizlet, etc.

Systematic Components and Experiential Components

As you already know, gamification is a game mechanism applied in other contexts, as described by Terill. Game mechanics is the systematic component of the game, the construction of the game, and how the gaming systems are made. Most of it is a mechanical and quantifiable part. The experiential component is very important as it is related to the human component of the game. It is more abstract and is related to student involvement. The system is the game rules, and all the objectives are part of a systematic component; however, what the student experiences is the motivation he feels and the learning he gets after playing the game, all received in the experiential part of the game. This is why all games are unique. Then, we combine both the systematic and experiential parts of the game. Only then can we get a particular outcome that we aim to get from the game. It combines all the mechanics, dynamics, and emotions of the learner.

Experiential Learning Outcomes

Learning by doing has been one of the main tactics in education. The students learn by reflecting on their experiences and working out activities. The teachers act as a facilitator, and students learn themselves. The students learn with the help of activities, also known as the engaged learning process. This process of learning is known as experiential learning. With the help of experiential learning, students get hands-on experience, can reflect better, and are able to connect theories and knowledge learned in the classroom. It is known that video games help in the ability of multitasking to improve the focus and working memory of the students. Some of the positive psychological aspects such as perception, motivation, satisfaction, attitude, engagement, and self-efficacy are improved with the help of gamification (Figure 10.1).

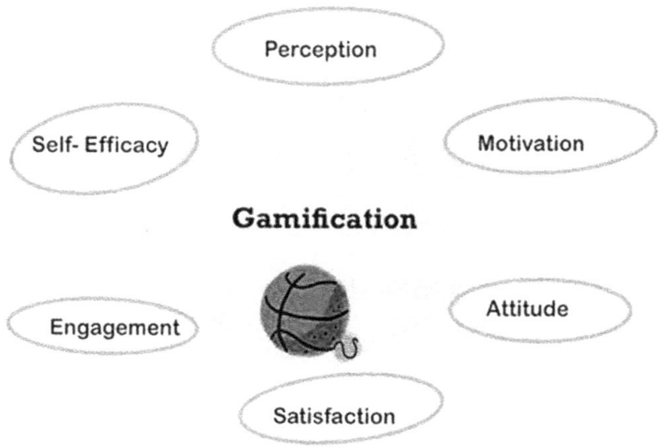

Figure 10.1 Psychological aspects that are improved through gamification.

Perception

Gaming provides a sensory experience to the students as it provides both stimulus and response to the students by giving them the environment and putting theory into practice through their actions in the game. Gamification helps in organising, selecting, and interpreting the data and also helps student with their mental representation of the subjects. It helps students to create a better self-concept and experience through the game the values, beliefs, and notions of the subject that they are studying.

Attitude

Jung defines 'attitude' as the 'readiness of the psyche to act or react in a certain way.' Gamification helps to bring a positive attitude to learning and also helps in improving the attention span of the learner. It lessens destructive behaviour and makes concepts more memorable compared to memorising the concepts from a book. Gamification enhances the learning of students.

Satisfaction

Satisfaction is also related to a positive attitude. Because students can get positive reinforcement and positive cognitive and emotional outcomes through the game, they feel satisfied while playing games. While providing positive experiences, gamification also provides learning. It provides gratification and contentment to the learner. It also provides emotional development as games are competitive, and some of the games also need cooperation while playing.

Engagement

Engaging students in traditional classrooms has been really difficult from the start as students naturally aren't able to focus a lot if they are not interested in the classroom or subject. Teachers have to think of many activities and programs so that learning can be enjoyable and students can be engaged in the class. Gamification can help to engage students as games provide various levels of advancement, and students desire to continue to play the games over a long period. The complexity of the game increases as the levels are crossed by students, and students are provided with more difficulty. They are more motivated to learn through the game.

Self-efficacy

Bandura referred to self-efficacy as individuals' expectations about their ability to perform a task successfully. As games help students to achieve and motivate them, with each task students are given reinforcement after performing a task successfully. Games also help students to improve their performance, and they increase learners' interest in various subjects as students can associate better while experiencing the game.

Motivation

Motivation is a very important part of education. Gamification provides both extrinsic and extrinsic motivation. Students play the game because it motivates them to perform better. All the games have this type of system in which students have to achieve better. With increasing levels, they have to match the difficulty of the level for their growth in the game. In games, this psychological need of players is fulfilled. Event-related education brings out the desired outcomes and motivation in students.

Conclusion

Gamification is a multidisciplinary field and helps students understand difficult topics. The association with education gamification can bring about positive psychological and behavioural changes in students. It can help in increasing motivation, self-efficacy, and other positive aspects of their cognitive ability. Although this field has a lot more to discover and many researchers are still waiting to be done on this topic, the impact of gamification on education has been seen to be positive until now. Gamification provides a positive learning environment to students and helps them to focus. As the traditional classroom is unable to provide them with various experiences, this new technology can help them improve their ability to learn and sustain motivation for a long time.

References

Ahmad, A., et al., (2020). The impact of gamification on learning outcomes of computer science majors. *ACM Transactions on Computing Education*, *20*(2), 1–25. 10.1145/3383456

Cheng, V. W. S., Davenport, T., Johnson, D., Vella, K., & Hickie, I. B. (2019). Gamification in apps and technologies for improving mental health and well-being: Systematic review. *JMIR Mental Health*, *6*(6), e13717. 10.2196/13717

Hursen, C., & Bas, C. (2019). Use of gamification applications in science education. *International Journal of Emerging Technologies in Learning (IJET)*, *14*(01), 10.3991/ijet.v14i01.8894

Lau, A., & Borchert, M. (2020). Gamification. *WiSt – Wirtschaftswissenschaftliches Studium*, *49*(5), 5–10. 10.15358/0340-1650-2020-5-5

Ofosu-Ampong, K., Boateng, R., Anning-Dorson, T., & Kolog, E. A. (2020). Are we ready for Gamification? An exploratory analysis in a developing country. *Education and Information Technologies*, *25*(3), 1723–1742. 10.1007/s10639-019-10057-7

Saleem, A. N., Noori, N. M., & Ozdamli, F. (2021). Gamification applications in e learning: A literature review. *Technology, Knowledge and Learning*. 10.1007/s10758020-09487-x

What "Gamification" is and what it's not. (2017). *European Journal of Contemporary Education*, *6*(2). 10.13187/ejced.2017.2.221

Chapter 11

Flipped Learning: A Strategy for Focused Group and Personalised Learning

M. Poorani

Biological Science Education, Bosco College of Teacher Education, Dimapur, Nagaland, India

Introduction

Irrespective of whether a nation is developed or in the course of development, there has been a remarkable change in the process of learning whereby the incorporation of technology has become inevitable. For instance, in a developing country like India, the progress from Operation Blackboard (1987) to the present day's Operation Digital Blackboard – ODB (2019) is one such note-worthy phase. A step ahead, it has been proposed that there will be around nine lakh classrooms (including schools, universities, and colleges) with digital boards by 2022. In Leamnson's (2000) view, learning is mostly influenced or stimulated by external agents whereby teaching becomes critical. The transformation from regular boards to digital boards constructively improves the quality of education, enables the learners' easier access to e-resource materials, promotes personalised learning, alters the teachers into versatile facilitators, and encourages exploring

DOI: 10.1201/9781032675176-11

the newest technologies. Further, initiatives like e-Pathshala, SWAYAM, DIKSHA, National Programme on Technology Enhanced Learning (NPTEL), National Repository of Open Educational Resources (NROER), etc. provide suitable and quality content, thus facilitating blended and flipped learning (Drishti, 2019, February 21).

A flipped classroom is referred to as an instructional strategy that offers greater scope for the teachers to spotlight each individual learner. In this pedagogical approach, learning instruction is transferred from a group to individual learners. Ultimately, flipped learning aims to provide a dynamic and interactive learning environment to enable learners' active engagement, reflective learning, peer discussion, and enriching problem-solving skills with a pedagogical approach. Though Jonathan Bergmann and Aaron Sams (high school teachers) are regarded as pioneers in using flipped learning by posting video tutorials online, now there are numerous online flipped learning course providers who sustain the veracity of flipped learning like Khan Academy, TeacherTube, Coursera, TED-ED, etc. Millennial learners have the utmost ease of access and prefer to learn in action as well as in collaborative learning environments (Vaughan, 2014), and they expect communications to be constant in all aspects of their lives, including education (Prensky, 2005). Taking into consideration the present-day learners who are often referred to as digital natives and the transforming digital learning environment, flipped learning has been found to have an important place.

Flipped Learning – A Reverse Approach to Learning

The flipped classroom model, as per Nouri (2016), is the idea of inverse traditional teaching with what students generally do out of class. In flipped learning, teachers intentionally provide the students with digital content or short video lectures before experiencing the traditional classroom. This allows the learner to gain basic knowledge essential to participate actively during the classroom activity. Thus, the learner becomes more interactive and collaborative during the flipped classroom process. As stated by Abeysekera and Dawson (2015), students engage in learning under the instructor's guidance only after watching online or video lectures, collaborating during online discussions, or performing research activities at home. In this, there is an intentional shift from teacher-led instruction where the students are more passive to a learner-centric model where the students are active learners, and teachers are facilitators. In other words, there is an alteration in the activities that took place at school and home in the traditional classroom; they could be explained in two stages.

i) ***At-home learning:*** Learning at school has shifted to learning at home with the aid of the content given by the teachers, and

ii) ***In-class activities:*** Homework given by teachers in traditional classes has transformed into various activities practiced in the classroom according to the guidance of the facilitator or teacher and through peer learning after the completion of stage one.

This attempt to switch over or reverse the activities taking place in class and at home could be related to shifting or flipping the sides of a coin. The value and purpose of the coin even after shuffling its two sides remain unchanged. Likewise, the purpose of education or the learning outcomes remain constant even after replacing the teacher-led instruction at school with digital content to be learned at home, and replacing homework in the traditional form with student–teacher collaborative practices/activities in the classroom.

Four Pillars of FLIP

Muir and Geiger (2016) used a framework of four pillars or features of FLIP, namely a flexible environment, a shift in the learning culture, intentional content, and professional educators (Figure 11.1). Additionally, these four elements are considered to be conducive for learning to happen in a flipped classroom. These four factors are the major components that hold and elevate the standard of flipped learning. In other words, the quality of flipped learning relies on the provision of the infrastructure, curriculum, and efficiency of the teachers.

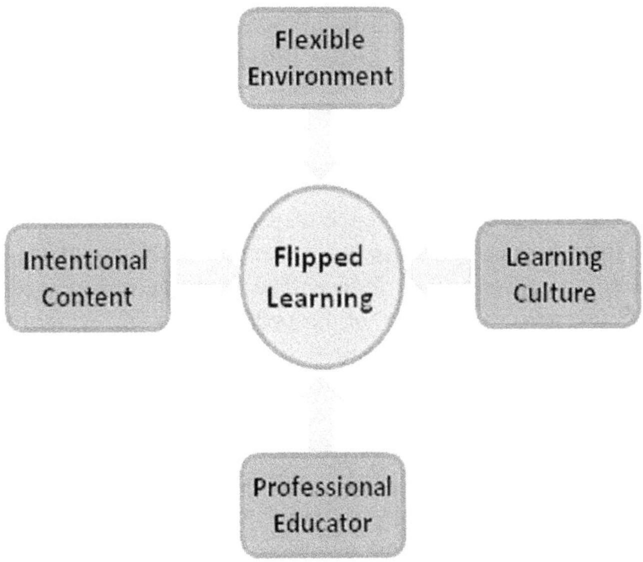

Figure 11.1 Four pillars of FLIP (Voss and Kostka, 2019).

- **Flexible environment:** In flipped learning, the learners are free to choose their own convenient time and place for learning. Thus, the teachers or facilitators provide ample flexibility to the students and offer an amicable environment. Also, teachers maintain flexibility in timelines based on the abilities of the students and allow them to master the content at their own pace.
- **Learning culture:** Learning both in class and at home is efficiently managed in a way that keeps the learner motivated and engaged. The time spent during classroom learning is devoted to learning concepts in-depth through varied activities. Though both the learning patterns vary outwardly, the learning culture at home and in class is in sync with each other and offers a constructive learning culture.
- **Intentional content:** As mentioned earlier, the teacher or the facilitator intentionally provides the learners with digital content or videos before they step into the normal classroom. The teacher pre-determines what must be taught to whom along with the materials required for individual learning and classroom activities. Pre-determination of the learning content is based on the continuous assessment made by the teachers.
- **Professional educator:** Though the role of teachers or educators may seem to be less visible, their profile seeks more expertise in both the technical end and subjects. Their role is more demanding and challenging compared to that of traditional classroom teachers. They equip themselves to multitask, monitor, guide through flipped learning videos, and assess students' performance. They dedicate their entire time to in-class activities to enable students to explore new knowledge and skills, which makes them key driving forces of flipped learning.

Evidential Highlights on Flipped Classroom

While attempting to examine the flipped classroom application and its efficacy in teacher education programs, Umam, Nusantara, Parta, Hidayanto, and Mulyono (2019) reported that it promoted independent learning, encouraged peer group learning, and improved awareness of flipped learning. In a multi-perspective assessment, Malto, Dalida, and Lagunzad (2017) showed that teacher-observers reported the flipped-classroom approach to be novel and encourage collaboration and active interactions between student–teacher and student–student, along with opportunities for scaffolding and differentiation. In an analytical review, Ngo and Yunus (2021) highlighted that English teachers and learners mostly agreed that flipped learning was beneficial to them. In a study on the effectiveness of Flipped PBL in mathematics learning among collegiate students, Kim (2018) found that the performance and interest of the experimental group were higher than the control group. Lo and Hew (2021) reported that using the flipped classroom approach, a considerable number of mathematics instructors have redesigned their courses, and that resulted in the increased behavioural, emotional, and cognitive engagement of students. Apart from maths, Iyer (2019) found that while teaching English as a Second Language (ESL) using a flipped approach to first-year Tamil medium learners at the university level, the students' proficiency level intensely progressed.

Nevertheless, flipped learning not only improves the performance or achievement of the students but also enables overall development. Fernández-Martín, Romero-Rodríguez, Gómez-García, and Navas-Parejo (2020) indicated that flipped classrooms improved students' knowledge and attitudes toward mathematics along with collaborative work, autonomy, and self-regulation toward learning. In 2016, Bhagat, Cheng-Nan, and Chun-Yen reported that those students who learned maths through the flipped classroom approach had gained significantly better attention, relevance, confidence, satisfaction, and positivity, and higher motivation than the group learned through the traditional method. This result substantiates the findings of Clark (2015) and Katsa, Sergis, and Sampson (2016) that there was increased learning outcomes, better motivation, and more engagement of students through the flipped classroom model (FCM). Also, Malto et al. (2017) reported that students showed more interest and greater confidence in learning a subject, and they actively engaged in activities like discussions, projects, debates, etc. It is important to understand that the variation in the outcomes of some studies may be due to the homogeneity or heterogeneity of the group involved in the experiment.

Flipped Classroom and Mastery Learning

According to Hattie (2013), gifted students in a flipped classroom can opt to learn via video tutorials more quickly, and it also enables them to escape from boredom due to the slow pace of their less gifted or slow-learning peers. This could be reversely understood that in flipped classrooms slow learners can learn and master the lessons freely at their own pace without being forced or compared with gifted learners, unlike in traditional classrooms. Mastery learning is a concept widely spoken way back at the beginning of the 20th century. There are four major differences between the traditional classroom and mastery learning model based on a) the mastery level of each student, b) time, c) strategy, and d) the role of the teacher. Mastery learning when used singly identified itself to be impractical, and lots of issues, like providing diverse lectures to diverse groups of students, evaluation, sharing of test items by gifted learners, etc., popped up. However, these issues were rectified when mastery learning was merged with the flipped classroom. Rosenberg (2013) pertinently stated that while some teachers are now reviving mastery learning, flipped classroom is making it feasible. Flipped classrooms focus on the mastery learning model to achieve equality among students in gaining content command. This is evident from the study by Ferriman (2020) on Clintondale High School, where classroom flipping that was done in 2010 reduced the failure rate from 44% to 13%. Also, Eugenia (2021) reported that the success of flipped classrooms relied on the appropriateness of learning material or content and teachers' pedagogical knowledge, rather than just technical competence.

Personalised and Focused Group Models

Any novel approach in the educational system should cater to the needs of all kinds of learners (gifted, average, and slow learners) and allow them to excel. It is no surprise that an innovation optimises the performance of gifted learners. Conversely, it must equally encourage and improve the achievement of slow learners. Thus, both personalised and focused group flipped learning could be initiated for effective learning to happen among various groups of learners. Personalised learning enables customising the learning content and the learning process according to the interest, skills, and needs of each learner. In the case of focused group learning, the main aspect to be remembered while grouping the learners is that they should be homogeneous, especially based on their performance or ability. For example, the grouping of the learners based on their I.Q., mathematical ability, communication skills, examination scores, etc. To understand better, here are some of the sample groups, namely gifted learners, slow learners, students with intellectual disability, autism, and ADHD.

Focused Group Flipped Learning (FGFL) for Slow Learners

The focused group flipped learning primarily relies on what is known to the slow learners (Vygotsky's ZPD) and what knowledge has to be acquired by them with regard to Bloom's taxonomy. Here is an illustration of the effective use of FGFL for slow learners. (Figure 11.2)

Generally, gifted learners and average learners can speed up their learning by attaining mastery over the content. Likewise, slow learners can also be guided to keep pace in learning with their peers by concentrating on their mastery level in the subject. Excluding the time difference in learning, if they are given an optimal learning environment slow learners can also excel. From the words of Rosenberg (2013), it is evident that teachers are shifting from flipped learning as it allows the students to master the content. Additionally, the research carried out at

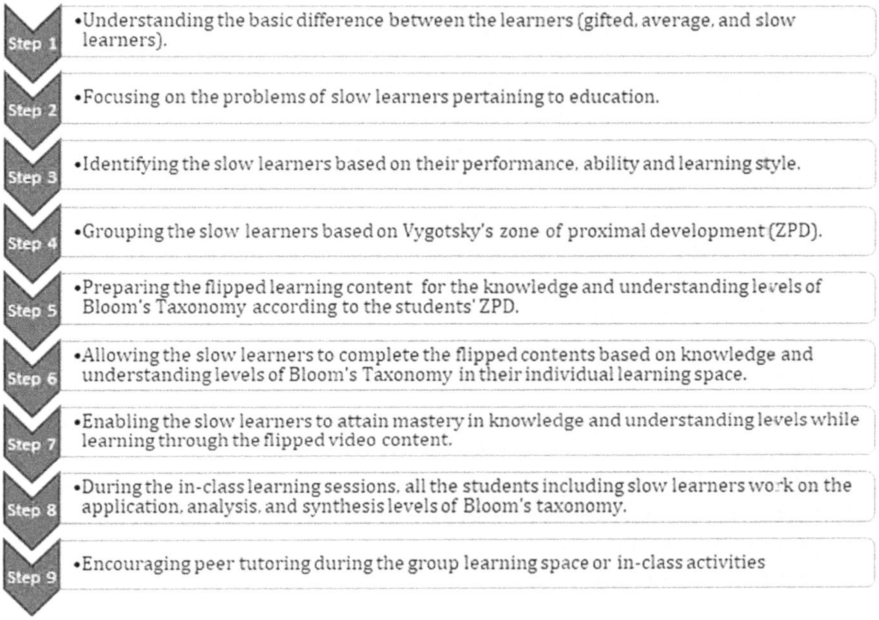

Figure 11.2 Steps in FGFL for slow learners.

Clintondale High School (2010) showed that classroom flipping reduced the failure rate by 21%. While investigating the impact of flipped learning, Nouri (2016) revealed that there was a substantial improvement in the attitude and learning of the low achievers. Thus, by adopting the focused group flipped classrooms, equality among students in achievement can be attained, and slow learners will also be equally benefited like others. The main element leading to an effective focused group flipped classroom is technology-enabled learning, which relies on teachers' knowledge of technology as well as the content.

Another important aspect to be remembered by the teacher while converting the normal classroom into a focus group flipped class is that the teacher does not need to convert the entire class. Instead, they can have groups of students based on their ability and provide learning content as required or demanded by the groups. Thus, the gifted learners who learn quickly may not receive the remedial videos, but the slow learners may receive them apart from focused group flipped learning and learn them to match the mastery level of other students in the class. This enables the weaker students to perform well and with ease during in-class activities. Thus, if the bias in the learning of diverse students existing in the traditional classroom must be eradicated then a teacher should boldly opt for focused or personalised flipped learning models.

Regular Benefits of Flipped Learning

Irrespective of the pedagogy and the nature of learners in a group, flipped learning provides some common benefits as below:

- Self-paced learning by students.
- Provides an opportunity for in-depth as well as diverse learning.
- Encourages collaborative and peer learning.
- Both students and teachers get familiarised with various digital tools and technologies.
- Apt for dynamic teachers who have abundant knowledge and expertise in technology.
- Allows the students to self-evaluate and improve their efficacy.
- Parents are the indirect beneficiaries who passively learn the content and technology.
- Teachers can easily judge the level and difficulties of the students.
- Active classroom/interactive learning environment that allows better classroom management.
- Improves students' accountability.
- In-class focus is on more exploration, discovery, and application of new knowledge.
- Motivating and challenging for dynamic teachers.
- Cost-effective, richer, and infinite subject content.
- Can periodically upgrade the content with some additions and deletions.
- Facilitates better teacher–student interaction.

Specific Advantages of Flipped Learning for Focused Group and Personalised Learning

1 **Enables a strong foundation for all:** By this, even the slow learners or those who need individualised attention are privileged to watch the digital content like videos provided by their teachers as many times as they want during at-home learning. This gives the learners a more personalised experience due to which they understand the concept well; boost content command, problem-solving ability, and logical reasoning; and are able to critically evaluate just like the gifted students or other students of the class do.

2 **Additional/Remedial lectures for slow learners:** Teachers can provide additional or remedial digital materials/videos for the students who are grouped under the 'focus group,' (i.e., those who need special attention) along with the routine videos given to the entire class to learn by themselves

while at home. This enhances their memory strength, abstract reasoning, imagination, transfer learning, and life skills.

3 **Both focus group and personalised learning:** In this, the video content given to learn at home could be customised as per the requirement of a group of students or for individual learners. Thus, it widens the chance of better learning for even those who are weak.

4 **Content mastery:** Mastery learning becomes inevitably possible with the successful implementation of focused group flipped learning, which could cater even to the need of slow learners during problem solving. As per Rosenberg (2013), even some of the students who do not get through the entire year's study material were able to demonstrate competency in the portions that they did complete.

5 **Increased participation of learners in in-class activities:** Since focused group flipped learning enables students to be strong and confident in what they know (even if it is a little), it allows them to liberally participate in classroom activities like discussion, projects, games, drills, puzzles, illustrations, etc.

6 **Evaluating different learners:** Learning Management Systems (LMS) like Moodle, Google Classroom, Canvas, ILIAS, etc. provide a versatile platform to manage content as well as evaluate in flipped learning. Testing through LMS becomes easier as it allows sorting different sets of questions for students from a pool of questions.

7 **Personalised instruction vs independent projects:** Personalised instruction enables slow learners to gain understanding at their own pace and attain mastery; at the same time, the gifted students can work on independent projects that allow them to be engaged and productive so that they do not disturb the slow learners.

8 **In-depth foundation:** It is advantageous for learners since they gain an in-depth understanding of the concepts, theories, and principles while learning through videos at home and in-class practice with their peers and optimal guidance from their teachers. Lo et al. (2017) identified three main benefits that learners get while learning through flipped classrooms, namely increased in-class time for tasks or assignments/practice, integration of new knowledge with existing knowledge, perception or beliefs, and real-time feedback.

9 **Higher-order skills:** Unlike the traditional classroom that takes you only to the knowledge, understanding, and application, flipping takes you to the advanced levels of Bloom's educational objectives, namely creating, analysing, and evaluating during the in-class activities. Thus, the primary two to three levels are already crossed at home or outside the classroom.

10 **Ample time and opportunity for in-depth learning:** Due to the at-home self-learning process, basics will be clear for the students. Thus, the students

find more time to discuss, explore, and take up new projects or activities in the classroom.

11 **Being voluntarily regular and dedicated to class:** Due to feasibility and better learning experience, even students who are irregular or slow will also gradually show regularity and active participation in learning. Also, those students who are unable to attend classes due to other school activities like sports and culture need not miss any of these classes.

Supporting Tools for Flipped Learning

There are various tools like video editors, gaming applications, LMS, websites, online educational channels, and editing software that could be used for flipped classrooms. LMS like Moodle, Canvas, Google Classroom, ILIAS, Edmodo, or in some cases, Zoom and Google Meet, are being extensively used, especially during this epidemic situation. Numerous online and offline applications for games like bingo, Soduku, and memory development are available. An LMS, PlayPosit is recognised by the National Science Foundation for bringing positively significant student learning outcomes and knowledge attainment. This permits educators to slot questions directly into a video's timeline and that can be answered by the learners in a synchronised fashion. LiveTiles Mosaic is an app for K-12 students and schools that forms an interface layer over Microsoft Office 365 and offers seamless online integration. Some examples of YouTube channels are 3Blue1Brown, Math Antics, and Numberphile. Teachers can make their instructional videos and upload them. Khan Academy is a typical example of digital blackboards and instructional videos. There are various tools to aid a teacher in the production of video content for learners like Electa, Audacity, Ink2Go, Windows Movie Maker (e.g., interpreting graphs), and screen recorders like Camtasia, which is also a video editor.

Problems Encountered in Implementing Flipped Learning

In developing countries like India, infrastructure is the major barrier to implementing flipped learning. Particularly, the financial assistance to establish flipped learning in all the government schools across the nation brings a question mark to our faces. Also, the availability of technically sound teachers along with superior content command who can showcase versatility in developing diverse learning content for diverse groups is a long way to go. Umam et al. (2019) highlighted some challenges in the application of flipped classrooms like technical issues, skills required for editing and recording, and time consumption.

Another problem that India might be facing is poor networks and slow internet connectivity. The challenges in the flipped classroom as reported by Lo et al. (2017) were i) the unfamiliarity of students with flipped learning and ii) the lack of instructors' striking start-up effort. Other severe threats to any novel technology in education are the digital divide and the socio-economic background that hinders a person from experiencing it, for which flipped learning is not exclusive. Even if we overcome all these barriers, the administrative authorities should understand the effectiveness of flipped learning and speed up its implementation process.

Conclusion

Although the flipped classroom approach may not work for every class, this model signifies an innovative approach to the teaching–learning process with the possibility to craft active, engaged, and learning-centred classrooms. In flipped learning, the slow learners obtain some prior knowledge and form a base before learning in the classroom. This enables them to think beyond and stimulates their inquiry mode before meeting their teacher. It also avoids the vagueness among them that originally existed in the monotonous traditional classes. Instead, it allows the students to be excited about the session and prepare various questions to discuss with their teacher and peers. On the other end, the teachers will also transform from being mere disseminators of information to innovative and inspiring teachers who can no more be referred to as monotonous teachers who stick to the blackboard. Flipped learning has enabled teachers to explore a new arena of the learning process whereby they represent themselves more as learners and less as teachers. In short, learning takes place as per the students' preferences, and the actual classroom is replaced with an efficient and intellectual discussion room for teachers and students.

References

Abeysekera, L., & Dawson, P. (2015). Motivation and cognitive load in the flipped classroom: definition, rationale and a call for research. *Higher Education Research & Development*, 1–14.

Bhagat, K. K., Cheng-Nan, C., & Chun-Yen, C. (2016). The impact of the flipped classroom on mathematics concept learning in high school. *Journal of Educational Technology & Society*, *19*(3), 134–142. https://www.jstor.org/stable/jeductechsoci.19.3.134

Charunphankaseam, R. (2018). Developing the application for learning place value. *The International Journal of Multimedia & Its Applications*, *10*(1/2/3), 53–61. 10.5121/ijma.2018.10305

Clark, K. R. (2015). The effects of the flipped model of instruction on student engagement and performance in the secondary mathematics classroom. *Journal of Educators Online*, *12*(1), 91–115. 10.9743/jeo.2015.1.5

Corbat, J. (2020, July 28). 7 steps to a flipped classroom. TeachThought. https://www.teachthought.com/learning/6-steps-to-a-flipped-classroom/

Corbat, J. (2020, July 28). How to flip your classroom in 7 steps. Teach Thought. https://www.teachthought.com/learning/6-steps-to-a-flipped-classroom/

Eugenia, M. W. Ng. (2021). Reflecting on leading flipped classroom practices in a liberal arts university in Hong Kong. *International Journal for Academic Development*, 1–5. 10.1080/1360144x.2021.1895169

Fernández-Martín, F., Romero-Rodríguez, J., Gómez-García, G., & Ramos Navas-Parejo, M. (2020). Impact of the flipped classroom method in the mathematical area: A systematic review. *Mathematics*, *8*(12), 2162. 10.3390/math8122162

Ferriman, J. (2020, January 14). 6 steps for flipping your classroom. LearnDash. https://www.learndash.com/6-steps-for-flipping-your-classroom/

Ferriman, J. (2020, January 10). Flipped classroom facts and figures. LearnDash. https://www.learndash.com/flipped- classroom-facts-and-figures/

Flip your classroom in 6 simple steps. (2017, July 11). Edmentum blog | An education blog. https://blog.edmentum.com/flip-your-classroom-6-simple-steps

Hattie, J. (2013). *Visible learning: A synthesis of over 800 meta-analyses relating to achievement.* Routledge.

Iyer, M. S. (2019). Flipped English as a Second Language (ESL) Classroom Approach to Scaffold the Slow Learners. *Language in India*, *19*(2), 114–119.

Jonathan, T. (2021, April 12). *Flipping your math classroom: A beginner's guide*. Mathspace Blog. https://blog.mathspace.co/flipping-the-classroom-without-flipping-a-table-a-blog-of-three-parts-c61f4df63d1a/

Katsa, M., Sergis, S., & Sampson, D. G. (2016). *Investigating the potential of the flipped classroom model in K-12 mathematics teaching and learning* [paper presentation]. 13th International Conference on Cognition and Exploratory Learning in Digital Age (CELDA 2016). https://files.eric.ed.gov/fulltext/ED571429.pdf

Khan, S. M. (2008). *Education of slow learner.* Retrieved from http://researcheducationedu

Kim, D. (2018). Study on flipped learning and flipped PBL effectiveness of college general mathematics. *Journal of the Korea Convergence Society*, *9*(6), 209–215. https://www.koreascience.or.kr/article/JAKO201819352297827.jsp-kj=SSMHB4&py=2012&vnc=v27n6&sp=588

Leamnson, R. (2000) Learning as biological brain change. *Change: The Magazine of Higher Learning*, *32*(6), 34–40. 10.1080/00091380009601765

Lo, C. K., & Hew, K. F. (2021) Student engagement in mathematics flipped classrooms: Implications of journal publications from 2011 to 2020. *Front. Psychol.* 12: 672610. 10.3389/fpsyg.2021.672610

Lo, C. K., Hew, K. F., & Chen, G. (2017). Toward a set of design principles for mathematics flipped classrooms: A synthesis of research in mathematics education. *Educational Research Review*, *22*, 50–73. 10.1016/j.edurev.2017.08.002

Lynch, M. (2015, November 3). The four pillars of flipped learning. The Edvocate. https://www.theedadvocate.org/the-four-pillars-of-flipped-learning/

Malto, G. A., Dalida, C. S., & Lagunzad, C. G. (2017). Flipped classroom approach in teaching biology: Assessing students' academic achievement and attitude towards biology. *KnE Social Sciences*, 3(6), 540. 10.18502/kss.v3i6.2403

Muir, T., & Geiger, V. (2016). The affordances of using a flipped classroom approach in the teaching of mathematics: A case study of a grade 10 mathematics class. *Mathematics Education Research Journal*, *28*(1), 149–171. http://dx.doi.org.ezproxy.nwciowa.edu/10.1007/s13394-015-0165-8

Mukerjee, S. (2014). Agility: A crucial capability for universities in times of disruptive change and innovation. *Australian Universities' Review*, 56(1), 56–60. Retrieved from https://www.learntechlib.org/p/154480

Mukunthan, T. (2013). A study on students' errors in word problem. *International Journal of Management, IT and Engineering*, *10*(3), 205–214.

Our Bureau. (2019, February 20). *HRD ministry launches operation digital board.* @businessline. https://www.thehindubusinessline.com/news/education/hrd-ministry-launches-operation-digital-board/article26319604.ece

Operation digital board. (2019, February 21). Drishti IAS. https://www.drishtiias.com/daily-updates/daily-news-analysis/operation-digital-board

Ngo, H. K., & Yunus, M. M. (2021). Flipped classroom in english language teaching and learning: A systematic literature review. *International Journal of Academic Research in Business and Social Sciences*, 11(3), 185–196. 10.6007/IJARBSS/v11-i3/8622

Nouri, J. (2016). The flipped classroom: For active, effective and increased learning – especially for low achievers. *International Journal of Educational Technology in Higher Education*, 13(1). 10.1186/s41239-016-0032-z

Prensky, M. (2005). Listening to the natives. Educational leadership, *63*(4), 8–13. Retrieved from http://www.ascd.org/ASCD/pdf/journals/ed_lead/el200512_prensky.pdf.

Rajkumar, R., & Hema, G. (2017). Teaching slow Learners in Mathematics: Innovative Technologies and Strategies. In M. Harikrishnan (Ed). *Education for Slow Learners*. Paper presented at the International Conference on Education for Slow Learners organized by Department of Education, Annamalai University, Annamalainagar (pp. 120). Chidambaram: Sri VelanPathippagam. (ISBN: 978-93-81236-33-8).

Ramakrishnan, & Priya, J. (2016). Effectiveness of flipped classroom in mathematics teaching. *International Journal of Research -GRANTHAALAYAH*, *4*(10(SE)), 57–62. 10.29121/granthaalayah.v4.i10(se).2016.2469

Rosenberg, T. (2013, October 23). *In 'Flipped' classrooms, a method for mastery*. Opinionator. https://opinionator.blogs.nytimes.com/2013/10/23/in-flipped-classrooms-a-method-for-mastery

Sebba, J., & Ainscow, M. (2001). International developments in inclusive schooling: mapping the issues. *Cambridge Journal of Education*, *26*(2), 5–I 8.

Shulman, L. S. (2002). Those who understand: Knowledge growth in teaching. *Educational Researcher*, *15*(2), 4–14.

Thakare, R. (2021, May 12). 8 Types of Flipped Learning Classrooms and Tools to Build Them. eLearning Industry. https://elearningindustry.com/flipped-learning-classrooms-tools-build-types

Umam, K., Nusantara, T., Parta, I. N., Hidayanto, E., & Mulyono, H. (2019). An application of flipped classroom in mathematics teacher education programme. *International Journal of Interactive Mobile Technologies (iJIM)*, *13*(03), 68. 10.3991/ijim.v13i03.10207

Vandivier, P. L., & Vandivier, S. C. (2002). Teacher attitudes toward main streaming exceptional students. *Journal for Special Educators*, *7*(3), 381–388.

Vaughan, M. (2014). Flipping the learning: An investigation into the use of the flipped classroom model in an introductory teaching course. *Education Research and Perspectives*, *41*, 25–41.

Voss, E., & Kostka, I. (2019). *Flipping academic English language learning: Experiences from an American University*. Springer.

Wei, X., Cheng, I., Chen, N., Yang, X., Liu, Y., Dong, Y., Zhai, X., & Kinshuk. (2020). Effect of the flipped classroom on the mathematics performance of middle school students. *Educational Technology Research and Development*, *68*(3), 1461–1484. 10.1007/s11423-020-09752-x

https://aiworldschool.com/how-is-the-flipped-classroom-model-bringing-about-a-revolution-in-education/

https://en.wikipedia.org/wiki/Flipped_classroom

https://lesley.edu/article/an-introduction-to-flipped-learning

https://livetilesglobal.com/9-helpful-tips-designing-flipped-classroom/

http://pedagogybyvasu.blogspot.com/2018/04/gifted-slow-learners-in-mathematics.html

https://sites.google.com/site/flippedlearning101/home

https://www.teacherspd.net/7-ways-flipped-learning-can-moderise-your-classroom-and-improve-student-learning/

https://www.teachthought.com/learning/6-steps-to-a-flipped-classroom/

https://www.winjigo.com/the-advantages-of-a-flipped-classroom/

Chapter 12

Need-Based Mobile Education and Care for Differently-Abled Students: Facilitating Flexible Learning

Shiba Khatoon and Vanitha C.
Department of Education, Central University of Kerala Kasaragod, Kerala, India

Introduction

The COVID-19 pandemic has caused stark changes in the face of the education system worldwide, disrupting normal functioning. Educational institutes have taken to online classes through digital applications. However, the digital divide caused by geographical differences, technological illiteracy, and lack of digital aids created barriers to the smooth functioning of regular online classes for all students. The most affected are the differently-abled students, which calls for more flexibility and customised learning. For the purpose and clarity of this study, differently-abled students here implies students with a disability that includes students with

DOI: 10.1201/9781032675176-12

hearing impairment, students with visual impairment, students with orthopaedic disability, and students with developmental disorders.

This chapterattempted to bring forth an idea to bridge the gaps associated with web-based teaching–learning in the context of differently-abled students and the COVID-19 pandemic. Many educational institutes have already shifted to a blended mode of teaching–learning. However, it is not as easy for differently-abled students, affecting their learning, retention, and motivation. Differently-abled groups of students need more flexibility in teaching–learning. This paper, therefore, sought an adaptive teaching–learning strategy, thereby giving shape to an evolved idea of blended learning. Various isolated concepts and principles of flexible learning, bookmobile, mobile learning, mobile teachers, and Therapy on Wheels were studied and integrated to shape a new idea of need-based mobile education and care for differently-abled students.

Theoretical Background of the Study

Flexible Learning

Naidu (2017) expressed flexible learning as 'a state of being' in his editorial. That is a state in which students have the freedom to choose the time, place, pace of learning, entry–exit points, learning activities, assessment tasks, and utilisation of educational resources. For teachers, this freedom is in the context of time management, mode, and methods of communication.

Flexibility in learning is seen as a valuable and potent principle in the educational field and society in general, like the significance of diversity and equality. Flexible learning evolved in terminologies over time. Blended learning and e-learning are synonymously used to imply flexible learning strategies. Flexible learning means flexibility and freedom in access to learning opportunities and approaches to teaching–learning (Naidu, 2016).

According to Shurville et al. (2008), flexible learning encompasses educational philosophies with wide choices, convenience, and individualised instruction for learners. In particular, flexible learning provides learners with choices about where, when, and how learning occurs.

For this chapter, Hart (2000)'s Flexible Learning Strategy was identified and summarised (as given below); it was instrumental in shaping the idea of need-based mobile education and care.

- Flexibility in access to education, resources, participation, teaching–learning methods, assessment, and choice of content
- Prior learning awareness
- Continuous evaluation

Bookmobile

Wikipedia describes a bookmobile or mobile library as a vehicle designed to suit the purpose of a library extending services to the doorsteps, in the streets, and to any underserved groups of people and remote areas. Bookmobile thus brings a customised service for the learners and those in need either in print books/ audiobooks, internet access, or both. Bookmobiles include varied modes of conveyance like wagons, motor vehicles, bicycles, camels, elephants, horses, donkeys, and mules (Bashaw, 2010). Even boats, India being an instance, are used as bookmobiles under the initiative of Paturi Nagabhushanam in 1935 as part of the Andhra Pradesh Library Movement (BL, 2023).

The West Bengal Transport Corporation launched Boat Library in collaboration with the Heritage Bookstore to promote the reading culture in Kolkata, West Bengal. The library consists of books in English and Bengali and comes with a Wi-Fi facility. Boat Library is a one-of-a-kind initiative in Kolkata (GKToday, 2021).

Similarly, 24 September 2020 witnessed the launch of the Tram Library Service in Kolkata (OT Staff, 2020).

Mobile Learning, Mobile Teachers and Teaching, Mobile Therapy (Therapy on Wheels)

Hockly (2013) studied mobile learning, its significance for English language teachers, and mobile literacy's concept, which brought to light the possible meanings of mobile learning subject to diverse interpretations and expressions. Mobile learning is traditionally implied using mobile as a technological aid or digital aid to support teaching-learning either through distance mode, in the classroom, or outside the classroom. Over the years, the term 'mobile learning' has evolved by exploring the diverse meaning of the term 'mobile,' si the specific meaning of 'mobile learning' is thus debatable (Kukulska-Hulme, 2009; Traxler, 2009).

For instance, mobile learning could mean learning involved using a mobile device in hand. Alternatively, mobile learning could mean flexibility in the learning space, mobility of place, and time of learning. This debate leads to a discussion on alternative concepts like mobile teachers and teaching or simply alternative meanings for the existing idea of the concept of mobile learning.

Few research studies and articles on mobile teachers and teaching suggest the similarity of the concepts with bookmobile or library on wheels In this respect, mobile teachers are 'teachers on wheels,' and mobile teaching is 'teaching on wheels,' making way for an alternative way to bring learning to the doorstep of the learners (Pinca, 2015).

The mobile teachers and teaching concept in India is new, and its first instance or execution was reported by The Better India (Raja, 2021) in the Kullu region of

Himachal Pradesh. As per the report, the Samphia Foundation in Himachal Pradesh launched a Therapy on Wheels programme on 3 December 2020, making it India's first mobile van therapy unit for the differently-abled. It is interesting to know that the mobile van was designed to meet the needs of children with disabilities. This programme was supported by The Indian Renewable Energy Development Agency Limited (IREDA).

The gist of the concepts of mobile teacher, mobile teaching, and mobile therapy expressed in a few of the articles available on websites suggest the following core ideas of mobile teaching learning and therapy:

- Bringing teachers to the doorstep of the learners.
- Facilitating flexibility in teaching-learning.
- Bringing therapy units to the doorstep of the learners.
- Suitability of the idea of learning at the doorstep to cater to the diverse needs of differently-abled students.

It is to be noted that the concept of mobile teachers and teaching is new to India, and a few studies have been conducted abroad.

The Emergence of the Idea, Concept, and Principles of 'Need-Based Mobile Education and Care'

The core concepts and principles of Bookmobile, Mobile Teachers, Mobile Teaching and Mobile Therapy are clubbed together to explain the concept of need-based mobile education and care. It is based on the principles of flexible learning to facilitate a blended mode of online and offline teaching–learning, whenever required, customised especially for different categories of differently-abled students and their individual needs. In addition to the existing ideas and concepts discussed above, the emergence of the idea of need-based mobile education and care for differently-abled students involves the introduction of the following innovative ideas:

Recreation and Creativity on Wheels

The idea is to design mobile vehicles well-equipped with tools and instruments, with adequate recreational and creative pursuits space. Resources such as art and craft papers, colours, stationery, musical instruments, plants for gardening, wooden planks, needles, and wool for stitching and embroidery, yoga mats, or equipment for physical exercises can be planned, adjusted, and brought on wheels. Such well-equipped vehicles should reach the learners to cater to their individual recreational and creative needs. It is vital to maintain COVID-19 safety measures while providing recreational and creative resources to differently-abled students.

Mobile Reinforcement Drive

The idea is to motivate, encourage, and inspire differently-abled students and their families to attend online classes and activities and come forward with a zest for both online and the wheels learning activities wherever online classes and activities are not feasible. For this purpose, a mobile reinforcement drive, including incentives like chocolates, stationeries, play tools, photo frames, a selfie with the favourite teacher, teaching aids, books, and the like, can be planned and distributed. It would also help provide the much-needed physical presence of the teachers before the students for their psycho-social well-being, especially in this COVID-19 pandemic time.

Principles of Need-based Mobile Education and Care

- **CUSTOMISED LEARNING:** Different categories of differently-abled students have different learning, psycho-social, and developmental needs, which again differ from individual to individual. Thus, one of the principles is to keep track of the changing or evolving needs of differently-abled students and to customise teaching–learning materials and activities accordingly.
- **FLEXIBILITY and MOBILITY:** Need-based mobile education and care is based on the principle of flexibility and mobility of teachers, teacher assistants, and students – when needed, and as needed, on wheels. Mobility is in terms of persons, vehicles, time, space, distance, pace, needs, and interests.
- **HEALTH and CARE:** Well-equipped mobile vehicles provide health and rehabilitation services to differently-abled students, and the presence of mobile teachers provides an 'empathetic' and 'cared for' environment to the students to promote their overall well-being in this pandemic.
- **RECREATION and CREATIVITY:** To make education fun, engaging, and exciting, recreational and creative activities should be brought to the doorsteps of the differently-abled students.
- **REINFORCEMENT and INCENTIVE:** To motivate and reinforce students and guardians to attend online classes, incentives at the doorstep of the learners for healthy attitude development towards learning in this pandemic time should be considered.
- **SAFETY MEASURES:** This principle calls for the maintenance of social distance while catering to the individual learning, creative, recreational, and health needs of differently-abled students. This principle implies following COVID-19 safety protocols of wearing masks, taking care of sanitisation, and motivating students and their family members to follow the safety measures.

- **BLENDED Mode:** Mobile education and care aims to beautifully blend distance, online mobile learning, desktop or laptop learning, and 'on the wheel' learning experiences filling in the gaps of either or both as per the need of the learners.
- **HAPPINESS and SATISFACTION in LEARNING:** If the needs of the students are met, students are likely to be happy and satisfied. Therefore, the focus of need-based mobile education and car' is to cater to the student's overall well-being by providing therapeutic services, guidance, and online and offline counselling through the 'therapy on wheels' concept.
- **INCLUSIVE EDUCATION and CARE:** Rethink and restructure education and care of differently-abled students in this pandemic time to promote and shape inclusive education and inclusive care.
- **RECORD MAINTENANCE:** Maintaining records of differently-abled students needing mobile education and care, their performance, progress and development, and the issues and positive changes associated with mobile education and care.

Benefits

The idea of need-based mobile education and care is to mitigate the problems causing hindrances to the smooth learning and development of differently-abled students. A review of the literature suggests various issues associated with the existing online-based distance learning system. The problems listed below strongly back the idea of introducing and executing mobile education and care and its benefits in overcoming these problems.

Akcil & Ünlücan (2018) conducted a study on mobile-based learning and brought to light the lack of adapted technologies for students with hearing impairment, visual impairment, and orthopaedic impairment.

As cited in the work of Mantzikos & Lappa (2020), distance learning is not free from issues like technical problems such as the absence of transcription and subtitles on video clips of teachers' lessons, making it difficult for students with hearing impairment to follow the classes. Other issues include delays in providing immediate feedback, trouble engaging students actively throughout the online lesson, and lack of collaborative strategies for the overall development of the learners.

Stepanović (2020) brought to light varied problems associated with shutting down schools like digital handicaps, the digital divide, shortage of necessities of life like food, health care, and child care, and loss of jobs. Rotarou et al. (2021) identified the need for protection, inclusion, and provision of employment, education, health, and care as comprehensive, inclusive measures for disabled people during this COVID-19 pandemic.

Studying the problems mentioned above in the context of distance learning for differently-abled students, as well as the need, significance, and merits of need-based mobile education and care can be realised based on the principles of flexibility, mobility, and customised blended learning. Where distance education and telehealth are next to impossible, 'mobile education' and 'mobile care', that is, 'care and education on wheels' at the doorstep of the learners will prove to be fruitful in bridging the learning, recreational, therapeutic, and developmental gaps of the differently-abled students.

Drawbacks or Limitations

1. One of the problems associated with the execution of mobile education and care is to identify the needs of differently-abled students, putting more pressure on teachers and guardians to keep a more vigilant watch on the learning developments and health of the students online and offline.
2. Mobile education and care units require heavy financial investment from government and non-government organisations.
3. The mental health of the faculty and students is to be actively considered and regulated from time to time while switching from online distance learning to learning on wheels, which otherwise may break down smooth communication.
4. Consistent investment of added time and energy is required to locate students' places of stay and the availability of teacher assistants in the vicinity to facilitate mobile education and care, which might not always be possible.

Conclusion

The idea of need-based mobile education and care is a step towards more flexible inclusive education and provision of inclusive care in this COVID-19 pandemic time and beyond. The potential benefits and drawbacks listed above provide scope for further study. Nevertheless, the new concepts, principles, and merits of the emerging idea of need-based mobile education and care substantiates the gaps in online and offline teaching–learning in a more flexible and innovative blended manner.

The idea is supported by the concepts and principles in similar lines of study as mentioned in the theoretical background section. Since the paper is theoretical, and as is the need of the hour to bring theory into practice, the feasibility and practicability of the idea presented can be analysed critically and tested empirically. Need-based mobile education and care should be promoted not only for differently-abled students but also for academia in general.

References

Akcil, U. & Ünlücan, Ç. (2018) The problems disabled people face in mobile and web-based e-learning phases in a developing country. *Qual Quant, 52*(suppl 2), 1201–1210. 10.1007/s11135-018-0683-z

Bashaw, D. (2010). On the road again: A look at bookmobiles, then and now. *Children & Libraries: The Journal of the Association for Library Service to Children.* p. 33.

Hart, I. (2000). Learning and the 'F' word. *Educational Media International, 37*(2), 98–101. 10.1080/095239800410388

Hockly, N. (2013). Mobile learning. *ELT Journal, 67*(1), 80–84. 10.1093/elt/ccs064

Kukulska-Hulme, A. (2009). Will mobile learning change language learning? *ReCALL, 21*(2), 157–165. 10.1017/s0958344009000202

Mantzikos, C. N. & Lappa, C. S. (2020). Difficulties and barriers in the education of deaf and hard of hearing individuals in the era of covid-19: The case of Greece – a viewpoint article. *European Journal of Special Education Research, 6*(3). 10.46827/ejse.v6i3.3357

Naidu, S. (2016) The case for open educational practice, *Distance Education, 37*(1), 1–3. 10.1080/01587919.2016.1157010

Naidu, S. (2017). How flexible is flexible learning, who is to decide and what are its implications? *Distance Education, 38*(3), 269–272. 10.1080/01587919.2017.1371831

Pinca, E. C. (2015). The mobile teachers' profile, competencies, performance and problems in the Department of Education, Division of Northern Samar, Philippines. *International Journal of Scientific & Technology Research, 4*(12), 45–50.

Rotarou, E. S., Sakellariou, D., Kakoullis, E. J., & Warren, N. (2021). Disabled people in the time of COVID-19: identifying needs, promoting inclusivity. *Journal of Global Health, 11*, 1–4. 10.7189/jogh.11.03007

Shurville, S., O'Grady, T., & Mayall, P. (2008). Educational and institutional flexibility of Australian Educational Software. *Campus-Wide Information Systems, Emerald Group Publishing Limited, 25*(2), 74–84. 10.1108/10650740810866576

Stepanović, S. (2020). The impact of the COVID-19 Pandemic on education. *NastavaiVaspitanje, 69*(2), 183–196. 10.5937/nasvas2002183s

Traxler, J. (2009). Learning in a Mobile Age. *International Journal of Mobile and Blended Learning, 1*, 1–12. 10.4018/jmbl.2009010101

Websites referred to

BL (2023, October 17). Boat Libraries. https://en.wikipedia.org/wiki/Boat_Libraries

GKToday (2021, January 27). *Kolkata's First Young Readers' Boat Library.* Kolkata's First Young Readers' Boat Library – GKToday

OT Staff (2020, September 26). Outlook Traveller. *Kolkata has the world's first tram library.* https://www.outlookindia.com/outlooktraveller/travelnews/story/70660/kolkata-has-the-worlds-tram-library

Raja, V. (2021, February 10). *India's First Mobile Therapy Van Has Helped 80 Diff-Abled Kids Access Therapy in Lockdown.* The Better India. India's First Mobile Therapy Van Has Helped 80 Diff-Abled Kids Access Therapy In Lockdown (thebetterindia.com)

Chapter 13

M-learning: A New Definition in Technology-Based Learning

Swapna Sikha Das and Nil Ratan Roy
Department of Education, Tezpur Univeristy (A central University), Tezpur, Assam, India

Chapter Objectives

1. To shed light on m-learning and characteristics of m-learning (mobile-based learning)
2. To identify the value of mobile learning with technological advancement
3. To understand the role of m-learning during the COVID-19 era
4. To know about the different m-learning apps in India that are playing a great role in digital learning
5. To throw light on the challenges of this type of learning in any educational system

Introduction to M-learning

Change is difficult, but the rapid development and adoption of new technology, as well as social changes, are likely to make changes in educational provision unavoidable (Cavus, 2011). Anyone, at any time, and from any location may now access information and communicate using a variety of devices. Digital learning can transform the performance of your learners and businesses in today's world.

DOI: 10.1201/9781032675176-13

M-learning is the use of mobile technology to help someone learn, research, or explore knowledge that is pertinent to them at the time or in a particular situation, according to its definition (Feser, 2010). Mobile-based learning, often known as m-learning, is the use of mobile devices to access educational online learning resources. It is a way of teaching and learning that uses wireless and mobile technology. It is a style of teaching that uses mobile technology wholly or primarily. It inspires people to continue learning throughout their lives, and a rising number of students throughout the world are choosing to learn using convenient mobile devices.

The rapid development of mobile technology and devices draws attention to the idea of mobile learning. M-learning is only accessible online or through a downloadable app. Using a compact, portable digital device that they always have with them, has dependable connectivity, and can fit in their pocket or purse, people can be more productive while consuming, participating with, or generating knowledge (Batsila & Tsihouridis) (2021).

According to Skui and Suki (2017), 'M-learning refers to the new possibilities, available to people as a result of widespread deployment of technological devices that everyone now has in their hands and the upcoming connectivity.' According to Keegan (2002, 2005), 'No other technology has invaded the world with the depth and speed of mobile telecommunications.' The difficulty for distance educators, according to him, is to realise this fact and provide learning environments for mobile devices right now. M-learning allows students to blend their learning experiences in a collaborative setting (Wagner, 2008). From e-learning, m-learning is a natural next step. It can change when, where, and how students study and succeed in a variety of areas. M-learning has evolved into a more cost-effective and relaxing way of communication.

M-learning, or mobile-based learning, is a new type of education that is developing from today's mobile technology and is beginning to offer 'striking new technical possibilities.' There is a high demand for information that is structured, organised, and accessible at any time and any place for learners. This new type of learning is being heralded as a revolutionary phase in educational technology. The use of mobile devices to access electronic materials and resources exclusively to support teaching and learning is therefore referred to as mobile learning (Perryman, 2020). A new and rapidly expanding field of educational practice is m-learning.

Features of M-learning

Mobile phones are the most popular and commonly utilised m-learning devices. Mobile phones have made our lives easier, and life without them is impossible to imagine because people have grown accustomed to them (Cui & Wang, 2008). Institutions, organisations, and others that seek to fulfil the needs and interests of learners are increasingly obtaining access to mobile learning. Anytime, anywhere learning is now an option because of the development of personal digital assistants and telecommunications networks. Advances in wireless communication technologies, such as mobile phones, have given educators the possibility to develop new instructional areas. The essential elements of m-learning that allow students to be in the appropriate location at the appropriate time to enjoy learning are as follows:

- **Wireless networking:** Wireless networking technology on mobile phones allows users to roam around considerably more freely and without restriction. A wireless network allows devices to remain connected to the network even if they are not connected via cables. Telecommunications and personal communications, as well as remote appliance control and internet access, are all possible with a mobile phone. Mobile phone networks provide the infrastructure that connects individual access points to terminal devices.
- **Portable size:** Another essential feature is the ability to easily move a mobile device within a learning environment or to different surroundings. It is small enough to fit in our pockets and bags and is always with us. It may be used anywhere and can be used with just one hand, with the thumb doing the functions. Learners can use their mobile devices to learn anywhere there is a network, and they can instantaneously snap a photo, send a message, or share any information.
- **Private:** M-learning is fully private and tailored to the individual. Students can use the device's functions to obtain information, connect, and download content on their own (Virvou & Alepis, 2005; Chidi, 2002; BenMoussa, 2003; Zhang, 2003). It can provide individualised learning opportunities as well as peer-to-peer learning and support. Mobile phones have become a personal item for students, assisting them in a variety of activities. In the worldwide landscape for individualised learning, a new form of learning, known as m-learning, has arisen with mobile devices.
- **Social connectivity:** With m-learning, sharing data and cooperating or collaborating with other students is easy. Communication between students and professors is aided by mobile devices. M-learning focuses on information sharing to provide learners with authentic learning experiences through group work and partnerships. Increased social interaction is aided by m-learning tools. M-learning technologies support increased social interaction with peers and teachers (Bansal & Joshi, 2014). Group chatting is one of the advantages of m-learning tools, where group members may share data without any barriers or limitations (WhatsApp Inc., 2017). M-learning has a positive social impact. It allows learners to participate in creative activities, social networking, organising and reorganising social content, learner-created cognitive space, and managing social acts using mobile technology at any time and from any location (Hsiung Tut al., 2013).
- **Instant information:** Learners can learn at their own pace and in a location that is convenient for them using m-learning. Because most students have

their smartphones with them at all times, they can access their courses or learning materials from anywhere at any time. Speed is essential when utilising a mobile tool (Eteokleous & Ktoridou, 2009; Cavus & Ibrahim, 2009). M-learning gives learners an instant response to a problem and deep insight into an issue through rapid dialogues, online lectures, videos, and repetition of learned topics. According to Cohen (2010), there is a need for simple solutions to specific questions. Access to learning resources at any time is a noteworthy benefit of mobile learning technologies. M-learning enables quick communication of educational activities such as notifications on teaching techniques, classroom management, participant questions or problems, and administrative updates.

- **Content delivery-dased learning:** Learning materials for m-learning can be supplied as e-books and files that can be viewed on mobile devices. The majority of these methods are only available on smartphones. Users can access information in and out of any work using small pieces of content. The goal of mobile content delivery is to give structured and appropriate content that is appropriate for a developed learning scenario.
- **Game-based learning:** Mobile technologies and gamification have the power to engage students and start mobile-friendly educational experiences. A very successful teaching method that guarantees maximal memory retention is game-based learning. This approach is frequently used in both traditional and online education. Thanks to improvements in mobile technology, it is now also available via mobile.

Need for M-learning in Technology-Based Learning

Technology is advancing rapidly in all facets of society. Information and communication technology (ICT) is being used in more and more educational activities as a teaching and learning tool (Matimbwa & Anney, 2016). One of the many devices that have been acknowledged for their capacity to provide students with significant learning opportunities from any location is mobile phones (Traxler, 2009). A new paradigm of technology-assisted teaching and learning known as mobile learning has emerged. Mobile technologies offer unique and innovative methods to teach and learn both inside and beyond the classroom. Portability, immediacy, connectedness, ubiquity, and adaptability are the technical characteristics of m-learning, according to Valero et al. (2012). It promotes student engagement, knowledge development, and information searching, and teacher–student communication easier. Additionally, it makes it easier to use a variety of educational apps and stay connected, allowing you to access education at any time and from any location. One of the most essential educational technologies has been identified as mobile learning (Johnson, Adams, & Cummins, 2012). Educational institutions all around the world are increasingly using mobile technology to deliver online training as a result of the growth of mobile-based applications (Jimoyiannis et al., 2013).

Language learning, ecological and environmental education, computer and engineering education, and historical and cultural education are the top m-learning applications. With the proper use of mobile technology and instructional strategies, as well as with the right support and strategy, these applications can enhance students' learning accomplishments, motivations, and interests. Smartphones are the most often used m-learning devices, which are increasingly being used in both professional and informal settings. The ability of mobile learning to enable the improvement of problem solving, interactive learning, critical thinking, and lifelong communication skills as well as the transmission of knowledge without regard to location or time restrictions are its defining features (Abidin and Tho, 2018). The rapid expansion of mobile learning in the technology sector has increased awareness of and acceptance of mobile learning (Ilci, 2014).

Because mobile phones are used more extensively than desktops and laptops and have access to popular websites like Facebook, Youtube, and Twitter, they have the potential to be used in educational settings. Due to the effectiveness of constructivism as a learning approach, the shift from computer-based to web-based learning, and technical advancements, mobile learning has emerged as one of the most widely used learning strategies in recent years (Göksu & Atici, 2013).

Mobile devices can be used by educators to monitor, record, and report on student performance in a classroom context. Students should be evaluated using a variety of tools, including databases, software, online quizzes, chat rooms, discussion forums, and project evaluations. It has all the components required to evaluate a learner's knowledge, skills, creativity, and manners. Therefore, it is essential to understand the significance of m-learning in the educational environment.

Students who participate in interactive content and simulate in flexible settings with the knowledge that applies to the actual world learn effectively. Laptops, tablet devices, and smartphones can be easily incorporated into an active learning environment because of their portability. Students become more motivated to learn as they have more control over how they study, what they learn, and how they participate in m-learning projects. As a skill for the digital age, m-learning gives students the assurance to master new tools and, eventually, the job.

Learning is thorough when students participate in virtual visits and simulations in flexible settings with content that is applied to the real world. Laptops, tablets, and smartphones may easily be incorporated into an active learning environment due to their portability and mobility. As students make choices about how they study, what they learn, and how they participate in projects with m-learning, they become more motivated in their learning. M-learning, as a digital era skill, offers students the confidence to master new tools and, eventually, the job.

Role of M-learning during COVID-19 Era

The rapid evolution of COVID-19, a devastating disease that was proclaimed a pandemic by the World Health Organization, startled the entire world. A range of preventive steps has been adopted in response to the pandemic to combat the virus's global spread. Quarantine is in force over much of the world, including schools, colleges, and institutions. In such situations, transitioning to distant learning was an inescapable option. The issue posed a challenge to the educational system around the world, prompting a transition to online mode. In times of difficulty, online learning has proven to be a lifesaver (Dhawan, 2020). Educational institutions have been compelled to accept new technology as a result of the crisis. Recognising the critical nature of the current situation, educational institutions were forced to digitalise their operations. The key concern was not whether online teaching–learning techniques can deliver high-quality education during this challenging COVID-19 period, but rather how academic institutions will be able to adopt online learning on such a massive scale (Carey, 2020). Online learning environments have evolved into the new norm for both students and teachers throughout the prolonged COVID-19 pandemic. As a result, instructors can now teach via online technology. Moodle and other virtual meetings systems, such as Zoom, Microsoft Teams, Google Meet, and other educational portals, have made learning and teaching easier. WhatsApp on mobile devices provides a platform for communicating, studying, sharing videos, and quickly capturing and uploading educational materials.

One of the technologies that has been essential during this pandemic was mobile learning (m-learning). M-learning is stepping forward as a saviour amid this uncertainty. Throughout the whole lockdown, the majority of students accessed educational resources on their mobile devices. The primary factor was the instantaneous and widespread functionality of mobile devices, which enabled students to access their course materials at any time or location. The teaching–learning process was significantly aided by mobile technology. To minimise academic setbacks for students, institutions started offering lesson courses online (by computer, laptop).

Due to many socio-economic conditions, students and teachers in India are rapidly adopting mobile devices to learn. Smartphones are popular among students because of their easy accessibility, affordability, and portability. Smartphones' quick accessibility and mobility make it possible for students to study whenever and wherever they want. During the COVID-19 pandemic, students chose mobile devices as their primary learning tool. Teachers and students used to meet electronically for e-classes using these online platforms. Teachers and students chose an online platform depending on their preferences. Mobile apps for online education let students learn topics in fun ways, making learning more enjoyable.

Mobile learning has resulted in a high level of learning flexibility. This means that students will be able to access learning materials at any time and on several occasions. Students can talk to their professors at any time. Information or any kind of notification can be instantly accessible by utilising the internet on a mobile device. India's educational system, according to the National Council of Educational Research and Training (NCERT), during the COVID-19 pandemic was heavily reliant on mobile phones, with 80–90% of students in central schools using mobile phones to access digital schooling during the pandemic rather than other technological devices.

Different M-learning Apps in India

A mobile learning app is a software program that can be downloaded to a mobile device and utilised to access educational materials. Developing a mobile learning app can have several advantages, including a simple and appealing user experience with consistent branding and the ability to access training materials offline *(Dashe & Thomson)*. Mobile learning applications give consumers the option to learn whenever and wherever it is most convenient for them. Utilising free time and leisure activities is highly helpful.

M-learning apps are being developed to allow learners to learn anywhere, at any time, according to their needs, and they are free to use. A wide range of apps is available for download and use, depending on the learner's needs. Many disadvantaged students in India lack access to adequate resources and training institutions. Furthermore, some metro area colleges are so overcrowded that learning is difficult for all students. In such circumstances, India's mobile apps have ushered in a revolution. They have not only made studying easier for students, but they have also made parenting less stressful. In India, the following are some of the most popular apps:

A. Diksha is an initiative of the National Council of Educational Research and Traning (NCERT) India to help school students. Here, learners can get resources such as lesson plans, concepts, videos, and worksheets, mapped to the curriculum. Teachers will have their personalised workspace where they can plan and track their progress, including courses completed, performance in tests, etc.
B. SWAYAM is a project of the Indian government aiming to improve quality, access, and equity. All of the courses are interactive, created by some of the greatest teachers in the country, and are available to citizens of India at no cost. Over 1,000 highly selected faculty and teachers from across the country contributed to the development of these courses. There is a video lesson; well-prepared reading material that may be downloaded/printed; self-assessment tests in the form of tests and quizzes, and an online discussion forum where any questions can be addressed.

C. Byju's: It is an online learning environment to ensure that students like and find learning engaging. This app is regarded as one of India's most popular and effective educational apps. This software contains key videos, complete mock tests, and sample papers for all board exams, assisting in the preparation of competitive exams such as IIT-JEE, CAT, and NEET. BYJU'S combines the best professors, technology, content, and media to provide each student with a seamless, world-class learning experience.
D. Toppr is an educational app that personalises learning for all pupils. It offers a diverse choice of courses, as well as the best live classes feature, which greatly aids students in resolving their problems in real time. It also offers students a timetable so that they are aware of their classes. Machine learning based on artificial intelligence is utilised in this software to build tailored learning routes for millions of pupils. Adaptive methods are utilised with pupils to see what works best for them. Mock tests on Toppr helped develop exam strategy.
E. The most popular online learning platform in India, Unacademy has helped students advance their knowledge and verbal and written communication skills. This app offers video lectures and specialised courses on a variety of competitive tests, and it has benefited students from all around the country. In this app on a subscription, teachers can access all of their live and recorded classes, which students can view on any of their devices.
F. Brainly is a helpful application with a knowledge-sharing community where 350 million students and experts share their resources to solve their most difficult assignment problems. Brainly assists students in locating answers to all of their inquiries on a variety of topics. It allows students to connect with an online community of teachers and tutors who are eager to assist kids in need of academic assistance in just a few minutes.
G. Kahoot is a technologically driven educational application that encourages student involvement in a virtual classroom by using games. Teachers can design quizzes, hold live games, and more with Kahoot. They can apply games and enjoyable tasks to help students understand each lesson since all of these activities will be based on the school's fundamentals. With Kahoot training, presentations, meetings, and events on any video conferencing platform become simple.
H. Zoom is one of the greatest cloud video conferencing online software for organising meetings, tutoring lectures, and communicating with many students, among other things. Teachers can boost student engagement during remote learning by using fantastic features like one-click document sharing, digital whiteboarding, and more.
I. Google Classroom: An essential learning tool for online courses is this application. In light of recent events, Google Classroom has become an essential learning software for mobile devices. With the help of this software, students may communicate with their teacher, start a discussion, and turn in assignments without being present.

Challenges of M-learning

The Digital Age is changing the way pupils study and will have a significant impact on their future chances, and COVID-19 has ushered in a new era of online learning, along with many issues. Despite its numerous benefits and prospects, m-learning also came with several drawbacks. In terms of m-learning, India still has a lot of issues to work out. A few problems with mobile learning include a lack of support for curriculum design, an insufficient number of institutional m-learning strategies, and a lack of infrastructure and technical support (Awadhiya & Miglani).

a. Network issue: Network concerns among the students are a significant disadvantage of mobile learning in rural areas of India. Even if they have obtained a mobile device, many students from underdeveloped regions cannot attend online classes due to inadequate network access. In online classes, there has been a lot of absenteeism. With these kinds of problems, teachers are unable to come up with an alternative method of instruction for students who are having network problems. Some students struggle to fully benefit from mobile learning because they lack experience with these devices. These students are unaware of how to download educational resources from the internet.
b. Socio-economic conditions: Numerous students who cannot afford to take online classes suffer greatly. The resources required for online education are difficult to access for many students. Many people in India have only one smartphone and no other devices with which to take online lessons. In certain cases, the smartphone is mostly operated by the older member of the household who is away working; there is no smart device for the student to use to access the internet and, eventually, digital education. Because not all students have the same smartphone, some applications may be more suitable for one student than for another. Furthermore, many learners will be unwilling to accept m-learning due to the expenses of equipment and materials.
c. During the COVID-19 pandemic, there was no physical interaction between students and instructors, internet problems, no work, lack of readiness, and social isolation. Apart from that, using these online modes over the phone leads to a lot of cheating, which has and will continue to impair students' learning results and degrade education quality. Teachers, parents, and students face institutional and personal hurdles when it comes to adopting m-learning.
d. Some instructors have inadequate training and knowledge with inflexible attitudes towards digital learning. They are reluctant the use technology. As a result, m-learning can be a challenge for both the learner and

instructor. Computer and digital literacy are not satisfactory among parents, teachers, and students in some parts of India. Teachers need proper time to learn the use of technology, and it may also help that they find it difficult to deal with students' behaviour when technologies are in use. Although teachers are new to digital teaching, teachers with experience in Blackboard, Chalk, Books, and classroom instruction are swiftly adapting and handling it like a pro to assist students in their present situation.

e. Students are usually distracted by their mobile devices, and during class, they text, play games, watch humorous videos, search social media channels, or even accept calls. The excessive usage of mobile phones hurts the pupils' health. Long-term mobile exposure can hurt the learner's vision.

Although mobile devices have become an integral part of daily life in many countries, such as India, certain students from lower socioeconomic backgrounds may not have access to them. This is a problem for disadvantaged students that must be acknowledged and addressed. To remain competitive in the global economy and keep their students, schools must successfully integrate mobile learning into their teaching–learning process. M-learning is still developing and has a ways to go.

New challenges will emerge as a result of rapid technological progress, which must be tracked and addressed.

Conclusion

The number of people who own a mobile device is growing. Today's students are time-crunched, technologically smart, and constantly connected. Using mobile devices as learning tools has become a need for bridging the divide between old and new. Mobile learning satisfies this demand by allowing learners to acquire little chunks of information at their speed. Learners can now study wherever they want, whenever they want. We need to train ourselves to make proper use of this technology. We need to broaden our m-learning commitments, and in this new atmosphere, both the learner and the instructor must now collaborate to learn. Mobile learning is one medium that has come as a saviour, especially during the COVID-19 pandemic.

Although a good number of studies have pointed to the positive impact of mobile devices as a tool to access educational content, more analysis and outlook should be pointed out for m-learning. It might yield more significant beneficial educational outcomes. It is important to have a deeper knowledge of the underlying factors that compel academics to use mobile learning's features and traits.

References

Abas, Z. W., Chng, L. P., & Mansor, N. (2009). A study on learner readiness for mobile learning at Open University Malaysia. *In Proceedings of IADIS International Conference Mobile Learning* 151–157.

Abidin, N. Z., & Tho, S. (2018). The development of an innovative resonance experiment using smartphones with free mobile software applications for tertiary education. *International Journal of Education and Development using Information and Communication Technology, 14*(1), 164–176.

Ally, M., & Tsinakos, A. (Eds.). (2014). *Increasing access through mobile learning.* Vancouver, BC: Commonwealth of Learning

Awadhiya & Miglan (2016). Mobile learning: Challenges for teachers of Indian open universities. *Journal of learning for development.* https://files.eric.ed.gov/fulltext/EJ1108182.pdf

Bansal & Joshi, D. (2014). A study of students experiences of WhatsApp mobile learning. *Global Journal of Human-Social Science, 14*(4), 27–33. Retrieved from: https://socialscienceresearch.org/index.php/GJHSS/article/view/1326

Basak, Wotto, & Paul. (2018). E-learning, M-learning and D-learning: Conceptual definition and comparative analysis. Retrieved from: 10.1177/2042753018785180

BenMoussa, C. (2003). Workers on the move: New opportunities through mobile commerce. Presented at the International Conference e-Society (IADIS), 3–6 June, Lisbon, Portugal, 251–256.

Brown, D. (2006). Personalised learning – the technology challenge. Global Summit 2006 Technology Connected Futures. Retrived from: http://www.groups.edna.edu.au/file.php/1030/GS2006_BROWN.pdf.

Carey, K. (2020). Is everybody ready for the big migration to online college? Actually, no. The New York Times. https://www.nytimes.com

Cavus, N., & Ibrahim, D. (2009, December 23). m-Learning: An experiment in using SMS to support learning new English language words. *British Journal of Educational Technology, 40*(1), 78–91. https://doi.org/10.1111/j.1467-8535.2007.00801.x

Chidi, G.A. (2002). AT&T wireless launches mobile web service in US. Wireless IT World. Retrieved June 08, 2020, from: http://www.itworld.com/020416attwireless

Clark, J. (2007). Learning and teaching in mobile learning environment of 21st century.

Cohen, A. (2010). Characteristics of effective mobile learning.

Crompton, H. (2013). The benefits and challenges of mobile learning. *Learning and Leading with Technology, 41*, 38–39.

Cui, G., & Wang, S. (2008). Adopting cell phones in EFL teaching and learning. *Journal of Educational Technology Development and Exchange, 1*(1). 10.18785/jetde.0101.06

Dhawan, S. (2020). Online learning: A panacea in the time of COVID-19 crisis. *Journal of Educational Technology Systems, 49*, 5–22. 10.1177/0047239520934018

Eteokleous, N. & Ktoridou, D. (2009). Investigating mobile devices integration in higher education in Cyprus: faculty perspectives. *International Journal of Interactive Mobile Technologies, 3*(1), 38–48.

Evans, C. (2008). The effectiveness of m-learning in the form of podcast revision lectures in higher education. *Computers& Education, 50*, 491–498

Feser, J. (2014). M Learning is not e-Learning on a mobile device. Mastering Mobile Learning, 35–42.

Gikas, J., & Grant, M. (2013). Mobile computing devices in higher education: Student perspectives on learning with cellphones, smartphones & social media. *Internet and Higher Education, 19*, 18–26.

Göksu, İ., & Atici, B. (2013). Need for Mobile Learning: Technologies and Opportunities. *Procedia – Social and Behavioral Sciences*, 103, 685–694. 10.1016/j.sbspro.2013.10.388

Hsiung, C. M. (2012, January). The Effectiveness of Cooperative Learning. *Journal of Engineering Education, 101*(1), 119–137. https://doi.org/10.1002/j.2168-9830.2012.tb00044.x

Huang et al., (2009). Developing argumentation processing agents for computer-supported collaborative learning. *Expert Systems with Applications, 36*, 2615–2624

Ilci, A. (2014). Investigation of pre-service teachers' mobile learning readiness levels and mobile learning acceptance levels. A Thesis Submitted to The Graduate School of Natural and Applied Sciences of Middle East Technical University, METU, Ankara, Turkey.

Johnson, L., Adams, S., & Cummins, M. (2012). NMC Horizon Report: 2012 Higher Education Edition. Austin, Texas: The New Media Consortium. Retrieved August, 2020 from: https://www.learntechlib.org/p/48964/

Jimoyiannis, A., Tsiotakis, P., Roussinos, D., & Siorenta, A. (2013). Preparing teachers to integrate Web 2.0 in school practice: Toward a framework for Pedagogy 2.0. *Australasian Journal of Educational Technology, 29*(2). 10.14742/ajet.157

Keegan, D. (2002). The future of learning: From eLearning to m Learning, ZIFF papiere 119. Retrieved from ERIC ED472435 database. Available from: http://www.fernunihagen.de/ZIFF/

Matimbwa, R., & Anney, V.N. (2016). Teachers' and students' perceptions of self-driven acceptance of mobile phone use as an ICT teaching tool. *Journal of Emerging Trends in Educational Research and Policy Studies, 7*, 91–106. https://hdl.handle.net/10520/EJC190056

Mohammadi, M, Sarvestani, M. S., & Nouroozi, S. (2020) Mobile phone use in education and learning by faculty members of technical-engineering groups: Concurrent mixed methods design. *Front. Educ.* 5:16. 10.3389/feduc.2020.00016

Motiwalla, L. F. (2007). Mobile learning: A framework and evaluation. *Computers & Education, 49*(3), 581–596.

Ozdamlia & Cavusb (2011). Basic elements and characteristics of mobile learning. *Procedia – Social and Behavioral Sciences, 28* 2011) 937–942

Pedro, Barbosa, et al. (2018). A critical review of mobile learning integration in formal educational contexts. *International Journal of Educational Technology in Higher Education*, 15(10)

Perryman. (2020). Evaluating MOOCs' Long-Term Impact: A Theory of Change Approach. In: Mishra, Sanjaya and Panda, Santosh eds. Technology-Enabled Learning: Policy, Pedagogy and Practice. *Perspectives on Open and Distance Learning*. Vancouver, Canada: Commonwealth of Learning, 143–164.

Sharples, M. (2013). Mobile learning: Research, practice and challenges. *Distance Education in China, 3*(5), 5–11.

Sihouridis, C., Batsila M., & Tsihouridis A. (2021). QRing Specialties' Mobile Course Elements to Support VET Learners' Cognitive Level. In: Auer M.E., Rüütmann T. (eds) *Educating Engineers for Future Industrial Revolutions. ICL 2020*. Advances in Intelligent Systems and Computing, vol 1328. Springer, Cham. 10.1007/978-3-030-68198-2_25

Suki, M. N., & Suki, M. N. (2017). Flight ticket booking app on mobile devices: Examining the determinants of individual intention to use. *Journal of Air Transport Management*, *62*, 146–154. 10.1016/j.jairtraman.2017.04.003

Traxler, J. (2007). Defining, discussing and evaluating mobile learning: The moving finger writes and having written *The International Review of Research in Open and Distributed Learning*, *8*. 10.19173/irrodl.v8i2.346

Valero, C. C., Redondo, M. R., & Palacín, A. S. (2012). Current trends in the use of mobile devices in education. *La Educación Digital Magazine*, *147*, 1–21. Retrieved from: http://educoas.org/portal/la_educacion_digital/147/pdf/ ART_UNNED_EN.pdf

Virvou, M., & Alepis, E. (2005). Mobile educational features in authoring tools for personalised tutoring. *Computers & Education*, *44*, 53–68. 10.1016/j.compedu.2003.12.020

Wagner, E. (2008). Realizing the promises of mobile learning. *Journal of Computing in Higher Education*, *20*(2), 4–14. 10.1007/s12528-008-9008-x

Hwang & Wu (2014). Applications, impacts and trends of mobile technology-enhanced learning: a review of 2008-2012 publications in selected SSCI journals. *International Journal of Mobile Learning and Organisation (IJMLO)*, *8*(2), 2014

WhatsApp Inc. (2017). WhatsApp features. Retrieved from: https://www.whatsapp.com/features/

Zhang, D. (2003). Delivery of personalized and adaptive content to mobile devices: A framework and enabling technology. *Communications of the Association for Information Systems*, *12*, 183–202.

Web Links

https://www.leolearning.com/blog/learning-content/what-is-mlearning/?cv=1
https://www.teachex.eu/modules/mobile-learning/. Accessed on 30/08/2021.
https://www.elearninglearning.com/learning-objectives/mobile/. Accessed on 20/8/2021
https://www.skillbuilderlms.com/top-benefits-challenges-mobile-learning/
https://docplayer.net/79803629-Educational-technology-society-an-international-journal.html?cv=1
https://journals.sagepub.com/doi/10.1177/2042753018785180
https://www.tandfonline.com/doi/full/10.1080/10494820.2022.2086267

Chapter 14

Augmented Reality in Education: Modern Technologies and Potentials

M. Balasubramaniam
Department of Education, Bharathiar University Coimbatore, Tamilnadu, India

Introduction

The development of information and communication technology (ICT) has provided a great amount of information in all aspects of life, providing new, improved, and instant options for individuals to communicate, network, ask for assistance, access information, and learn. According to Paul and Foray (2002), information exists within the kind of organised, structured records, that are passive and slow until they are employed by those who have the requisite skills. According to UNESCO (2005), everyone should be able to develop cognitive and critical thinking skills to differentiate between 'useful' and 'useless' information (1). Augmented reality (AR) is often considered a technological resource that will enable the changeover from an information to a knowledge society. Reality is 'superimposing the reflection of the stage on the physical world.' Thus, AR permits learners to determine the area with virtual objects.

 DOI: 10.1201/9781032675176-14

Background of AR

The term 'augmented reality' may have been created in the early 1990s by Thomas Caudell. The word 'augment' denotes the act of adding to something to make it more significant. It stems from the Latin root 'auger,' which means 'to increase. The definition of AR in the computer science community is superimposed graphics, sound, and other sensory-enhanced interactions in a real environment, shown in actual points and allied to a more wide-ranging idea called mediation. In reality, the word denotes a simple mixture of the actual world and virtual world (system produced). For actual objects shot with audio-visual or camera, this technique 'supplements' real-world images with an additional layer of digital info (e.g., sound), audio-visual, graphics, and GPS records. Therefore, technology is working hard to improve the existing acuity of reality. Addition usually occurs in real-time and in a semantic perspective with surrounding features, using innovative AR technology (e.g., the addition of computer visualisation and object recognition). Evidence about the actual world around the learner is controlled interactively as well as digitally.

Meaning of AR

The real-time integration of digital information with the environment of the user is known as AR. Instead of creating a virtual reality environment, AR leverages the real world and supplements new information. A broad conception is named intermediary reality. AR is a technology that pools digital facts with the actual world to improve 3D visuals, sounds, and things instead of normal objects. AR emphasises presenting additional visual information from the environment through user equipment, thereby providing a rich user experience.

Areas Where AR Technology Can Be Used

AR technology is used in several sectors such as the leisure industry, archaeology, art, business, manufacturing and renovation, teaching and learning, emergency management, entertaining and leisure, and health, to name just a few of the domains where AR technology is applied.

In the tourism field, the application of AR technology in tourist attractions uses technical tools such as mobile phone cameras and display software to integrate real-life scenes and reconstruct historical relics. Tourists can get additional information in addition to viewing the scenario.

This technology is commonly utilised in archaeology to transform cultural artefacts into authentic situations, allowing archaeologists to pinpoint their exact locations with greater accuracy. Consumers may see all about a product without opening it thanks to AR technology. They can access not only the custom parameter information but also other information about the product by scanning the image.

AR technology visually instructs workers, alerts workers of the schedule, and sketches in 3D to boost production efficiency in the automotive industry. Through visual presentations, AR technology allows automobile designers to improve vehicle design and mark well contrasts. People now have a better idea of how to perceive and interpret reality because of the use of AR technology in art.

AR technology can be used in civic care solutions and has a high degree of probability. For instance, an aerial camera is included with the AR exploration and associate degree rescue system, which can integrate the genuine picture with the detected forest road name and location. It is possible to save missing individuals more successfully.

Doctors can utilise AR technology to better and more precisely find a patient's surgical site in the medical field. With AR, they can get a clearer view of unborn babies in real time. Patients can also use AR technology to remind them to take their medication on time and to use the proper equipment.

AR in Education

Adopting AR with classroom settings could change daily learning into smart understanding. AR affords digital specimens and provides gaming factors to guide textbook resources. As an outcome, instructions grow to be extra interactive. AR helps learners remember the statistics they've learned.

In school, AR can work with some of the drives. It allows scholars to collect, process, and remember statistics without problems. Additionally, AR makes studying itself extra enticing and enjoyable. It is likewise now no longer constrained to the stage of schooling and may be used in all types of education – from pre-faculty schooling to college or maybe at work.

AR in schooling uses cutting-edge generation in exploration and classrooms, developing an immersive and unique studying possibility for youngsters. AR in schooling is virtual statistics incorporated with the learner's environments, performed in an actual stage. This forms future leaders and formulates them, targeted at coping with the needs of the future.

AR inside the classroom introduces a brand-new schooling method via an up-to-date technique and curricula. With this generation, youngsters can collect new knowledge via experiences, touch displays, and performances. Including AR in content material for instructors in mathematics and the physical sciences, is now no longer the most effective way to study; however, coaching may be faster, more enjoyable, and an additional resourceful.

The following applications are possible:

- **Object model**
  In this AR, an object can be immediately seen as a 3D virtual model that can be rotated and seen from all angles.
- **Simulation-oriented learning**
  AR leverages the existing world while adding additional information, in contrast to creating an artificial environment. AR aims to supplement the digital environment with physical objects, enabling a real-world user to interact with digital components without a glitch.
- **Gaming**
  AR is a blend of game visuals along with audio content for the user environment in real time, which supports the creation of an artificial setting.
- **Collaborative e-prints**
  AR permits the user to see virtual objects superimposed upon real-world sights through display devices such as PCs, laptops, pocket PCs, video projectors, or head-mounted displays (HMDs).
- **Learning and innovation**
  AR helps learners learn with modern technologies by empowering them to learn virtually in augmented ways on varied platforms.
- **Skills exercise**
  AR is implemented to encourage and motivate the user to perform the necessary exercises by producing skills such as comprehension, imagination, etc.

AR in the Classroom

AR technology may be brought into lecture rooms to complement present instructional resources. Teachers can take their students on a digital trip to notice ancient ruins at the same time as students sit at their desks in the classroom with headphones. By using AR applications, students can review pages of a book and a 3D hologram will display extra statistics approximately on the objects.

AR generation creates a similar environment but takes the whole thing deeper, supporting learners to imagine matters and further understand the idea. AR applications generate 3D holographic statistics at the form and sedation of the earth, length of family members, and different environmental pieces of information. Lab reports and tests also can end up extra immersive and powerful with the use of AR. For example, in reference to a cadaver, clinical college students can carry out surgical procedures anywhere and better comprehend complicated surgical procedures.

For any class, a minimal AR setup could include:

- Access to the internet
- Devices (i.e., digital gadgets)
- AR apps (for education)
- 'Provokes' or 'Indicators' (pictures, events, situations, and actions that cause an action to be performed on the device screen via the AR application)

Why Use AR in Education

- **Handle the technically unfeasible:** Learners bring materials to the class that may or may not be feasible.
- **Context the control:** At intervals of AR, learners may view 3D models from any angle, gap, or range.
- **User access interaction:** Learners can connect with AR content to have a better knowledge of a topic.
- **Increased participation:** Learners respond quickly to AR information and are expected to learn on their own.
- **Enhanced learning environment:** Learners use AR content to bring classroom displays to natural life.
- **Activate the sensory experiences:** Learners engage in a variety of sensory learning practices.
- **The profound impact:** Learners can see inside artefacts to discover what materials they are made of.
- **The economic ratio:** AR resources are relatively inexpensive, so more students can access information.

Benefits of AR in Education

In education, AR is used to improve problem solving, cooperation, and creative thinking skills that inadequately prepare students for the future. Conventional technical knowledge and skill-based education approaches are also supported.

- Trying to read
- Dealing with arithmetic
- Geospatial concepts
- Gaming
- Concept development
- Real-life places and circumstances

The following are some of the educational advantages of AR:

- **Learning materials that can be accessed at all times and from all places:** Printable books, object models, banners, and written manuals all will be replaced with AR. It provides learning resources that are handier and less expensive. Therefore, learning has become more portable.
- **No additional equipment is required:** AR does not necessitate the purchase of pricey technology. Most of the population can employ AR technology in the right way.
- **Increased student involvement and interest:** Learners benefit greatly from game-based AR learning. It retains their interest throughout the entire course and makes learning enjoyable and uncomplicated.
- **Enhances association:** AR applications open up a world of possibilities for diversifying and shaking up monotonous lessons. Teamwork skills are facilitated via interactive classes in which all learners are convoluted in the learning process.
- **More efficient, effective learning process:** Using mental imagery (visualisation) and complete immersion in the subject matter, AR in education helps students produce better results.
- **Practical learning:** The use of AR in skilled training could be very beneficial. Accurate recreation of in-field situations, for example, will make it easier to learn the practical skills required for a specific job.

Some AR applications can be used in K–12 classrooms to enhance and adapt learning. They are the following:

Elements 4D

Elements 4D employs AR to make chemistry more fun and engaging. To create, students/customers build paper cubes out of one-of-a-kind detail blocks. Then, they just place the cubes in front of their device's digital digicam to compare chemical factors, names, and atomic masses. Students can place cubes together to see if they react and observe the chemical reaction to uncover components.

Google Expeditions

Each VR and AR tour is presented by Google Expeditions, allowing instructors to employ AR in the classroom. Students can bring 3D products into the classroom via AR generation and cellular devices, then walk around and discover them. Google Expeditions covers a wide range of themes and includes over a hundred AR Expeditions on topics such as the circulatory system, generation records, and the moon landing.

3D Bear

Students can use the app's item collection or content material transferred from Thingiverse to create percentage situations, including the use of 3D fashion. Teachers use a web-based dashboard to design and assign classes, while students use the app to create scenarios. Pre-made lesson plans cover a wide range of topics.

Catchy Words AR

This program combines studying and movement, which appeals to school teachers. Students go around with smart devices 'catching' letters to solve phrase problems without touching the screen.

CoSpacesEdu

This application allows the students to create digital 3D worlds, make infographics, and share testimony through digital reveals and tours. Instructors make a category and add assignments to it. Images and 360-degree snapshots can be uploaded, and there is a companion application available.

Froggipedia

It enables biology students to learn about the life cycle and anatomy of a frog through a guided digital dissection using life-like images.

JigSpace

This app has a collection of information, and each 'Jig' might be a 3D representation of how everyday things work, defined in simple stages and viewed visually in augmented or digital reality. Students can examine the human heart, the solar system, innovations, and a variety of other topics from many perspectives.

MERGE Cube

Use the MERGE Cube to allow students to 'preserve a hologram' of their hands. When held in front of a device's digital digicam while using one of MERGE's apps, the dice morph into a virtual 3D item or scene that can be viewed from various perspectives by turning the dice. Instructors can use a MERGE Cube to develop instructions and sports to help students learn STEAM concepts, visualise complex systems, and 'experience' music or science.

Metaverse

This platform enables students to develop and proportion interactive multimedia material in AR. It is suggested for ages 13 and up. Tutors can use the gadget to make learning more fun for students by using preparation exercises, evaluation video games, and foundational evaluations. The learner can take part in games made by the teacher or other people, location-based activities like scavenger hunts and geocaching, and other things using the free mobile app.

Moatboat

Moatboat is AR and VR advent engine software. Brief instructions are given to the student to add objects and give them behaviour. Learners can then 'display' their creations on a table for others to see and enjoy.

Orb

Technophile young folks visualise locations with this software. Learners upload 3D shapes that appear to be part of the real environment when seen on the device's screen. Learners can practice custom colouring of the forms, as well as regulate and merge them using rotating equipment. The most recent advent can be retrieved, kept as a photograph or movie, shared, or printed out in 3D.

World Brush

Users have to 'paint' their surroundings in this AR game. Paintings are made within the application, remain anonymous, and are only visible in the location where they are reduced. Art lecturers could also ask learners to make digital drawings based on real-world objects and locations on the campus.

Obstacles of AR in Education

There are some obstacles to overcome while using AR:

- **A lack of adequate training:** Teachers may find it difficult to use this new technology because their earlier education did not provide them with the necessary skills. AR applications can only be used in the classroom by the most forward-thinking educators and cutting-edge institutions.
- **Hardware requirements:** AR in the classroom necessitates a robust resource basis.

- **Issues with resource adaptability:** The AR applications must run across all platforms and devices. However, it's practically impossible to produce the same quality of AR material across all platforms.

AR as the Future of Education

Since it enriches and provides advantages for students, instructors, organisations, and content producers, technology will be the future of education. A good resource for teachers looking to improve a student's learning experience is AR. It will better engage learners and make learning about STEM subjects more entertaining and interactive than ever before.

Using AR has several advantages, particularly for students, especially related to inspiring them to learn. It could offer a new learning platform and restructure classrooms to make them more shared. It may, however, assist students in better retaining material.

AR can alter conventional learning methodologies, especially in terms of addressing the diminished human attention span, which has become a problem over time. However, AR alone will not be able to tackle all of the difficulties that conventional teaching techniques cannot. As a result, publishers and institutions should be prepared to identify potential disruptors and devise strategies for gaining a competitive advantage to provide learners/end users with a better learning experience.

Furthermore, AR in the classroom has the prospects to improve a learner's participation, open-mindedness, subject involvement, depth of knowledge, and study interest in the future. Learners improve their learning with greater interest, commitment, and interaction.

Conclusion

AR continues to evolve to become more profitable, easier to get, simpler, effective, and more necessary, in addition to providing learners with the abilities and knowledge necessary to collaborate and develop future careers. AR makes the impossible possible and achieves its educational goals. The AR interface provides a seamless transition between the physical and, in turn, virtual worlds. With the help of a system, students will naturally interact with info, things, and 3D events. The education capability of AR is completely different for various reasons, as Billinghurst (2002) said: care for harmonious interaction of real and virtual environments. Tactile interface figures are used to govern objects. The ability to make the conversion from authenticity to virtuality is also needed. The coordination of a team of experts to solve the disadvantages of AR in education is essential. To attain a realistic solution, an interdisciplinary research project must be developed and coordinated to enhance the content and environment. Educators have to be compelled to collaborate with researchers in the development of AR interfaces. Hardware and software tools are fundamental to the production of AR applications. Some engineers can develop various AR environments. Though, learning material builders that can design a learning experience for AR are in high demand for educational technology learning.

References

Ariso, J. M. (2017). *Augmented reality: Reflections on its contribution to knowledge formation.* de Gruyter. Berlin

Augmented reality (AR) – A brief synopsis. (n.d.). Specbee - Digital Experiences Delivered | Drupal Development. https://www.specbee.com/blogs/augmented-reality-AR-brief-synopsis

Augmented reality in education. (2020). eLearning Industry. https://elearningindustry.com/augmented-reality-in-education-staggering-insight-into-future

Augmented reality in education: Interactive classrooms. (2021). Maryville Online. https://online.maryville.edu/blog/augmented-reality-in-education/

Augmented reality in education: The hottest EdTech trend and how to apply it to your business. (2021). Eastern Peak - Technology Consulting & Development Company. https://easternpeak.com/blog/augmented-reality-in-education-the-hottest-edtech-trend-and-how-to-apply-it-to-your-business/

Augmented reality in the classroom: 8 ideas for digitizing education & training. (2020). Overly. https://overlyapp.com/blog/augmented-reality-in-the-classroom-ideas-for-digitizing-education-and-training/

Billinghurst, M. (2002). Collaborative augmented reality. Canterbury-NZ. https://www.academia.edu/763015/Collaborative_Augmented_Reality

Blum, A. (2018, August 15). The multiple uses of augmented reality in education. Emerging Education Technologies | Engaging Students and Enhancing Learning Outcomes With Instructional Technologies and Active Learning. https://www.emergingedtech.com/2018/08/multiple-uses-of-augmented-reality-in-education/

Chen, Y., Wang, Q., Chen, H., Song, X., Tang, H., & Tian, M. (2019). An overview of augmented reality technology. *Journal of Physics: Conference Series, 1237*, 022082. 10.1088/1742-6596/1237/2/022082

Compliance, P. (n.d.). Augmented reality as the future of education. Planet Compliance. https://www.planetcompliance.com/augmented-reality-as-the-future-of-education/

Forbes. https://www.forbes.com/sites/bernardmarr/2021/04/19/extended-reality-in-education-the-5-ways-vr-and-ar-will-change-the-way-we-learn-at-school-at-work-and-in-our-personal-lives/?sh=43847bed1301

Kesim, M. & Ozarslan, Y. (2012). Augmented reality in education: Current technologies and the potential for education. *Procedia - Social and Behavioral Sciences, 47*, 297–302. https://www.sciencedirect.com/science/article/pii/S1877042812023907

Morozova, A. (2018). AR in education — Jasoren. Jasoren - AR and VR Apps Development Company. https://jasoren.com/augmented-reality-in-education/

Nextech. (n.d.). Augmented reality in education: The future of learning. Welcome to Nextech AR Solutions, Your Augmented Reality Provider. https://www.nextechar.com/blog/ar-in-education-the-future-of-learning

Panciroli, C., Macauda, A., & Russo, V. (2017) Educating about art by augmented reality: New didactic mediation. Perspectives at School and in Museums. *Proceedings, 1*, 1107.

Paul, A. D., & Foray, Dominique (2002). An introduction to the economy of the knowledge society. *International Social Science Journal, 54*(1). https://unesdoc.unesco.org/ark:/48223/pf0000125488.

Six benefits and Five examples of augmented reality in education. (2019). ViewSonic Library. https://www.viewsonic.com/library/education/6-benefits-and-5-examples-of-augmented-reality-in-education/

The future of VR & AR in education. (2020). Getting Smart. https://www.gettingsmart.com/2020/09/the-future-of-vr-ar-in-education/

Top 10 augmented reality tools for the classroom | EBSCOpost. (n.d.). EBSCO Information Services, Inc. | www.ebsco.com. https://www.ebsco.com/blogs/ebscopost/top-10-augmented-reality-tools-classroom

Use cases of augmented reality in education and training. (2019, January 18). Custom Software Development and Consulting Company | RubyGarage. https://rubygarage.org/blog/augmented-reality-in-education-and-training

UNESCO. Director-General, 1999–2009 (Matsuura, K.), & Bindé, Jérôme. (2005). Towards knowledge societies: UNESCO world report. United Nations Educational, Scientific and Cultural Organization. https://unesdoc.unesco.org/ark:/48223/pf0000141843

What is augmented reality (AR). (n.d.). IGI Global: International Academic Publisher. https://www.igi-global.com/dictionary/augmented-reality-framework-socialization-between/1859

Yuen, S. C., Yaoyuneyong, G., & Johnson, E. (2011). Augmented reality: An overview and five directions for AR in education. *Journal of Educational Technology Development and Exchange, 4*(1). 10.18785/jetde.0401.10

Chapter 15

Educational Augmented Reality Working Methodology, Opportunities, and Apps

R. Amsaveni[1] and M. Punithavalli[2]

[1]PSGR Krishnammal College for Women Coimbatore, Tamilnadu, India
[2]Department of Computer Applications, Bharathiar University, Coimbatore, Tamilnadu, India

Introduction

The workflow of teaching and learning is no longer confined to the classroom. As a result, teaching and learning can be done at any place, time, and location. As a medium for information and communication technology (ICT), a technological tool for education has been acknowledged to significantly impact human existence today. Augmented reality (AR) is a technology that mixes virtual objects with the real world and allows them to interact with one another. Although AR applications are used in several industries, education is by far the most important. AR expertise enables the grouping of actual items and virtual information to boost students' attention and interaction with physical environments and efficiently support their learning. Students now have access to new technology. Virtual reality (VR) gadgets allow students to learn hard topics pleasantly and easily thanks to recent technological advancements.

DOI: 10.1201/9781032675176-15

Today's learners are classified as Z generation and/or digital generation, and their features necessitate educators to keep up with technological changes and use the most relevant technological tools in the classroom. AR and VR applications in education are two of these new technologies.

Some of the most important uses of AR technology are listed below.

- The field of education
- The healthcare industry
- Marketing
- Interactive games
- Tourism promotion
- Structures for 3D-buildings
- Making a film
- Food science and technology
- Museums and art
- Automobile production
- Maintenance and support for all types of devices

In terms of delivery and outcomes, the current industrial revolution has had an impact on education. Many technical organisations have discussed the influence of the Industrial Revolution 4.0 (IR4.0) on the field of education, gender, and labour, as well as the need to gain skills to fulfill IR4.0 criteria. The proportions of IR4.0 are depicted in Figure 15.1.

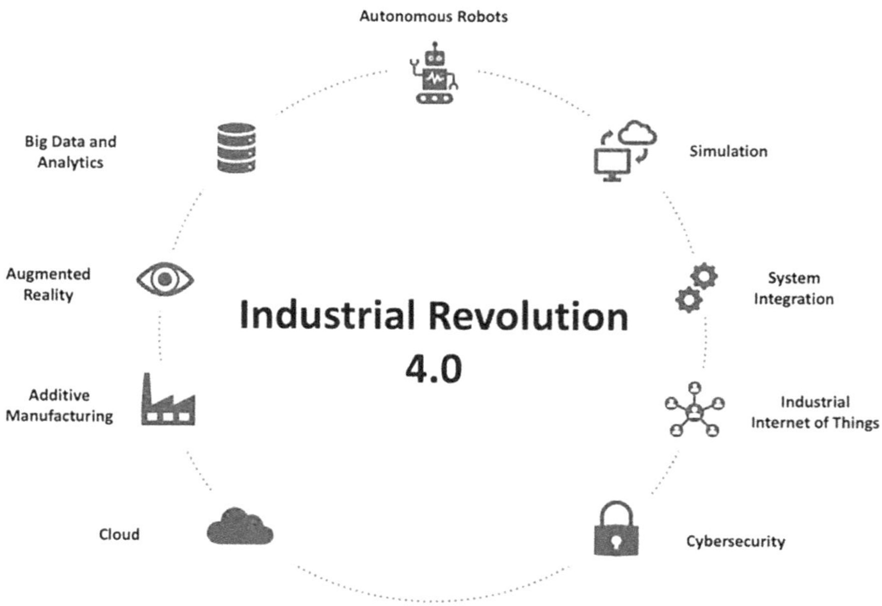

Figure 15.1 Industrial Revolution 4.0 (IR4.0) dimensions related work.

Related Work

AR has been slowly but steadily altering the education industry, digitising classroom teaching and learning, and making training more diverse and engaging, much like its forerunner VR. Current AR studies in the literature on the integration of AR applications into education are presented in this chapter.

AR is a tri-technology that allows humans to understand and view the actual environment while being surrounded by virtual objects (Alvin et al., 2020). In other terms, AR is a tri-visual framework that combines virtual and real-world surroundings for a variety of things (Diegmann et al., 2015).

AR-based products differ from VR applications, which are created in artificial environments with no connection to the real world, in that they allow for real-time interaction in which computer-generated and real-world components coexist (Carmigniani & Furht, 2011).

Some companies have adopted the concept of AR in business/industry, which was first used by Thomas Caudell and David Mizell for display, but with the advancement of technology, access to phones and computers has been much easier, and it has been used in a variety of ways (Johnson et al., 2010).

Scientific equipment and technologies are today employed in a variety of sectors, ranging from medicine to engineering, scientific study to creative endeavours (Kapur, 2019). AR-based applications have swiftly established themselves among these technology-based applications, and they are now being used in a wide range of enterprises and industries.

Digital natives, according to Prensky (2001), are people born after the turn of the 21st century. He says that instead of printed materials, these persons are encircled by PCs, phones, and downloadable games and that their constant exposure to these technologies causes them to think and act differently. To avoid these negative outcomes, technology should be employed in academic settings in a regulated manner. To do this, AR-based settings can be built under the supervision of a teacher (Harris et al., 2016).

AR-based applications have a considerable impact on student academic achievement, which is among the most important of these factors. Srakaya et al. (2018) suggested in their experimental research that AR-based technologies can assist pupils to excel in school. Figure 15.2 narrates AR history.

The following are some of the advantages of AR in education:

- **Availability of educational resources anywhere at any time and any place:** AR will completely replace printed textbooks, physical models, banners, and handwritten instructions. It is portable and does not require as many pricey learning resources. Finally, education is becoming more mobile and accessible.
- **No extra equipment needed:** Unlike VR, AR does not necessitate the development of sophisticated technology. Because 73% of all teens can own

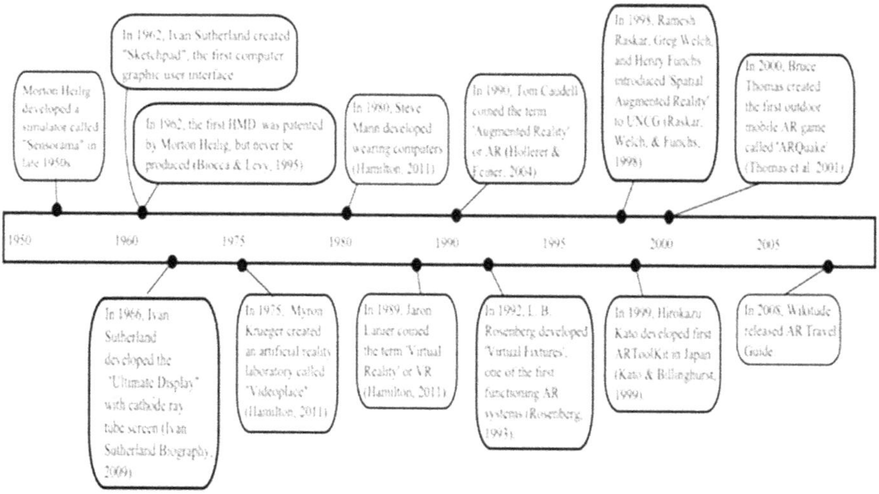

Figure 15.2 Augmented reality history, as Cited by Yuen et al. (2011).

a smartphone, AR applications are instantly accessible to the vast majority of the target demographic.

- **Increased learner interest and participation:** Students can benefit significantly from collaborative, gamified AR learning. AR keeps kids interested throughout the lesson.
- **Capabilities for collaboration have improved:** AR apps provide a wealth of opportunities to spice up and diversify routine classes. Teamwork skills are developed in the course through interactive sessions in which all students participate in the reading and writing system at all times.
- **A more interactive learning process:** Using AR in education, students may see and completely communicate with the subject matter, helping them to achieve superior outcomes. Isn't a picture worth a thousand words? As a consequence, instead of intelligence applied to something, students may see it in action firsthand.
- **Experiential learning:** In addition to education, specialised training may benefit greatly from the use of AR. As a consequence, perfect reproduction of in-field situations might aid in developing the practical skills necessary for a particular profession.
- **Safe and efficient workplace training:** Imagine trying to do cardiac surgery or shuttle program operations without harming others or risking significant damage when something goes wrong. With AR, it's possible.
- **Suitable for all stages of the learning process:** AR is not limited to a particular use case or industry, whether it is early childhood required learning experiences or on-the-job training.

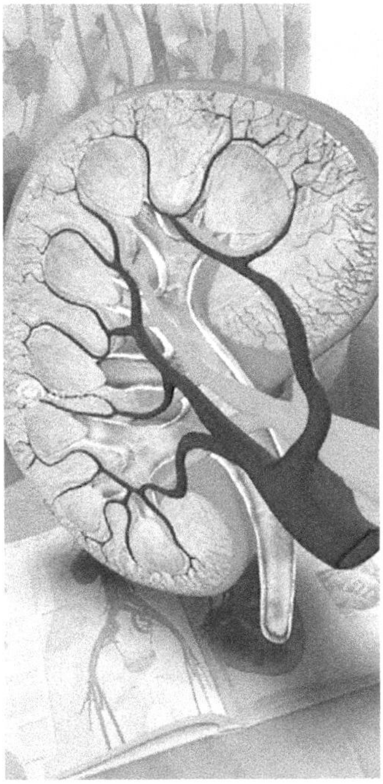

Figure 15.3 AR in reality.

Current AR/VR Technology Applications

AR/VR skills can enhance teaching and learning at all stages and across disciplines in education. As immersive skills mature, new capabilities in educational settings emerge. This section discusses some of the historic revolutions that are setting the basis for the future of immersive educational technology. Figure 15.3 shows AR in reality.

Controlling an Educational Process by Students and Teachers

Personalisation is the goal of the skill revolution that has been announced in the classroom. Students can go through the AR demonstration at their leisure and examine the directions and concepts they need to review. Figure 15.4 depicts an AR headset using controllers to interact with a 3D solar system.

AR programmes like HP Reveal make it easier to make your reality augmented. When a student or instructor takes a picture, it can be linked to internet content that shows in a floating window when the image is scanned.

Metaverse and Traces are two well-known AR apps that allow users to produce location or place-based information while also allowing them to travel between

Figure 15.4 Augmented reality with the solar system.

locations. Teachers, particularly in geography, can provide students with a live environment in which to learn. The widespread availability and cost-effectiveness of such solutions will undoubtedly expand shortly.

With the advancement of technology in the field of education, teachers now have the goal of enhancing students' skill sets through AR apps such as interactive games, puzzles, and 3D modelling for science subjects, as well as generating attention in the classroom and creating a more viable environment in colleges. As a result of technological advancements, the teaching–learning process will go to the next level, and students will receive individualised attention and a real-world environment while studying courses or concepts.

Teachers can create objectives for their students to improve their learning and share their knowledge through interactive games and quizzes, making discovery and learning much more enjoyable. They may provide special content for groups of students or individuals that require a more thorough or specific approach when necessary. As a result, the efficacy of the teaching–learning process will increase, and pupils will receive extra attention, which they may require to progress with a certain subject or concept.

AR can be used in a variety of settings, including schools, universities, and online or self-learning. AR could be combined with other technologies, such as VR, to produce mixed reality. The real world is merely a starting point for further investigation. Both in terms of the themes that may be investigated in AR settings and the demonstrations or information presentations that can be created using technology, the sky is the limit.

Types of Augmented Reality Used in Education

- Premade markers are one type of AR utilised in education.

Symbols are used to cause AR to appear on the surface that the device is capturing. There are numerous apps available for markers and triggers on the market. These markers are all directly relevant to the course's topic. By aiming their device camera at the website, pupils can find the material. Teachers do not need to engage in sophisticated technology labour to create bespoke markers while using programs with predesigned markers. This helps them save both time and money.

Having AR-enabled images on the walls of the school or other educational organisation is an excellent method to create more interactive AR content. Students will be able to scan these wallpapers to have access to the associated AR material. Wallpapers featuring intriguing facts, for example, can be presented. This strategy will push pupils to learn while also making learning more enjoyable. This technique can even be used in the faculty photo wall at the educational institution. A student or parent can scan a photograph and watch it come to life.

Experimentation with AR

Working with concentrated substances in science experiments can be hazardous. Students do not need to be directly involved in such experiments with the help of AR. Science teachers encourage pupils to use AR to guarantee a safe learning environment. Students can participate in and learn about a variety of experiments. Students can use this to scan a variety of lab instruments and acquire information such as what rules and safety precautions to take when working with the materials.

Augmented Reality's Educational Benefits

AR applications in education enable new methods of learning by connecting the online and offline worlds. They make information easy to grasp.

These are some of the advantages of AR in education:

- Learn location-based information
- Learn language

- Remember concepts for a long time
- Allow for practical training in a real-world environment
- Improve teamwork
- Improve student attention to classes

Tools and Platforms for Creating Augmented Reality Content in the Classroom

Students can not only interact with technology using **augmented reality tools**, but they can also produce their material.

This is necessary to foster 21st-century skills such as problem-solving, real concern, critical reasoning, analytical skills, scripting, and iteration testing, which is the technique of establishing tests on insights gained from previous tests in addition to making progressive, evidence-based improvements.

EBSCO, a library services pioneer, has compiled a list of 10 well-chosen virtual environments for classroom materials that might assist K-12 students in improving and personalising their learning. If you intend to start as a developer, there are two possibilities on the list that are multi-platform and suitable for people of all ages:

- **CoSpacesEdu:** It is a tool available for students who know how to code and wish to create virtual 3D environments. They may also create infographics and communicate tales through virtual displays and tours. UsingCoSpacesEdu, teachers may form courses and assign homework. Images and 360-degree images may be uploaded, and a companion app is available.
- **MERGECube:** This is an AR multi-platform mobile gadget that makes you feel like you'll be attempting to hold a hologram in your hand. It may evolve into a multitude of things depending on the MERGE programmes you acquire. Teachers may utilise Merge Cube to develop STEM instruction, and also explore history and science, while students can create content and applications, and watch their creative works come to life in AR. This is an excellent way for students to see the outcomes of their effort, which is the first step in motivating future developers. You can also utilise Google Sky Map in this handheld planetarium to obtain a stunningly perfect view of planets and stars.

The Importance of Augmented Reality and Virtual Reality in Education

Students can interact with tangible objects visually with the use of AR and MR (mixed reality) technology, which improves student attention. Because of this sort of technological innovation, users will be able to interact with virtual items while maintaining spatial awareness of their actual surroundings. Students might, for instance, follow digital patches of guidelines for complex operations like learning how to repair a sophisticated machine or performing a medical procedure. AR, like VR, allows the user to view static virtual elements or information within actual space, but less dynamically. This is most beneficial when the object has the most teaching merit, such as in a lecture with a simulated environment of a statue or historical artefact, or on a heritage site with additional text or images.

Immersive technologies are becoming increasingly popular as teaching tools among students and instructors, as well as caregivers, administrators, and institutions.

In a 2016 poll of 1,000 teachers conducted by Samsung and GfK, 93% of participants claimed that their pupils would be excited to use AR and VR, and 83% believed that these technologies may help improve learning outcomes.

- According to a 2017 survey conducted by digitised and VR entertainment providers and the digital academic network, 70% of US children aged 8 to 15 and 64% of caregivers are fascinated by VR experiences.
- According to a 2018 Sensible Media survey, 62% of parents overall—and 84% of caregivers who had used VR themselves—believed it can provide instructional experiences for their children.
- In a 2016 study of 1,000 instructors done by Samsung Electronics and GfK, 93% of respondents stated their children would be thrilled to use AR and VR, and 83% thought these technologies may enhance learning results.
- According to a 2018 study, slightly over 50% of institutions of higher learning have employed VR in some capacity.
- Education is the second most probable sector to be touched by interactive technology soon, according to respondents in a 2020 research performed by Perkins Coie and the XR Association.

AR/VR-based education tools have the potential to completely change the way students of all ages and disciplines learn.

AR Apps for Education Environments

Narrator AR

With the advancement of technology in this industry, various AR has developed a variety of hands-on experiences for students to grasp concepts more quickly. The narrator is another fantastic app that assists children to learn engagingly writing in several dimensions. This AR programme animates the handwritten words on a page authored by kids. This sort of animation attracts children's attention and pushes them to use critical cognitive abilities to boost early literacy and neurodevelopment. Students will gain a deeper knowledge of how to write the word by watching animated handwritten words on the Narrator APP.

Clever Books

Students of all levels may be using the CleverBooks Geographical AR app to find ready-to-use AR knowledge. This programme contains 3D nation representations along with info about geographical distinctiveness, political systems, fauna, vegetation, and heritage sites. CleverBooks Geographic is one of the best AR applications for kids because it engages learners in a new way of thinking about problems and seeing the planet and all of its beauties through an immersive learning opportunity in a real-life setting. It applies to a wide range of courses and grades.

Quiver Education

It was one of the best AR applications for education, and it'll blend physical colouring with virtual colouring technology to give pupils an extraordinarily magical experience. It allows you to use a 3D colouring programme to animate your material. This AR programme is primarily utilised in biology, planets, and mathematical operations.

Curiscope Virutali-Tee

Curiscope's Virtuali-Tee app exhibits science in a novel method for kids to learn about the human psyche in a realistic context. The main benefit of this software is that it is well-designed, with a 3D experience that allows students to examine the human body structure and immersive 360-degree films. **Curiscope's Virtuali-Tee** is a wonderful AR app for kids to track the heart rates of themselves and their patients, and bring their imagination to life in real time.

Wildlife 4D+

Wildlife 4D+ is now one of the greatest AR applications for integrating the majesty of rich biodiversity into the planet's surface. Using the miracle of AR, several creatures are mysteriously immortalised in realistic-looking simulators for the students to explore, complete with their unique noises and motions. It's one of the greatest AR applications for teaching, created to increase children's understanding of wildlife diversity and the need for maintaining, safeguarding, and safeguarding the ecological balance.

The Galaxy 4D+

The Galaxy 4D+ software is a simplistic but excellent 3D virtual application that transfers children to the outer fringes of our solar system, where students may observe and learn about various celestial objects and space expeditions. It's one of the greatest AR applications for education, intending to inspire children with the marvels of the cosmos.

Catchy Word

Catchy Word employs 3D virtual technology to allow kids to 'grab letters' while roaming through their residences, classrooms, and other venues. After capturing the elements, they can be arranged to form a word. It's an excellent programme for children who have difficulty spelling. It was one of the best innovative features for learning because it allows parents and teachers to create their lists of words and solve them a few at a time or all at once.

ANSTO XR

ANSTO XR is an AR software for pupils that assists them in solving the periodic table to unveil the universe of a proton, neutron, and electron and demonstrate their significance in research and economics in the 21st century. By navigating the gadgets on the ANSTO chemical elements poster, students may discover new and intriguing information about the most significant elements, including how the atom is formed and how the elements are utilised in everyday life.

Geogebra Augmented Reality

When it comes to mathematical and scientific space, GeoGebra Augmented Reality fosters critical reasoning and attention in the real world. This programme provides students with a variety of 3D geometric objects that they may arrange on a tabletop, the ground, or any flat in their near surroundings. It's one of the best AR apps for learning as it permits students to work in groups to learn 3D functions, shapes, and more. They can also rotate their camera to penetrate a Klein bottle or join a Penrose triangle. Students can also take screenshots from different points of view, evaluate facts with the other learners, and then exhibit and debate their results in class.

Bookful

By merging AR and 3D components to bring characters and storylines to life, Bookful creates a fascinating experience. Parents and kids will be delighted at how this programme transforms reading habits into chances for active learning.

The nation's biggest 3D/AR catalogue includes hundreds of titles from recognised publishers and brands such as The Legend of Peter Rabbit, DK's Encyclopaedia, and children's favorites such as Barbie, My Little Pony, Thomas & Associates, Inductors, and The Smurfs.

Geometry Cleverbooks

CleverBooks Geometry allows students to learn geometrical solids in AR, sparking their enthusiasm for 3D geometry. It's one of the best AR applications for education since it has 3D representations of the five most frequent 2D geometrical forms (circle, rectangle, cube, hexagon, and triangle) and it allows teachers to see abstract geometry concepts in 3D. Users can integrate their apps with CleverBooks Geometric Construction Masonry blocks to create an interesting and entertaining learning atmosphere at home or in geometry class for kids aged 5 to 12 (K-6).

World Brush

Global Brush is an interactive virtual feature that enables children to sketch in the actual world with brushes. It's one of the best AR apps for learning since it allows kids to exhibit creative artwork with their classmates and professors. Every artwork is anonymous, and the approximate GPS coordinates of where it was drawn are saved.

Translate With Google

Students may use Google Translate simply by directing their hands and fingers at the phrase they want to convert, and the translation will appear in real time on the picture display. It's one of the greatest AR applications for education since it allows kids to learn the language without having to write the phrases they wish to translate.

Conclusion

A full analysis of the AR environments and applications that are widely utilised in the creation of learning and teaching environments in the education field with the making of the digital process is included in this research review editorial about VR. As part of the global examination of this AR in education research, many tools and resources have begun to be employed in teaching practices as a result of the integration of technologies into educational environments. In this case, it can be seen that the use of mobile tools and applications in educational settings has recently grown more prevalent.

Today's AR in the classroom is a little messed up. Although researchers have made progress in identifying some of the best strategies for integrating AR into educational settings, it remains one of the most recent disciplines in education. As a result, educators are still coming up with new ways to successfully incorporate technology into the classroom.

References

Alvin, L., Pratik, T., Wei, Y. T., & Indranil, B. (2020). "Can touch interaction predict product-related emotion? A study on mobile augmented reality". Proceedings AMCIS 2020, Human-Computer Interaction (SIGHCI) Aug 10th, Association for Information Systems AIS Electronic Library (AISeL), pp. 1–5.

Carmigniani, J. & Furht, B. (2011). "Augmented Reality: An Overview". In: Furht, B., Ed., *Handbook of Augmented Reality*, Springer, New York, 3–46. https://doi.org/10.1007/978-1-4614-0064-6_1

Diegmann, P., Schmidt-Kraepelin, M., Van den Eynden, S., & Basten, D. (2015). "Benefits of augmented reality in educational environments - A systematic literature review". *Wirtschaftsinformatik Proceedings*, 2015.103. https://aisel.aisnet.org/wi2015/103

Harris, L. J., Al-Bataineh, T. M., & Al-Bataineh, A. (2016). "One to one technology and its effect on student academic achievement and motivation". *Contemporary Educational Technology*, *7*(4), pp 368–381.

Johnson, L., Levine, A., Smith, R., & Stone, S. (2010). "Simple augmented reality. The 2010 Horizon Report". *The New Media Consortium*, pp 21–24.

Kapur, R. (2019). "Advantages of technology". https://www.researchgate.net/publication/333395640_Advantages_of_Technology

Prensky, M. (2001). "Digital natives, digital immigrants part 2: Do they really think differently?". *On the Horizon*, *9*(6), pp. 1–6. 10.1108/10748120110424843

Sırakaya, M. & KilicCakmak, E. (2018). "Effects of augmented reality on student achievement and self-efficacy in vocational education and training". *International Journal for Research in Vocational Education and Training*, *5*(1), pp 1–18. 10.13152/IJRVET.5.1.1

Yuen, S., Yaoyuneyong, G., & Johnson E. (2011). "Augmented reality: An overview and five directions for AR in education". *Journal of Educational Technology Development and Exchange*, *4*(1), pp 119–140.

https://www.ebsco.com/blogs/ebscopost/top-10-augmented-reality-tools-classroom

https://technologyeduc.com/15-best-ar-apps-for-education/

https://www.intechopen.com/chapters/78230

https://www.ncbi.nlm.nih.gov/pmc/articles/PMC8279104/

Chapter 16

Teaching and Learning Mathematics Using Augmented Reality

P. Dhanalakshmi and E. Shrilekha

Department of Applied Mathematics, Bharathiar University, Coimbatore, Tamilnadu, India

Introduction

Technology advancement has upgraded human life and enabled us to attain efficiency in all aspects of life. It is the driving force of development and has made our life comfortable. Technological development is a long-term process that involves modernisation, widespread creativity, technique, and skill. It is a whole combination of effective usage of method, innovation, and process. From the historic period of the basic tool being made from stone to the present digitalisation age, the technology has gone through a lot of development. The different technological tools originated from the effective ideas of science. The research, experiment, and project in the lab have become a medium for technology development. Even though technology has been progressing rapidly, people (especially the younger generation) get familiarised in no time. Technology has elevated the economy and has increased the potency of the manufacturing sector. It has accomplished massive progress in the medical field, notably decreasing the death rate. Technology development often comes in a wave pattern rather than a continuous or consecutive pattern. The personal computer was the first wave of technology that became

DOI: 10.1201/9781032675176-16

stronger after the internet, the second wave. The popular technology growth, mobile technology, is the third wave of technology. Currently, augmented reality (AR) and virtual reality (VR) are considered the fourth wave of technology. Evaluating those three waves that have transformed human lives, we can conclude that the fourth wave will have a positive effect.

Digitalisation is the process of converting physical information to digital form. It spreads knowledge and information everywhere, such as rural, urban, suburban, and metropolitan areas. It is a progressive transformation that made human life easier. We can perform other work in a reduced time. It comprises technology such as mobile, internet, computers, and other features. The physical components used for educational purposes, such as books, journals, and newspapers, are converted to digital information, for the ease of the learner to read from anywhere. It also has an impact on other fields, such as the banking and finance sector, tourism, and entertainment. It has left its footprint in almost all the fields that are required in human life. The technology that made an astonishing breakthrough is undifferentiated from magic. If a person from this century time travels with a mobile phone to the ancient period, he would be considered a magician with some magic box in his hand. This digitalisation and technological development will completely transform the future and where society is headed.

Digital learning has become inevitable in contemporary education. It helps students to collect various information about the concept. Digital education can also be referred to as technology-enhanced learning, as it enhances learning and teaching through technology. The coexistence of technology with learning has contributed to the advancement of active learning outside the classroom. The various digital resources such as software, mobile applications, online resources, etc, promote the speed and depth of learning [1]. It is convenient to use digital resources as they can be easily acquired anywhere. It is evident that digital learning has elevated students' academic performance. Also, technology has the capability of creating deep learning. Digital resources have a longer lifetime than physical things, and they are not damaged or faded over time, like books and journals. Digital learning is a vast area and offers diverse learning technique, which is not limited to AR and VR. Learning mixed with digital technology may take place in other forms, too, such as blended learning, badging, and gamification; open educational resources; differentiated learning; adaptive learning; etc. In the future, digitalisation will be widespread in most fields; thus, skills based on technology will become a necessity, and these digital skills must be learned along with education.

VR means stepping into a virtual world entirely. It blocks us from the outside (real) world and builds a new environment. These new environments may depend on real or imaginary ones. AR is viewing computer-generated objects in the real environment. AR includes the real environment rather than building a wholly virtual environment. It superimposes computer-generated objects on reality.

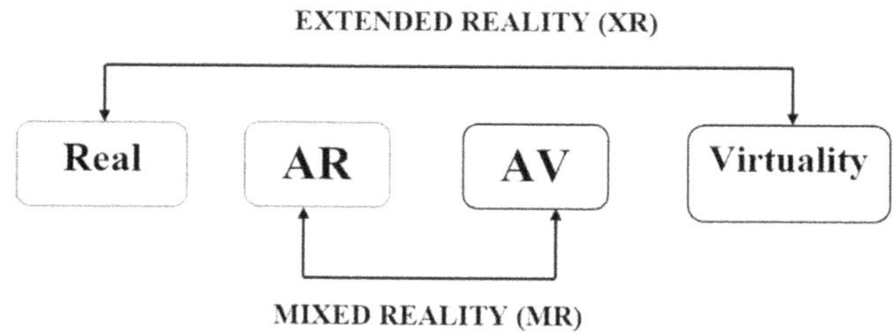

Figure 16.1 AR, VR, and MR.

AR has evolved and introduced mixed reality (MR) to the world. MR is the technology in which reality and virtually improved objects can interact. In MR, we can either view the real world with digital objects or view the real-time object in a virtual environment. Thus, MR can act as both AR and VR. In MR based on AR, it appears as if the virtual object no longer exists and blends into the real world. For instance, if we throw a ball (digital object) on the wall, we can view the ball bouncing back. We can also view the shadows caused by digital objects and adjust the brightness and contrast depending on the real world. Augmented virtuality (AV), also known as merged reality, is contrary to AR. AR generally uses virtual objects in the physical world, whereas AV incorporates physical elements in the virtual environment. Extended reality (XR) is a collective term that comprises AR, VR, and AV as shown as a scale (Figure 16.1). Virtuality continuum, [2] is utilised to calculate the amount of reality and virtuality of the technology. The end of this scale is occupied by the entire real environment, whereas the other end is occupied by the entire virtuality. XR ranges from the entire real to an entirely virtual environment, that is, it covers the entire scale. AR and VR are the most common technology.

Earlier, the HMD (head-mounted display) used in VR was huge, had less visible range, and had high cost. To overcome these limitations, Palmer Luckey created a prototype HMD [2], that is available at a minimal cost with greater visible range. This accelerated the virtual technology in the industrial and marketing field. AR amazed users as it was predicted that such technology can be accessed by mobile phones. AR also went through some crises, but the upsurge of VR constructively supported the growth of AR.

Mathematical Learning

Mathematics education must occur as an approach to gaining knowledge by self-learning, and it should involve real-life problems modelled mathematically to equip the student to face society. For proper learning, one must be able to summarise the concept, give examples to represent the mathematical concept, and choose the appropriate procedures to solve and apply the concept. The main objective of learning mathematics is to be able to apply the concept to solve problems in multidiscipline and real-time problems. One of the ways to learn mathematics is by solving problems and practicing them again and again. Another method of learning is understanding the concept using digital resources. Using technology in education enables students to deepen their learning. Both technology and mathematics are inseparable.

There are four eminent methods of learning under the mathematical learning inventory, namely mastery, understanding, interpersonal, and self-expressive. Based on the student's interest we can customise the teaching style with the above methods. Such teaching will increase the attention of the student and reduce boredom. The following information will help to distinguish the student based on their preference. We can also recognise the student by a survey or by providing four different types of activities on the same topic.

Mastery

Students of this type prefer realistic data and creative approaches. The problems must be solved by using the approach previously learned, and it must lead to a unique solution. They like to solve problems step by step. They experience the abstract part of mathematics as complicated. The teaching for such students must involve personalised coaching, adequate time to learn, design skills, and feedback.

Understanding

Math students who are of this type like to understand how math works. They prefer the math problems to be demonstrated and illustrated. They solve the problems by examining the pattern and sequence, and by analysing and classifying the question, and they may not be strong in teamwork or solving the problem while partnering with others. The active teaching style of the student will be questioned, and their thinking ability will be provoked.

Interpersonal

This type chooses to learn mathematics in abstract form and by teamwork. Application-oriented and real-life-based problems encourage students of this type. Since they like teamwork, they appreciate problems that involve others' opinions when solving. They face hardship when they are asked to perform individually or when the problem is not based on a real situation, and they like to solve the complex problem with the guidance of their teacher.

Self-Expressive

The imaginative student who investigates and examines math concepts belongs to this type. These students are interested in problems that are unusual and activity based. They solve the problem by visualising it, collecting the appropriate solution, and examining it. The learning gets complicated when there is routine practice or memorisation problem solving. They desire to be educated in solving imaginative and innovative problems.

Mostly, the preference of the student will be a combination of two methods, and thus the teaching method must incorporate all four methods. Even though this incorporated method may not be their preference, it will train them to view a different perspective. It is not a standard or compulsory procedure. It is one of the perspectives in which learning can take place.

Augmented Reality

The term 'augmented reality' was given by Tom Caudell and David Mizell. They commenced AR technology in the industrial field. AR is an interaction between reality and virtual objects. VR shifts the real environment to virtuality, whereas AR employs virtual images in the real-world environment. VR and AR are usually called the 'fourth wave' of revolution in technology after the computer, internet, and mobile technology. All the 'three-wave' technologies had a great impact on the lives of humans and are inevitable in our daily routine. We can say that the fourth wave – AR and VR – will also have an enormous effect on our life. AR is an extension of VR, which are much alike [3]. The impact of those waves will be unpredictable and their length cannot be estimated.

Imagine, just by staying in your home comfortably and wearing a headset, you can be in your desired place, maybe a stadium, concert, zoo, or museum. You can travel to other countries, bounce from planet to planet, and even explore space and experience everything just by sitting on your couch.

This learning using technology increases long-term memory recollection, content understanding, and enriched physical task performance. It plays a remarkable role in the fields that involve experimenting and are more practical. Also, it enlarges digital literacy and collaborative skills, and is easily intractable.

AR in Education

Technology keeps flourishing in the educational world. The development of technology and ever-present access to mobile devices has gained recognition of AR. It is a technology that imports virtual objects in real time using digital tools such as smartphones, computers, AR Toolkits, etc. It provides personalised learning and collaboration of virtual content outside the classroom environment.

In many fields such as medicine, engineering, science, etc., AR is used in learning and teaching, which has proved to be effective. Although AR learning is in the budding stage, it has a progressive result. Students' creativity, innovation, and productivity skills can be enriched. It plays an important role in increasing mathematical literacy, such as constructing, analysing, and using mathematics in different areas [4].

AR in Learning

Education has taken new progress through the development of e-learning. A major part of our learning takes place from the objects we see. The integration of virtual objects of two and three-dimensions into the three-dimensional (3D) real environment is AR. Often, different types of technology assist the progress of learning and the word 'technology' itself motivates the students. The virtual object renders a lot more information than a physical book with words.

Using AR technology with a suitable device not only visualises the objects in printed materials but also projects them in three dimensions with video and sound. It can also be used in the form of cards with the Android application for learning. AR learning does not require extensive knowledge about technology or technical devices, students can interact normally without any discomfort. Classroom education usually takes place with books, formulas, and the depiction of equations, which is usually bi-dimensional. Adding virtual objects to classroom education through AR supports exploring mathematical and technological concepts.

Some students choose to learn with fixed images, whereas others prefer dynamic images. In AR learning, the student can individually select their way of learning. In a properly developed learning circumstance, the students can learn using the technology to formulate, calculate, represent, and identify problems and also make decisions. Using this technology in learning has proved to increase focused concentration in students because it provides interaction with virtual objects. Further, this technology is remarkable for facilitating learning connected with the location. Since the technology allows students to handle virtual objects on their own, it strengthens their motivation and interest to study. In this AR learning, students receive customised learning, which helps them to distinguish what they know and what they don't know.

AR in Teaching

Unlike other educational fields, mathematics has a long tradition of teaching with physical objects. Some objects are created in the course of teaching for students to grasp various mathematical concepts, and these objects are known as manipulatives. Such manipulative objects have been used for a long time, such as the abacus, Cuisenaire rods, pattern blocks, base ten blocks, etc. The development of technology has progressed physical manipulatives to a new form of virtual manipulatives. The incorporation of printed books with technology enables teachers to demonstrate the geometric concept digitally and instill knowledge of geometry based on 3D space. Since AR technology is easily intractable, it is convenient for teachers to create an augmented learning environment [5]. In AR learning, we can programme the information to be displayed along with the model.

Digital technology has justified that education can happen anywhere, anytime, and the teaching methods get progressed accordingly. The present generation being familiar with technology increases the need for teachers to enlarge their technology skills. An efficient teacher can teach students of different classes to understand the usage of technology (e.g., AR) along with the mathematical concepts and improve problem solving as well as computational skills. With the increasing utilisation of technology, the teacher must be equipped with technical and conceptual knowledge.

When teaching a complex concept in mathematics that is difficult to understand by traditional classroom method, learning it by using AR technology allows the students to interact and explore practically the objects, rendering a new perspective of the concept. Since the model is 3D and can be viewed in real time enables the students to gain experience by exploring it and gathering more information regarding the concept. The main objective of AR in the teaching process is not to replace the teachers but instead to support the teachers to deliver the concept effectively using technology. The merging of concepts from the physical book and the virtual objects enables the teacher to demonstrate the concept in real time and instigates the motivation and interest for learning.

Geometry Using AR

Learning and teaching are two-way processes. Many concepts in geometrical mathematics are necessary to be viewed as real-time models. Geometry is a fundamental part of mathematics [6] and has a long history. It involves the distance, shape, and position of objects. These concepts are used throughout mathematics learning. It has an efficient role in arithmetic and algebra, differential equations, and topology. The art and architecture field also uses geometry.

Learning geometry can be difficult sometimes, but once we learn and master the geometrical concept, it becomes amusing. The faces, edges, or vertices of the geometrical objects may not be seen while using the blackboard and chalk to illustrate the objects. By using AR technology, we can overcome this hurdle and the students can understand the concepts and create their models. AR will be a stepping-stone in combining geometric concepts with technology. The principal objective of using AR in geometry is visualising 3D models, which would drastically improve geometrical learning among students. The geometry concepts, such as conic section, elementary geometry, vector analysis, and construction of 3D models from 2D, can be learned effectively through AR. While learning with such realistic technology, the students are interested in attending more AR classes. Geometry is not a difficult subject, but it needs practicing [7]. While learning through AR technology, the students obtain creative ideas to construct 3D and 2D objects. Although AR has not been developed for all geometric concepts, it keeps progressing.

Creating a 3D Model

Geometry in classroom learning needs imagination of objects in a 3D way, which is complicated and provokes fear in many students. This limitation can be reduced by using technology. Learning geometry through AR makes the concept interesting and reduces the uneasiness.

There is plenty of software for creating 3D objects that is available on websites for the learning process [8]. Such software is compatible and can be accessed with mobile devices and laptops. Download the appropriate software from the website, and set up the installation on your device. Now, the object can be created by choosing the primary shapes or creating your convenient model from primary shapes. The following Cube (Figure 16.2) and Icosahedral Sphere (Figure 16.3) are primary 3D models constructed using the software.

We can reshape them, assign colour, adjust brightness, and perform any operations to acquire the desired objects. We can also remove faces, and edges, to create the desired model. From these objects, students can understand the concepts

Figure 16.2 Cube.

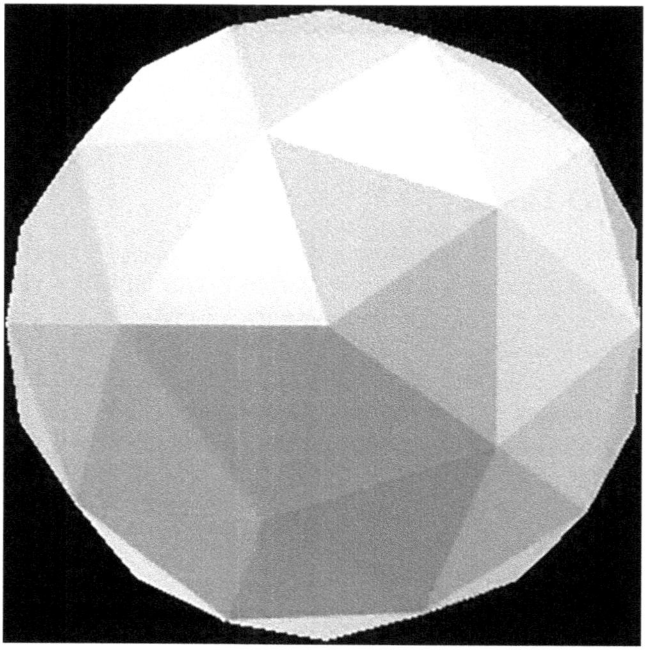

Figure 16.3 Icosahedral sphere.

clearly, especially the faces, edges, and vertexes, which can be observed instead of imagining them. The icosahedral sphere is a complex shape that is difficult to draw and calculate. The essential part of learning by AR is that students can learn about the object by zooming and rotating the object. Concepts learned by communicating with the object have proved efficient [9,10].

By combining two primary or simple models we can form a complex model. For instance, one of the faces of the cuboid model given in Figure 16.5 is removed. The created models must be exported to Wavefront (.obj) which saves the files in.obj format in the designated folder. This format expresses both colour and geometry. There are other available formats too, which can be applied if needed. Such files can be viewed in 3D format from your device. Here, by a similar process, the following 3D sphere with plane and cuboid with hollow face are created by using the software Blender (Figure 16.4 and Figure 16.5).

Three-Dimensional to AR

To convert these 3D models to augmented ones, another software is used. Sometimes the same software can convert your model into 3D, AR, and even VR. Otherwise, we can create a model and register it in another software that converts our 3D models to AR. After choosing the software we need to browse our model

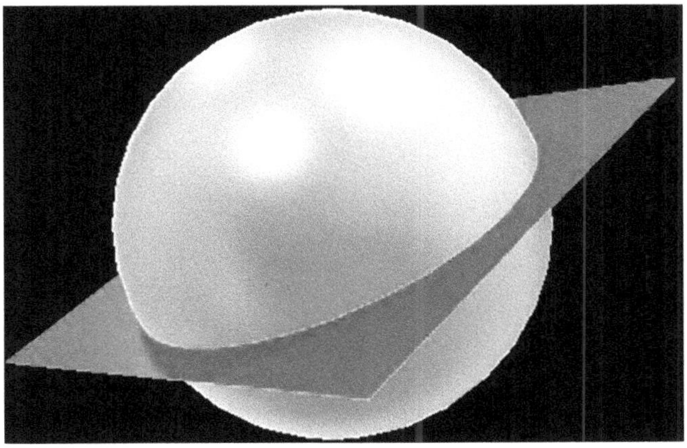

Figure 16.4 Sphere with plane.

Figure 16.5 Cuboid with hollow face.

and upload it. It will be saved as a project under the title you provide. Here also we can choose our colour, brightness, and other features provided. Eventually, when the project is completed, we must export and publish it. This action may differ for each software. Now, the QR code will be generated for your project. We can also edit the model whenever required. The QR code can be downloaded or copied as a link and provided to the students. Here we have provided the link and image for a sphere with the plane.

Link for Sphere with Plane: https://briovr.com/6a44b4ee-b74f-4ce4–86b0-cfb934c39c21/sphere-and-plane

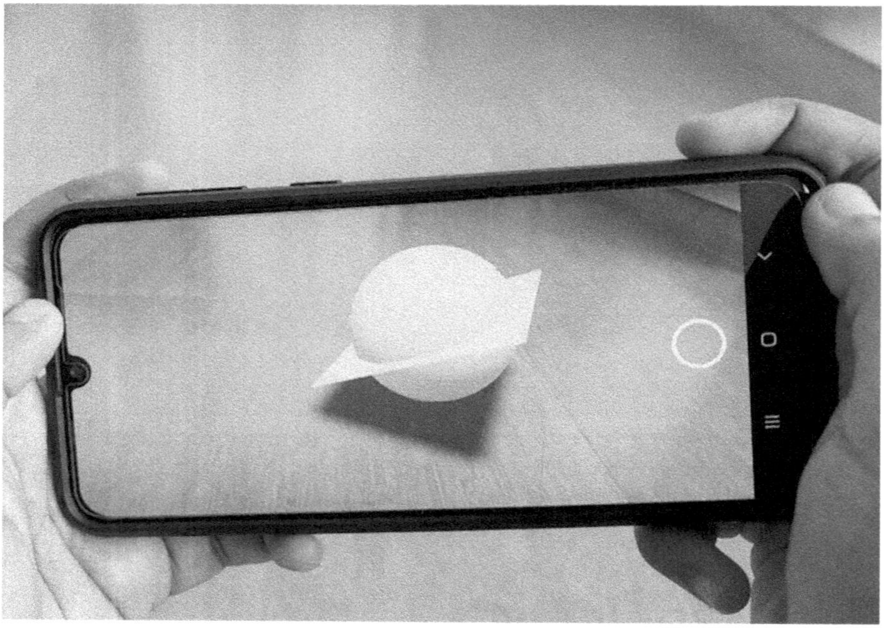

Figure 16.6 AR model of sphere with a plane.

The generated AR model can be viewed as a 3D model suspended in the air with your selected environment as background [8]. By using the link or QR code the student can view the AR model after scanning their desired environment using their mobile phone or computer. The different view of the sphere with a plane model exhibited in AR form is given here. (Figures 16.6 and 16.7).

The student can move the object and rotate the object virtually to get a proper view from all sides. They can zoom the model to fill the screen or pinch the screen to zoom in. All these operations can be performed with the fingers and slightly moving the phone alone; no other external devices are needed.

The geometrical concepts have always required a lot of attention because the student has to imagine the other side of the geometrical figures, which cannot be illustrated on the blackboard. For instance, suppose a teacher is explaining the faces, edges and vertexes of the cuboid. It is not easy to illustrate the side view or posterior view of the cuboid. The students also find it confusing to follow up on the illustration. In AR, the students can rotate the cuboid and calculate the faces and vertexes themselves. But in blackboard illustration, the students can view at most four faces. By dissecting one of the faces, they can easily calculate the edges of the cuboid also (Figure 16.8).

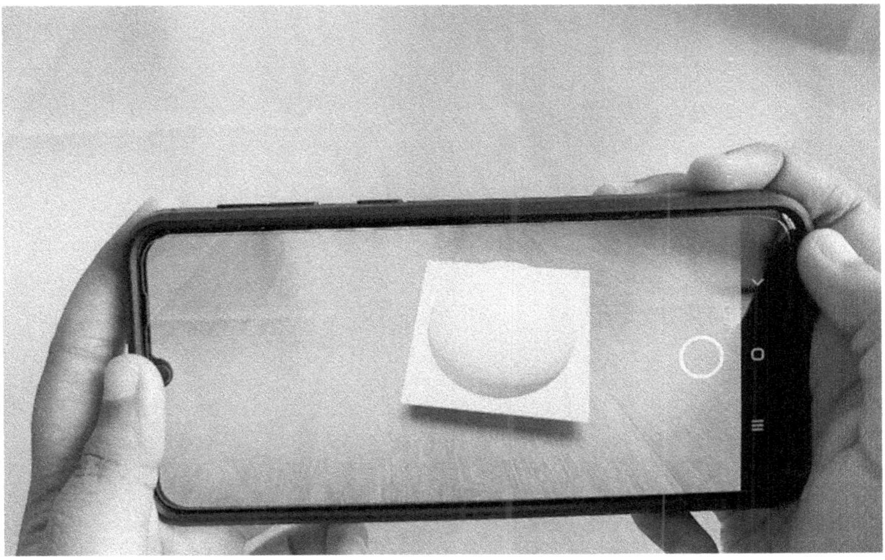

Figure 16.7 AR model of sphere with a plane.

Link for Cuboid with Hollow Face: https://briovr.com/f77dc9a9–3478-4ee5-b8d9-07bd857db67e/cuboid-with-hollow-face

Thus, the AR model can be explored by the students, and the teacher can demonstrate the models conveniently rather than the traditional classroom method. It enables the teachers to promote the interest of the student to examine more about the models and enhance self-learning. Also, space geometry can be learned digitally by interacting the digital component with the real object using real-time interactive display. There are many software and applications available, which can create both 3D and AR, instead of creating them using separate software.

Advantages of Learning Using AR

AR is ubiquitous and has altered the circumstances of both teachers and learners. Methods of learning and teaching are changing constantly. The skills of learners and the skills required in society are also enlarging. Implementing AR in education will be a golden opportunity for students to become familiarised with technology and employ it in various fields. It can be created in remote learning as the contents can be viewed by anyone, anytime, and anywhere. The availability of AR in mobile technology is another reason for its far-reaching recognition. Using AR technology,

Figure 16.8 Cuboid with a hollow face.

for learning mathematics, especially geometrical concepts, helped the students to absorb the content easily and use this technology with no difficulty. Further, to develop AR in education, it must be developed and tested at all levels of education. AR has set an example for the promising future of technology application in the educational field. Students also show great interest in creating their own AR models for visualising and learning.

To understand that AR in learning can have a positive influence on education and students' learning, we need to know about its prominent role in the educational field.

- AR learning increases teamwork, creative skills, and motivation to learn deeply and enables the student to individually access various content according to their curiosity.
- It consumes less time, leads to more retention of knowledge, and increases the motivation to learn mathematics.
- The students feel comfortable learning outside the classroom and also receive individualised instruction. It helps in visualising the concept and also plays a major role in minimising cognitive difficulties in learning.
- It allows the students to implement the knowledge already gained from the real world along with the educational concepts. Based on the student's age and the technology used, it has a great impact on learning mathematics.
- AR learning allows the student to promote involvement in the content; be present in the moment; and boost mathematical, technical, and conceptual ability.
- This type of learning gives a personalised experience. In traditional classroom learning, the student may get uninterested when they are unable to follow the concept along with the teacher, but AR learning technology helps students overcome this obstacle.
- Since AR learning comprises videos, images, and 3D models, it elevates student engagement to learn.
- The students may be forced to imagine objects in the traditional classroom, but in AR learning, they can view the model without difficulty.

Psychological Perspective

AR technology will have a significant role in all fields, especially in the educational sector. Since this technology is inevitable, let us view the constructive outcome of AR learning associated with the mind. Learning in the classroom environment and learning in the virtual environment have their benefits. The AR that provides virtuality in a real environment enables us to experience the advantage of both spaces. The AR models allow the students to make natural interactions, such as zoom in/out to vary the size, move the model, and examine it by changing the environment.

Students get motivated and interested to learn, as this kind of learning is more fun and interesting. They are able to pick their way of learning, which facilitates long-term memory recollection [11]. They can move physically in AR learning, to change the viewpoint of the model to examine the educational concepts. Location of learning also improves learning and memory retention. Their learning ability, creativity, and interaction flourishes, as the learning is not restricted within the classroom and can take place in fields, streets, playgrounds, etc., Students learning with this technology have higher adaptability in real time. AR learning encourages students to apply the educational concept learned by technology in real-time application [12].

AR in Diverse Fields

AR has played a major role in the education field, especially since it is a blessing for mathematics as it helps in visualising complex concepts. Even though we have only discussed the AR technology being used in the geometrical field, this technology can be extended to other fields, too. AR technology in mathematics is developing but is in a promising stage. Technology certainly reforms the learning, teaching, and educational structure.

AR transforms the way of connecting with the real world. In many fields such as medicine, engineering, science, etc., AR is used in learning and teaching, which has proved to be effective. In the engineering field, AR is used in manufacturing processes and projects. In the future, most of the process may be replaced by digital objects. Adapting AR has various effects based on the likeability of consumers. Still, the success or future of AR is unpredictable [13]. It is also applied in electronic engineering [14], architecture [15], etc., and AR technology is also growing in the fields of advertising and marketing, the environment, the medical field, the military, travel, and gaming. Some of the fields are explained in this chapter.

Problem-Based Learning

A real-time problem is constructed mathematically to enrich the students' scientific learning. This type of learning inspires students to develop hypotheses, which leads to obtaining the solution to the constructed problem [16]. To strengthen the mathematical skill of students, the help of interesting technology (e.g., AR) is used for problem-based learning. AR is easy to apply in studying, and students can understand the working of AR effortlessly. It doesn't involve complicated coding or operations. It especially focuses on involving a student to engage their knowledge. The 3D models can be created mathematically based on real problems, which impacts positively learning problem-based questions. This type of learning mathematics encourages the students to visualise the new concept using AR and increases their achievement. This technology needs to be improved in other areas of problem formulation and fields of mathematics.

Construct3D

Construct3D is a 3D geometric construction tool especially devised for geometry [17]. It is associated with Studierstube. It provides primary shapes such as spheres, cubes, cylinders, and planes and also has normal lines and symmetric operations. Using this tool improves spatial recognition [9] and includes parts such as AR, method of teaching, psychology, and geometrical mathematics. The size of the geometric object created can be raised or lowered, which allows users to examine the object entirely. This tool contains three types of modes – independent mode, collaborative mode, and teacher mode. With the help of this Construct3D tool, the teacher can work and manipulate the model, which can be viewed and examined by the whole group of students using head-mounted displays. If the teacher requires the student to create a model, the teacher changes it to independent mode, which enables the student to work on their model. This progresses the teacher–student interaction.

Interactive Printing & AR Books

Interactive printing is an association of AR technology with print resources. It combines a digital content layer, such as audio, video, or 3D models, with the printing material [18]. The recent software can recognise the outline and design of the page as an entire piece to convert it into an interactive document. The combination of AR technology and interactive print has invoked the motivation, curiosity, and interest to learn geometry and dimensional analysis. With this technology, any content can be instilled from printing to mobile devices. Such combined systems are powerful, conceptualised manipulatives and result in extensive grasping of contents. The exploration of AR with interactive print is in the basic stage.

The interactive and easily accessible AR books are a novel path of learning. It presumably plays a great role in combining the physical book and virtuality [19]. It affords 3D interactive learning for students. AR books deliver remarkable progress for primary education. These AR books are being created for various subjects. It undoubtedly provides an amazing experience for learners of any age. The characters of the book come out lively, and by adjusting the book, the characters can move.

Medical Field

Using AR in the medical field facilitates doctors to act effectively in emergencies. It has revolutionised various medical areas, especially surgery. During surgery, the surgeons were required to focus on the patient's body as well as the LCD monitor. In some crises of surgery, this little diversion may cause danger. AR supports medical professionals to virtually observe the anatomical parts and even project the surgical situation using an HMD. The blending of virtual images in real-time upgrades the training simulators to the next level. The unforeseen crisis creates stress and pressure during surgery. By the use of AR, such cases can be trained beforehand [19]. It allows the surgeons and residents to visualise the problems and come up with a solution before surgery. By saving time during surgery and having a beforehand experience, many lives can be saved. The expert surgeon can guide their resident with this technology. In addition, surgery AR can be used in clinical settings also. Technology in the medical field can protect life and minimise time.

Military

AR can project a real battlefield and display the annotation details. HMDs can be used in visualising the real battlefield and provide other information. The soldiers can exchange information with the base about their enemy's position [19]. This technology is used in flight simulation, battlefield combat simulation, battlefield medical response simulation, military weapon usage, bomb disposal, remote maintenance, and vehicle simulation. AR has reduced the time and cost and also provides the experience of the engine failing in flight simulation. In bomb disposal simulation, the bomb disposal squads can train to neutralise the explosives without any damage. Thus, AR has shown its presence in the military also.

Industry

Compared to other areas, AR progress is enormous in the industrial field [2]. It is applied extensively, especially in minimising maintenance or production time and faults. It has raised production, and the faults are minimised when correlated to the previous method. The customers can view their objects before buying [19]. It is widely used in the gaming industry [20,21]. The AR games enable the user to view objects in the real world and control them from the device screen. Rather than any other technology, AR requires the limited usage of hardware. With the help of mobile and laptops, AR can be created or used anywhere.

The Future of AR & AR Learning

Digitalisation and technology development will play a major role in the 21st century. In this technological era, students must be skilled in digitalisation. Estimating the future of AR in learning can be hard. We can either anticipate or presume. It is a new model for learners to get used to. The mobile phone is a widely used technology. Even though the learners may not own a mobile phone, they are aware of operating it. Similarly, AR may be an unfamiliar method of learning, which shows a different perspective of the physical world, but learners can get trained in it and use AR effectively. Regardless of the benefits of AR, if AR learning was initiated immediately in the classroom, it will be a hardship for the students. At first, the teacher must get familiarised with AR learning technology, and then it is passed down to the students. With proper instruction in technology and practice, students can learn better. Though AR learning on mobile technology for a long duration may be discomforting, initiating this kind of learning process sooner will contribute to a familiar experience. In the future, when almost all fields employ AR-based technology, students can handle it with ease. The killer app is a term denoted to apps that urge the user to buy rapidly and provide satisfaction with the software or hardware acquired [2]. The AR hardware will have a difficult time when it is released in the market unless the apps perform better, and it becomes inevitable to delight the users. AR will have more progress in the industrial field, which focuses on users. The focus on enhancing the HMD and glasses might reduce some complications. The remarkable goods will become a failure if they are not used by the world. VR has met a large range of users, but AR has not met such a stage. AR is still in its initial stage, and it is early to predict its success or failure. AR development in the future may even replace mobile technology. Since AR can combine the physical world with a virtual object, it provides a leading sign rather than the VR required to adjust to the whole environment. Even though both have potential, AR can easily alter its present surroundings more than VR.

Thus, AR has an upper hand over VR. VR is an enclosed technology; it may be placed in a complicated situation. One of the hurdles is that the user devotes most of their time to virtuality. Likewise, AR could suffer similar drawbacks. These technologies such as network, AR, and VR link all the users and students. The AR development in the world will be faster than you expect. It is better to learn about the technology and handle it in the early stage. And, when the technology reaches its peak, learners will be well-versed in using this technology. At some stage, we can see the users attend their work with AR glasses and, after returning home, watch entertainment shows at home leisurely with AR glasses.

Conclusion

With or without our acknowledgement, AR will be the future. There may be a circumstance where we will use an HMD or AR glasses instead of a personal computer in our workspace. The capability of AR has a major advantage over VR and thus it will be employed before VR technology. Since technology is transforming, students must keep their knowledge and information up-to-date, or else they will be outperformed.

Being aware of the significance of AR and VR, it is natural to be curious which technology would have more influence in the future. Though AR and VR are separate technology, it is not possible to entirely side with one of the technologies. We cannot state that one of the technologies has a greater influence and the other has no impact. Both have their advantage and disadvantages. A headset or HMD that can combine both the technologies will have greater influence and will attract a large number of users. The development of both technologies is certain, but it will face some hurdles. The progress of AR apart from using mobile technology is limited at present. The expensive headset, adapting to the AR environment, and the shortage of contents are some of the barriers that need to be resolved.

Through AR learning, students are able to gather more knowledge versus the traditional method. Entrusting the student to create their model using AR, and apply the earlier acquired knowledge in their created model, permits them to understand the concept efficiently. Manipulating the object in their desired environment, performing their own actions with the objects, and repeating it any number of times increases their focused attention and self-learning, and immerses the student into the concepts. AR learning technology can be applied without any previous experience, technological skill, or instructions. Students can invest their time in learning AR technology, which has a bright future.

References

1. Joshi, D.R., & Rawal, M. (2021). Mathematics teachers standing on the utilization of digital resources in Kathmandu, Nepal. *Contemporary Mathematics and Science Education*, 2(1).
2. Mealy, P. (2018). Virtual & augmented reality for dummies.
3. Chang, M., Hwang, W.Y., Chen, M.P., & Müller, W. eds., (2011). Edutainment Technologies. Educational Games and Virtual Reality/Augmented Reality Applications: 6th International Conference on E-learning and Games, Edutainment 2011, Taipei, Taiwan, September 7–9, 2011, Proceedings, vol. 6872.
4. Sholikhah, B.U., & Cahyono, A.N. (2021). Augmented reality student worksheets for learning mathematics during the COVID-19 pandemic. *Journal of Physics: Conference Series*, 1918(4), 042063.
5. Navarro-Ibarra, L.A., Salazar, O.C., García, J.X.P., & Leyva, J.C.A. (2017). Teaching-learning mathematics in a virtual environment. Empirical evidence in scenarios of higher education. *International Electronic Journal of Mathematics Education*, 12(3), 397–408.
6. Auliya, R.N., & Munasiah, M. (2019). Mathematics learning instrument using augmented reality for learning 3D geometry. *Journal of Physics: Conference Series*, 1318(1), 012069.
7. Hendracipta, N., Rafianti, I., Pujiastuti, H., & Haryadi, R. (2021). The use of augmented reality to improve mathematics conceptual understanding of pre-service elementary education teachers. *Journal of Physics: Conference Series*, 1796(1), 012018.

8. Yingprayoon, J. (2015). Teaching Mathematics using Augmented Reality. Proceedings of the 20th Asian Technology Conference in Mathematics, vol. 20, p. 384–391.
9. Kaufmann, H., & Schmalstieg, D. (2003). Mathematics and geometry education with collaborative augmented reality. *Computers & Graphics*, 27(3), 339–345.
10. Liu, D., Dede, C., Huang, R., & Richards, J. eds., (2017). Virtual, augmented, and mixed realities in education.
11. Bujak, K.R., Radu, I., Catrambone, R., MacIntyre, B., Zheng, R., & Golubski, G. (2013). A psychological perspective on augmented reality in the mathematics classroom. *Computers & Education*, 68, 536–544.
12. Coimbra, M.T., Cardoso, T., & Mateus, A. (2015). Augmented reality: an enhancer for higher education students in math's learning? *Procedia Computer Science*, 67, 332–339.
13. Rauschnabel, P.A. (2021). Augmented reality is eating the real-world! The substitution of physical products by holograms. *International Journal of Information Management*, 57, 102279.
14. Boboc, R.G., Chiriac, R.L., & Antonya, C. (2021). How augmented reality could improve the student's attraction to learn mechanisms. *Electronics*, 10(2), 175.
15. Shumaker, R., & Stephanie, L. eds., (2014). Virtual, Augmented and Mixed Reality: Applications of Virtual and Augmented Reality: 6th International Conference, VAMR 2014, Held as Part of HCI International 2014, Heraklion, Crete, Greece, June 22–27, 2014, Proceedings, Part II, vol. 8526.
16. Cahyono, A.N., Sukestiyarno, Y.L., Asikin, M., Miftahudin., Ahsan, M.G.K., & Ludwig, M. (2020). Learning mathematical modelling with augmented reality mobile math trails program: How can it work? *Journal on Mathematics Education*, 11(2), 181–192.
17. Kaufmann, H. (2002). Construct 3D: An augmented reality application for mathematics and geometry education. Proceedings of the tenth ACM International Conference on Multimedia, p. 656–657.
18. Estapa, A., & Nadolny, L. (2015). The effect of an augmented reality enhanced mathematics lesson on student achievement and motivation. *Journal of STEM Education: Innovations and Research*, 16(3), 40.
19. Yuen, S., Yaoyuneyong, G., & Johnson, E. (2011). Augmented reality: An overview and five directions for AR in education. *Journal of Educational Technology Development and Exchange*, 4(1), 119–140.
20. Mekni, M., & Lemieux, A. (2014). Augmented reality: Applications, challenges and future trends. *Applied Computational Science*, 20, 205–214.
21. Monteiro Paulo, R., Pereira, A.L., & Pavanelo, E. (2021). The constitution of mathematical knowledge with augmented reality. *The Mathematics Enthusiast*, 18(3), 641–668.

Chapter 17

Artificial Intelligence in the Teaching–Learning Process: A Paradigm Shift in the Teacher's Role

Pranjal Das[1] and Nil Ratan Roy[2]

[1]*Department of Education, L.T.K. College, Lakhimpur, Assam, India*
[2]*Department of Education, Tezpur Univeristy (A central University), Assam, India*

Introduction

We are living in a globalised world where people can easily connect with other people through the help of technology within a very short period. It makes life easy for human beings. Nowadays technology also has entered the education field, where it has tried to modernise the education system to the level where maximum development of students can take place. Artificial intelligence (AI) is the most recent and great innovation that has come into existence in the life of humans. AI deals with making machines that find solutions to complex problems in human-like situations. AI borrows features from human intelligence and applies them as algorithms in a computer (Ahmed, 2018). AI also refers to a machine that thinks, understands languages, diagnoses medical conditions, solves problems, keeps cars on the highways, plays chess, etc. like an individual (Tuomi, 2018).

DOI: 10.1201/9781032675176-17

In our education system, we started giving importance to the activity-based approach, where students are the focus of the teaching–learning process. In the activity-based classroom, students are given some tasks that they need to perform to learn something new. In an activity-based classroom, the teacher plays different roles such as facilitator, planner, organiser, implementer, evaluator, etc., which eventually increases the workload of the teacher. Consequently, it reduces the effectiveness of the teacher in their day-to-day teaching–learning process. So, a lot of attempts were made to cut the workload of the teacher and thereby help them apply creativity in the classroom. AI is one of the means through which attempts are being made to solve this problem.

So, in this paper, the researchers tried to highlight the present practices of AI that are taking place around the world in the context of the activity-based classroom. And at the same time, they tried to highlight the practices of AI that are taking place in the context of fields other than education. This chapter is prepared based on secondary sources of data. The researchers used both content analysis and meta-analysis for this study.

Present Practices of Artificial Intelligence in the Education Field

AI already enters different aspects of education, starting from admission, assessment, individualised instruction, etc. In the following points, we will discuss it so that a better understanding can be developed regarding that. These are given below:

Teaching Robots

Ozobot is a kind of robot that teaches children how to code based on colour-coded patterns. This robot can be used for children ages 3 to 12 years (Ozobot & Evollve, 2019). Cubelets is a kind of robot that help students develop logic, which helps them to think and act depending upon the function of the different blocks (Cubelets Modular Robotics, 2012). At Wonder Workshop, Dash and Dot are used with age-appropriate apps that encourage the learners to do hands-on learning and make learning a creative, concrete problem-solving one. It was designed for the age group 6+ (Wonder Workshop, 2019). PLEO rb is a kind of robot pet that helps learners to learn biology by teaching the robot to react to the different aspects of the environment (Pleorb, innov labs, 2016, as cited in Stanford University, 2016). These kinds of robots are popular in the USA, where children love to learn with them, and they automatically help children's overall development process.

Telepresence robot is a tablet, computer, or smartphone-controlled robot that consists of a video camera, speakers, screen, and microphones so that people interacting with the robot can hear and view its operator, and the operator can simultaneously view what the robot is hearing and looking at (TelepresenceRobots.com, 2016). Telepresence robot helps special students to attend school or at a hospital or home and thereby helps in achieving the objective of inclusion (UNESCO, 2019).

In the year 2016, a primary school in China introduced a cute robot namely 'Xiao'pang' (Little Fat) in the classroom. It can interact with the children and is able to express the child's behaviour habits more effectively. It is also helpful in the development of a child's behaviour (Zhao and Liu, 2019).

At Different Educational Institutions

In an online AI course at Georgia Institute of Technology, a chatbot named Jill Watson was launched in 2016 as a teaching assistant to answer routine questions of students (The Chronicle of Higher Education, 2016). Carnegie Mellon University researchers created a chatbot system called Evorus, which answers a broad range of questions. Evorus is a kind of chatbot that can accommodate voice input, which can be accessed from smart watches, phones, and computers (Spice, 2018).

At Georgia State University, AI software named Pounce was used for admission to answer some 2,000 questions about things like registration, financial aid, and housing in an average of 7 seconds. This kind of chatbot provides information effectively and quickly, in some contexts more efficiently than human beings. Northeastern University and Arizona State University are experimenting with another kind of AI, which comprises dorm room voice-activated devices that answer questions from students about things like menus, dining hall, and campus activities. Some educational institutions use AI for non-academic activities; for example, the University of Texas uses AI to manage its landscape sprinklers, saving both money and water. The University of Michigan uses AI for testing the use of driverless campus buses. Santa Clara University uses AI to manage campus parking (The Chronicle of Higher Education, 2016).

For Assessments

Automated Essay Scoring is an advanced application of AI in education. In the 1990s, the E-rater engine (developed by Educational Testing Service) and Intellimetric (developed by Vantage Learning) reached the market, and under these, students' writing is scored, including different kinds of exams and assignments for lecture-based courses, which are used in the different educational institutes. Apart from them, there are some other massive open online courses, which include Coursera, EdX, and Udacity, which have integrated automated scoring systems into their platforms to score the writings of different students who may enrol in the course. Some software helps in increasing the overall writing quality of the students by providing model writing samples, feedback, and guidance. These are Turnitin's Revision Assistant, Chegg's WriteLab, and Grammarly (Murphy, 2019).

Edulai is an AI software that assesses how online learners develop employability skills such as critical thinking, communication, teamwork, leadership, and interculturalism. It suggests learners with high-quality target content based on the skills that are developed at the basic or intermediate level and helps the learners in their next target skill level (Smarthink, 2019).

M-write focuses on the implementation of writing-to-learn pedagogies in the enrolment courses in the multiple departments of the University of Michigan. First, the teacher identifies the key concepts (difficult to develop conceptual understanding) that students need to learn in the course, and then the M-Write staff works with the teachers to develop prompts that require students to write about those concepts. In this course, students write in response to the prompt, participate in the automated review, and revise their original draft in response to the peer review (Morris, 2019).

Gradescope is a platform where students need to submit their assignments and then receive feedback, which ultimately helps the teacher understand the students (Gradescope, 2019).

Peerceptiv® is an online peer assessment tool that allows learners to receive actionable and quick feedback from their peers to improve their writing. It offers analytics to confirm whether learning goals are achieved or not, identify whether learners require early intervention or not, and guide the instructor on rubric improvement. Under it, learners are learning not just by writing, but gaining new insights from reviewing the writing of their peers (Peerceptiv®, 2019).

China is testing a machine that uses AI to mark students' essays in one out of every four schools. It grades the work and provides suggestions in areas of theme, writing style, and structure (Chen, 2018).

AI Platform and Individualised Learning

MAThia is a smarter math learning AI software that provides a personalised learning experience and supports students who are struggling with some kind of problem and challenges those who are ready for more. It provides adaptive support to each learner based on how they are answering the problems (Business Wire, 2019).

ALEKS is a research-based, online program that uses AI and offers course products for mathematics, business, science, and behavioural science. It uses personalised learning and adaptive assessments and accurately and quickly determines exactly what a student is most ready to learn. It can be useful for different categories of learners such as students, teachers, parents, etc. (ALEKS, 2019). DreamBox uses AI to understand the students' actions and thereby provide them with personalised instruction at the right level, which promotes decision making and strategy development capacity among the students.

Achieve3000 employs AI, which provides daily differentiated instruction for non-fiction writing and reading, which is precisely designed for learners' Lexile reading level (Achieve3000, 2017).

In the United States, Betty's Brain was developed by a professor of education at Stanford University. Betty is a virtual character who plays with the children's companions in the learning activities and allows students to teach him learning biological knowledge. During the conversations, students' explanations are recorded and evaluated by Betty, who immediately provides feedback to them so that students can develop a deeper understanding of the knowledge (Zhao and Liu, 2019).

MATHiaU™ is a software platform that was developed by Carnegie Learning, which aimed to deliver a better math learning experience for every math student. It's affordable, easy to use, personalised, and meets the students' current needs according to their present condition. Through this platform, MATHiaU™ plays the role of a human coach and helps in achieving the goals that teachers and students are looking for. It has different components such as Personalised, Constructive Guidance, Thorough Assessment, and Thoughtful Design, and with the help of this math, learning becomes a more effective one for the students. MATHiaU™ is meant for higher education, and apart from this, Carnegie Learning also developed some other platforms such as MATHia® and Zulama™. MATHia® is meant for students who belong to grades 6 to 12, and Zulama™ is meant for computer science students (CARNEGIE LEARNING, 2019).

Carnegie Learning developed a programme called Cognitive Tutor that allows students to receive individualised attention by maximising the amount of time that is spent on active learning and mastering basic knowledge skills. It monitors the progress of students' knowledge regularly and modifies the course material based on continuous assessments (Carnegie Learning, 2019).

UTIFEN is an online learning platform based on AI through which training is provided to teachers. This platform takes into account of success and failure of its users and creates ideal intervention models for learners. It also provides personalised feedback to its users to get an insight into their progress (Karsenti, 2019).

WriteToLearn software of Pearson uses natural language processing technology, which gives students personalised feedback to improve their writing skills. It is software that rates students' writing in general areas such as idea development, style, and organisation and provides suggestions for improvement in these areas (NITI Aayog, 2018).

Mathematics Adaptive Platform is an online learning solution that provides personalised feedback according to a skill level based on the past experiences of students. It provides help to the students through a set of over 25,000 exercises and 2,800 feedback patterns (UNESCO, 2019).

In Australia, Smart Sparrow is an online adaptive education platform that assists teachers in designing adaptive teaching content according to the needs of different students. At present, this platform consists of different subjects such as medicine, science, engineering, etc. It combines the characteristics of these fields and provides a large number of simulation experiments in the course, where learning takes place through the principle of 'learning by doing' (Zhao and Liu, 2019).

In the United States, Desire2Learn is a cloud education learning management platform where individuals can read course materials, do test questions, submit assignments, and communicate with fellow students. After users perform these tasks, the platform has a large amount of raw data, and accordingly, it analyses the data to give feedback to the students and teachers about the learning progress in a graphical format. Based on the data, it can predict whether the students are suitable for the new programs or not, and help students in making good choices (Zhao and Liu, 2019).

Shadow Health uses AI is a program that simulates patient cases for nursing students to practice those skills that they will need for patients soon. It provides students and educators with a leading-edge technology that is centred on conversation-based learning across a cast of virtual patients (Shadow Health, 2019).

Duolingo is an AI platform that helps the learner to listen, speak, read, and write the language in a game-like lesson where it adapts to the learner's learning style and gives personalised feedback to the learners. It helps the learner in improving their vocabulary, which is very much necessary to learn a certain language (Duolingo, n.d.).

PopBot is an AI platform with a blocks-based programming interface that consists of pictures to help children who have not started reading yet. It can record time and current activity, which is performed by the child in a particular situation. It has an autonomous function to play an active role in the curriculum to explain its thinking to the children (Williams, Park, Oh, and Breazeal, 2019).

LAIX Inc. is an AI company in China that creates and delivers product services to popularise English learning through the 'English Liulishuo' app, which was launched in 2013. This app integrated AI technologies with diverse learning pedagogies, gamified features, and adaptive learning experiences so that English learning could become more interesting and fun (YuguanInforrmation Technology, 2019).

M-Shule is a learning management platform that is designed to improve the performance of primary school students across Africa. It uses an AI system to understand the competency of the child and delivers the right lesson at the right time to them. It delivers a personalised lesson to the students and parents through SMS at home and then analyses the performance of the student. After that, it shares insights and reports with the parent, teacher, and school through the Web and SMS, and it helps improve student performance (M-Shule, 2018).

Different Project Abstracts and Awards

EAGER (Early-concept Grant for Exploratory Research) records data and uses technology to tell the writer where they are looking (reading) and what they are typing. It can detect the writing process and thereby provide real-time feedback. The project is a prototype that provides an interactive online writing environment (Korelsky, 2015).

Cherniavsky (2015) took a project that uses a user-centred design approach to create a dashboard for teachers for intelligent tutoring systems in different realistic classroom environments. This project focuses on a freely available website named Mathtutor, which uses tutoring software for mathematics learning. This project includes design development, pilot testing, and classroom studies, which ultimately aim at improving student learning.

Baylor (2015) undertook a project that seeks to understand and capitalise on how teachers build rapport with learners and thereby build technologies that support rapport between learners and computers. It is a multimodal sensing rapport-detection system based on recent advances in computer vision, machine learning, and signal processing, which recognises visual and audio behaviours during learner interaction with an intelligent tutoring system.

Improvement of Classroom Communication

St. Thomas University, in partnership with Microsoft, conducted a pilot study where facial recognition software was used to measure the engagement level of the students within the classroom. This kind of AI helps in monitoring the faces in the classroom and identifies the emotions that are associated with engagement and then produces a report for the teacher in the real-time situation concerning the students' focus in the class. This kind of feedback helps the teacher to modify their teaching according to the needs of the students (Klutka, Ackerly, and Magda, n.d.).

Lexplore is a company that uses AI and eye-tracking technology to provide teachers with real-time data, which is helpful for the intervention that directly relates to the student's reading capability. With this kind of data, the teachers can decide what strategy and what resources could be used so that students can overcome their problems (Fast Company, 2019).

Emoti-OS assesses and visually represents the well-being and mood of the staff and learners in the school. It has two components: a chatbot and an emoji-based interface that helps the staff and learners to express their feelings about the school community, learning environment, and other issues. This helps in knowing the overall climate of the school, which will automatically improve the academic aspect of the school (Baker, Smith, and Anissa, 2019).

For Future Courses

Stellic is an AI application that helps students with their degree planning. Through the dynamic planning system of Stellic, students get empowered to make informed choices that help them to create a more intentional path towards graduation (Stellic, 2019). This AI software was used by the administrators to understand better when to offer certain courses in the future, which courses are to be offered, and how many sections are needed to meet the student demand (Klutka, Ackerly, and Magda, n.d.).

Conclusion

Today we cannot think of a day when we are not using any kind of device with AI. Starting in the morning, we use different gadgets such as mobile phones, laptops, etc. where we work with different apps through the help of the internet and it makes our life so simple and easy that we could not think of it a century ago. It is said that we have made incremental progress in AI and advocates that a lot of AI systems are filtered with general applications, and often are not called AI. The main reason behind this is once something becomes common and useful enough, then it is not labelled as AI (Woolf, 2015), and from this, we can understand how we are getting habituated in our day-to-day life to AI.

When it comes to the education field, we will find that automatically we are using AI in different parts of the world. Some countries are way ahead in applying this AI in their classrooms, and some have just started applying it. Studies are also conducted to understand the significance of using this AI in the education system. Among them, one such study was conducted by Alemi, Meghdari, and Ghazisaedy (2015) where it was found that robot-assisted language learning (RAIL) helped in developing a positive attitude and reduced the anxiety level among Iranian EFL junior high school learners in the area of English vocabulary acquisition.

After understanding the importance of AI, CBSE introduced AI as an optional subject in class IX from the session 2019–20 onwards (The Economic Times, 2019). So it is the need of the hour that teachers should start applying this in their day-to-day classroom and create awareness regarding it. With the changing times, teachers need to upgrade themselves, and if they do not do so, then in the near future they will get eliminated from this teaching–learning process (Zhao and Liu, 2019). At last, we may conclude by saying that we need to take necessary steps to improve our overall quality so that we can adjust to this modern-day education system.

References

Achieve3000 (2017). Retrieved from http://www.achieve3000.com/.

Ahmed, H. E. (2018). AI advantages & disadvantages. *International Journal of Scientific Engineering and Applied Science*, 4(4), 22–25.

Alemi, M., Meghdari, A., & Ghazisaedy, M. (2015). The impact of social robotics on L2 learners' anxiety and attitude in English vocabulary acquisition. *International Journal of Social Robotics*, 7, 523–535.

ALEKS (2019). Retrieved from https://www.aleks.com/independent.

Baker, T., Smith, L., & Anissa, N. (2019). *Educ-AI-tion rebooted? Exploring the future of artificial intelligence in schools and colleges*. Nesta. Retrieved from https://media.nesta.org.uk/documents/Future_of_AI_and_education_v5_WEB.pdf

Baylor, A. (2015). EXP: partners in learning: building rapport with a virtual peer tutor (Research Report No. 1523162). Retrieved from National Science foundation Where Discoveries Begin website: https://www.nsf.gov/awardsearch/showAward?AWD_ID=1523162

Business Wire (2019). *MATHia by Carnegie Learning Named "Best Artificial Intelligence Solution" in 2019 EdTech Awards*. Retrieved from https://www.businesswire.com/news/home/20190416005618/en/MATHia-Carnegie-Learning-Named-%E2%80%9CBest-Artificial-Intelligence

CARNEGIE LEARNING (2019). MATHiaU™. Retrieved from https://www.carnegielearning.com/products/software-platform/mathiau-learning-software/

The Economic Times, CBSE to introduce artificial intelligence, yoga as new subjects. (2019, March). Retrieved from https://economictimes.indiatimes.com/industry/services/education/cbse-to-introduce-artificial-intelligence-yoga-as-new-subjects/articleshow/68548174.cms

Chen, S. (2018). *China's schools are quietly using AI to mark students' essays … but do the robots make the grade?* Retrieved from https://www.scmp.com/news/china/society/article/2147833/chinas-schools-are-quietly-using-ai-mark-students-essays-do

Cherniavsky, J. (2015). EXP: helping teachers help their students: teachers' use of intelligent tutoring software analytics to improve student learning (Research Report No. 1530726). Retrieved from National Science foundation Where Discoveries Begin website: https://www.nsf.gov/awardsearch/showAward?AWD_ID=1530726&HistoricalAwards=false

Cubelets Modular Robotics (2012). Retrieved from https://www.modrobotics.com/

Fast Company (2019). *Most innovative companies Lexplore*. Retrieved from https://www.fastcompany.com/company/lexplore

Gradescope, (2019). Retrieved from https://www.gradescope.com/

Karsenti, T. (2019). Artificial intelligence in education: the urgent need to prepare teachers for tomorrow's schools. *Formation of Profession*, 27(1), 104–111.

Korelsky, T. (2015). *EAGER: exploiting keystroke logging and eye-tracking to support the learning and writing* (Research Report No. 1550122). Retrieved from National Science Foundation Where Discoveries Begin website: https://www.nsf.gov/awardsearch/showAward?AWD_ID=1550122

Morris, G. (2019). *M-Write*. University of Michigan. Retrieved from https://lsa.umich.edu/sweetland/m-write.html

M-Shule, (2018). Retrieved from https://m-shule.com/

Murphy, R. F. (2019). *Artificial intelligence applications to support k-12 teachers and teaching.* Retrieved from https://www.rand.org/content/dam/rand/pubs/perspectives/PE300/PE315/RAND_PE315.pdf

NITI Aayog (2018). National strategy for artificial intelligence. Retrieved from https://niti.gov.in/writereaddata/files/document_publication/NationalStrategy-for-AI-Discussion-Paper.pdf

Ozobot & Evollve (2019). Retrieved from https://ozobot.com/stem-education

Peerceptiv® (2019). Retrieved from https://www.peerceptiv.com/how-it-works/

Shadow Health (2019). Retrieved from https://www.shadowhealth.com/about/#mission

Smarthink (2019). *Edulai helping students to develop employability skills.* Retrieved from https://smarthink.org/edulai#new-page

Spice, B. (2018). *Crowd workers, AI make conversational agents smarter.* Retrieved from https://www.cmu.edu/news/stories/archives/2018/february/evorus.html

Stanford University (2016). *Artificial intelligence and life in 2030. One hundred year study on artificial intelligence.* Retrieved from https://ai100.stanford.edu/sites/g/files/sbiybj9861/f/ai_100_report_0831fnl.pdf

Stellic (2019). Retrieved from https://www.stellic.com/

TelepresenceRobots.com (2016). *What is a Telepresence Robot and what can they do?* Retrieved from https://telepresencerobots.com/what-telepresence-robot-and-what-can-they-do

The Chronicle of Higher Education (2016). *Artificial intelligence and chatbots in higher education.* Retrieved from https://www.vaughn.edu/wp-content/uploads/2018/10/Artificial-Intelligence-and-Chatbots-in-Higher-Education.pdf

Tuomi, I. (2018). *The impact of artificial intelligence on learning, teaching, and education.* Luxembourg: European Union. Retrieved from http://publications.jrc.ec.europa.eu/repository/bitstream/JRC113226/jrc113226_jrcb4_the_impact_of_artificial_intelligence_on_learning_final_2.pdf

UNESCO (2019). *Artificial Intelligence in education: Challenges and opportunities for sustainable development.* France: UNESCO. Retrieved from https://unesdoc.unesco.org/ark:/48223/pf0000366994

Woolf, B. P. (2015). AI and education: celebrating 30 years of marriage. *AIED 2015Workshop Proceedings*, 4. Retrieved from http://ceur-ws.org/Vol- 1432/ai_ed_pap5.pdf

Williams, R., Park, H. W., Oh, L., & Breazeal, C. (2019). PopBots: designing an artificial intelligence curriculum for early childhood education. *The Ninth AAAI Symposium on Educational Advances in Artificial Intelligence*, 9729–9736.

Wonder Workshop (2019). Retrieved from https://www.makewonder.com/

YuguanInforrmation Technology, (2019). *A leading "AI + Education" technology company.* Retrieved from https://www.liulishuo.com/en/aboutus.html

Zhao, Y., & Liu, G. (2019). How do teachers face educational changes in artificial intelligence era. *Advances in Social Science, Education and Humanities Research*, 300, 47–50.

Chapter 18

Cloud Computing in Education

A. Sivakumar and G. Singaravelu

Department of Education, Bharathiar University, Coimbatore, Tamilnadu, India

Introduction

Process education means theory and laboratory practices, self-study, projects, or experimental work with the equipment, software packages, and applications for laboratory work. To develop digital learning platforms for postgraduate and research scholars of various educational programs, modern methodologies may be taken into consideration: project, problem, and inquiry-based learning; digital laboratory, which requires laboratory infrastructure with remote access; or a virtual laboratory that means simulation of the existing laboratory and virtual environment implementation as close as possible to the real world. The use of cloud computing technology in an academic institution to support teaching and learning has changed the way education is being conducted in many nations. Educational institutions can collaborate, share resources and networks, and enhance enrolment because of advanced technology. It is common to see many online courses and degree programmes being offered in many academic bodies around the world. Academic institutions throughout the world have become highly dependent on advanced technology for teaching, learning, and research. They searched for ways to rationalise the ability to manage their resources, and due to *cloud computing*, these opportunities have become even better.

DOI: 10.1201/9781032675176-18

Cloud Computing

Cloud computing is the distribution of various services through the web, which includes tools and applications such as data stores, servers, databases, networks, and software applications. Instead of maintaining files routinely in local memory or on a proprietary drive, the memory based on the cloud saves files in a foreign database. While a device has access to the internet, the information is accessible; therefore, the programs related to that particular information can be executed in the software. Cloud computing could be a widespread option for individuals and industries for quite a lot of motives, inclusive of investments, safety, amplified manufacturing, speed, efficacy, and performance.

Cloud Computing Services

There are three service models – Infrastructure-as-a-Service (IaaS), Platform-as-a-Service (PaaS), and Software-as-a-Service (SaaS) – which are popular. A single company using all three models is not unusual. However, there is often confusion about the three models and what everyone receives.

Software-as-a-Service (SaaS)

SaaS is an application or software that is based on the cloud. The cloud hosts application software and provides access to a web browser. For this, a special client or an API is integrated into the desktop, i.e., the user's operating system. Generally, the users of SaaS pay monthly or annual subscriptions. Some can offer prices based on their actual use, or 'pay as you go'.

Platform-as-a-Service (PaaS)

PaaS offers software program developers a hardware source inclusive of an on-demand platform, a full stack of software, set-up, and even tools for development and management, as well as development and management of applications with no or low cost, no complexity, and enhanced flexibility to maintain the targeted platform.

Infrastructure-as-a-Service (IaaS)

IaaS affords access to the sources of the basic computer physical and virtual servers, networks, and internet memory based on the 'pay-as-you-go' system. IaaS allows the users at the other end to change the size and properties on a supported basis and requires a large investment of tasks, investments, or unnecessary entrepreneurs, or 'infrastructure holders,' to use the necessary resources for periodic peaks to reduce.

Serverless Computing

Serverless computing is a simple model that publishes the entire management process of the back-end system, including calls, planning, patching with the provider of the cloud setup, and sharing the time and efforts of the developers for the specific code and logic of a company focusing on applications.

Cloud Computing – Types

The Public Cloud

This is a kind of computing system in the cloud by which the service provider calculates the sources of a SaaS application, on VMS (i.e., individual virtual machines), hosted via exposed metal computers, to complete enterprise platforms for infrastructure and development that are available to users. These types of resources can be easily accessible, or permission to access could be sold based on the models for payment or pay-per-usage system.

The Private Cloud

This is an environment offered by the cloud in which all the setup, resources, and infrastructure are committed to a particular customer and can be reached via the customer. This system has many advantages, including pliability, scalability, and provision quota with admission to control, safety, and resource adjustment within the unframed infrastructure.

The Hybrid Cloud

This is a combination of both the cloud environments, namely public and private. Particularly, it is a hybrid form of a cloud that combines private organisational cloud services and public clouds into one adaptable infrastructure to carry out the functions and workload of the organisation.

Multi-cloud and Hybrid Multi-cloud

The use of more than one cloud of diverse providers is termed a multi-cloud. With this environment, the user finds it easy to e-mail SaaS providers and perform image editing of SaaS from others. However, while talking about multi-cloud, companies usually talk about the use of wide-ranging cloud services, encompassing services like IaaS, PaaS, and SaaS. A survey reports that 85% of organisations have adopted multi-cloud environments.

Cloud Security

Shared Responsibility for Security

Cloud providers, in general, are responsible for securing their infrastructure. On the other hand, users need to protect their data in the cloud. Nevertheless, it is equally vital to state the properties and regulations of both the third parties, namely private and public.

Data Encryption

The data are coded both during entry and during use. Customers must maintain complete control over the safety buttons and security module of hardware.

User Identity and Access Management

The users and teams who manage information technology require thorough knowledge and clarity on networks, equipment, various applications, and access to data.

Collaborative Management

Good communication, clarity, and comprehensiveness in the process are the key factors of a collaborative system. The teams of operations and security ensure unified cloud integrations that are safe as well as durable.

Security and Compliance Monitoring

To maintain the transparency of the data exchange between diverse cloud environments, like public, private, and hybrid, all the standards about regulatory compliance that apply to business as well as vigorous inspection of all associated systems based on the cloud must be the focus of the system.

Innovation in Education

Cloud computing denotes the organisation of computer properties that could be used everywhere, regardless of the location of the user. By implementing this, it becomes possible to bring facilitators and learners into a solo and uniform platform. Various educational establishments, namely schools, colleges, and universities, do not need to purchase and maintain their own cloud servers. On the contrary, they can use cloud computing to access current databases, memory, and other services if they need them. In addition, they can always be certain that their resources are safe in the cloud. Let's explore the wide-ranging advantages of cloud computing connected to the teaching–learning process.

Virtual Environments Strengthening Learning

Educational institutes could provide virtual learning environments to their learners via a cloud-based system. This reduces infrastructure costs primarily through the reduction of costs for faculty members. Expert coaches from afar can serve as teachers and be cost-effective resources. At the same time, they can manufacture and deliver online courses for learners, who can complete exams virtually, saving time and money.

Accessibility

The potential of the cloud is unique concerning accessibility. Learners can effortlessly access the contents of the course, the applications, and the data from anywhere. They can register for courses and also join group events. The barriers related to time do not exist as the cloud allows continuous delivery of content. In addition, it sends the content in mobile-friendly formats for ease of learning for students.

Extensive Cost Effectiveness

Another prominent advantage of this is the huge savings. Both students as well as providers experience countless benefits. Learners do not need to invest in books and applications that are costly because these items are accessible in the cloud. Also, providers can reduce administrative costs by streamlining processes like registration, product orders, infrastructure costs, etc.

Secure System for Data Storage

In addition, a cloud system offers the advantage of secured data memory. Educational institutions opting to learn using the cloud system can assume virtual private network (VPN) protocols to resolve data security and traffic issues. Thus, learning content could be transferred to users without difficulty and without the risk of attack. VPN also enables students to shield their privacy while learning using cloud-based applications.

Scalability

This refers to applications for many users, including schools, higher education institutions, and universities. This permits users to scale their experiences swiftly and effortlessly and to deal with additional learners. In addition, it helps to manage features related to traffic as a result of events such as training information and job comments. Similarly, the features can be assembled during the low or no activity period to avoid wastage of resources.

Agility and Novelty

This allows the user to trial frequently and quickly; in turn, enabling innovations for better learning experiences. In each application, novel tools and functions are developed, tested, and verified to make it better than earlier.

Better Reach among the Students

Undoubtedly, for the educational industry, cloud computing has brought the prospects to expand the vista. Those unsatisfied with traditional systems of learning can now explore the novel online learning system. Learners who wish to opt for learning through external mode or overseas mode are aided through this. Workers who cannot make use of conventional modes for learning to upgrade can also use this.

Nominal Hardware Requirements

These applications seek minimal resources concerning hardware; they effortlessly function on diverse browsers as well as on both PCs and mobile devices, thus reducing the need to invest in a computer. In addition, there is no need for external storage devices as a free cloudy store is ready for access. Learning cannot be easier than this. Thus, cloud computing offers immense advantages for educational sectors, due to which industries are rapidly implementing it to progress in services. Everyone in this sector, be it a student or a school or a higher education institute, experiences the best of the cloud, and its functionality is assumed to be superior and routinely improved.

Education Applications

Cloud computing in the education field becomes a paradigm shift in teaching–learning practice. It offers various distance and online learning platforms and academic information portals to students. The advantage of using it for educational purposes is that it offers powerful virtual environments, secure storage, accessibility, scalability, development for the students, and a smaller amount of hardware requirements for the applications.

Applications for Teaching and Learning

Slides from Google Sites

A program used for presentation is a feature of the Google Docs editor suite with Google Docs Editors. The service also contains documents, modules, designs, and

Google sites. It is available as both mobile (Android, BlackBerry, etc.) and web applications (iOS, Windows, etc.) and permits access to applications on a desktop in the operating system, namely Google Chrome. It is well-suited for the presentations of Microsoft PowerPoint. Through this, real-time creation and editing of files is possible and is stored as a revision in history. The position of a publisher is marked with a colour and a specific cursor editor and authorisation system controls. Updated functions with automatic learning include 'exploration,' layouts, and beat images for presentations, as well as 'elements of action' with which teachers can interact with students.

Apple Pages

Pages is a powerful Word processor that allows you to create breathtaking documents. It can be delivered to most Apple devices. With real-time collaboration, students can work together everywhere, regardless of whether they use it on Mac, iPad, iPhone, or a PC.

Apple Keynote

Apple Keynote has powerful tools and iridescent effects that make it easy to create breathtaking and unforgettable presentations on most Apple devices. The students can use Apple pencils on their iPads to create diagrams or illustrations that carry students' slides for learning purposes in all learning environments. With real-time cooperation, students can work together, whether they are using a PC, Mac, iPad, or iPhone.

Word Cloud

A word cloud is a visual representation of the frequency and value of the words used in a text. Students can use it to get insight into the most important conditions in their data. With the interactive experience of the word cloud in Power Bi, students do not have to use large amounts of text to find out which conditions are prominent or predominant. Educational institutes can easily visualise their students as a word cloud and create a picture of their interactivity to discover the topics behind the content. This visually brings them control of the appearance of the word cloud, regardless of whether it is the size or use of the room and dealing with the data. Students can choose to arrange the words in the text by frequency of the word or by value of the word in the text. Students can also choose to remove the original settings of the word cloud. By switching on rotation and playing with the permissible corners, users can become very creative with this view. They can also provide a measure to apply to the text. When 'No' measures are provided, the program simply uses frequency. Users can view the 'Format' window for more options.

Microsoft One-Drive

Microsoft One-Drive, which was previously known as SkyDrive, addresses synchronisation services that are managed by Microsoft Office related to the web. Its users save personal information such as settings, keys for recovery, and Android and Windows files. Teachers and students can upload files to One-Drive, which offers a free 5 Gigabyte storage space with 100 Gigabytes, 1 Terabyte, and 6 Terabyte memory options.

Dropbox

Dropbox offers a chief hub for the storage of files online and synchronising. Irrespective of whether the student is at an educational institution or on the street, the files on their devices are synchronised and retrievable in real time. Students and teachers can access the account Dropbox through various applications available for desktops on Windows and Mac, and mobile iOS or Androids.

Google Drive

With Google Drive, students can save files, synchronise, and release files to other devices. It offers offline features for Windows, MacOS, Androids, smartphones, and tablets. Google Drive contains Google and Google documents, which are part of Google Docs Suite Office Editors Creation of collaborative machining documents, spreadsheets, presentations, projects, forms, and potential publishing documents. Files created and modified via Google Docs Suite are stored on Google Drive.

Google Docs

This is a free online text processor through Google that includes sheets, slideshows, illustrations, forms, and sites. Documents can be reached via browsers and mobile applications. So, students can also save the data in the cloud.

Capture Cloud

The Capture Cloud platform incorporates safety, management, analysis, and threat intelligence in network security products, emails, devices, and clouds. This approach allows the entire high-performance hardware portfolio, virtual devices, and customers to use cloud performance, agility, and scalability.

Apple iCloud

iCloud is integrated with each Apple device. This means that all students' photos, files, notes, and more are secure and are up to date everywhere. It works automatically. All users receive 5 Gigabytes of free iCloud memory to start, and it's easy to add more at any time.

Amazon Cloud Drive

An Amazon account allows you to manage and release files from various devices, including browsers and desktop applications. It also allows users to order and print photos and photo books using Amazon's print service.

Memopal

Users can protect their entire computer with the online backup function of Memopal. If they need to share storage space on their hard drive and want to delete files from their computer, they can save a copy on Memopal. The student also receives a synchronised folder among all computers so that the latest version of their files is always available. Their synchronised files are safe.

SugarSync

SugarSync is a cloud-based service that proactively syncs files between computers and other devices to back up, access, sync, and share files from iOS, Mac OS X, Android, and Windows. An unofficial abandoned backpack client is available for Linux.

Cloud Printer

Cloud printing is a technology that provides access to printers on a network on cloud computing. There are two types of printing on the cloud in essence. On the one hand, cloud consumer printing is combined with every application for high-quality home printers to which people have or have access. With this technology, people can occupy digital media as a primary communication tool and create a printed page when they need content on fitness.

ZipCloud

With zipcloud, students can synchronise their files on multiple computers, deciding which files and folders they want to synchronise. They can also choose where to synchronise. zipcloud operates in the background and prompts cloud students to be ready to synchronise with other devices.

Benefits of Cloud Computing

Cost Savings in the Long-Term

Lowering costs is the main advantage of cloud learning software. Compared to the administration of data centres on-site, migration into the cloud supports the information technology (IT) ecosystem. This helps companies invest in predictable monthly operating costs. These predictable monthly costs bring organisations several benefits, including data storage cost reductions and minimum exposure centres. Less money is dedicated to the replacement of physical ageing of computer hardware to improve the environment and form new e-learning chances.

Collaboration

In education, collaborating in real time is an essential thing to be achieved by cloud computing. It helps: (i) Keep students connected, (ii) Create teacher management portals, and (iii) Provide distance learning by virtual mode. Managing education with a cloud-based setup creates many opportunities for collaboration that are effortless to generate the situation for teachers, students, and parents to be individualised.

Resource Availability and Easy Access

A cloud-based teaching and learning platform allows students to access live and digital sources no matter what device or web browser they are using. Cloud-like virtual resolutions offer lifelong educational opportunities to all; they are usually applied according to the guidelines for web content accessibility. Thus, it provides students with both mobility as well as a personalised learning curriculum that adequately meets their needs.

Flexibility

Compared to the size of conventional data centres, the BlackBased software can help reduce costs associated with the growth of universities. Whatever the number of students universities have, or when used as an unemployment service, this cloud system can guide visitors to the website.

Modernising Learning Environments

Solutions for education, such as VMware Cloud that are offered by Microsoft DaaS, will become the greatest means for educational organisations in the future. These innovations make the schools attractive to new learners and allow advanced-level learning.

A Few Cloud Computing Challenges in Education

Dependence on Internet Service Providers

The ill-fated truth about cloud computing is the need to access the internet. In contrast to traditional classrooms, service interruptions or very low ISP bandwidth can interrupt the learning taking place online. Yet, it is possible to implement a solution for better access and connections by managing issues with the users or the providers.

Less Control

While the benefits of the cloud are the availability of educational platforms and services, the problem lies with less or lack of control over the information updates, drills and training, and related characteristics.

Trader Commitment

The resolution of cloud computing concerning educational purposes depends totally on the services offered by the sole provider. Normally, service providers cannot be alternated; hence, MSP may allow selecting of the right supplier. If you move learning tasks to the cloud, it is important to choose the right supplier. A good salesperson who listens carefully, including to risks and management, starts at the end and resolves any unexpected problems that may arise. In most cases, users are blocked after signing their contract with the supplier. Although most of the sellers allow them to cancel the contract, they burden them with termination sanctions.

Safety

Cloud education technologies are safe when the technology is configured correctly, but when all resources are sent online, there are risks for intrinsic safety. Cloud systems that are inadequately secured can be susceptible to computer attacks, and data insecurity is an increasingly acute problem when data are accessed across various devices. When the device is stolen, including the saved authorisations, then the cloud is available to unauthorised and unlicensed users. Thus, giving priority to security is a must. Teachers start with the correct configuration of learners' cloud infrastructure to ensure that all the students are designed for best practices with cloud safety. The cloud should also further protect the susceptibility of the end-user device.

Upfront Costs

Although the cost is minimised, there are predictions about its' benefits in the field of education. Migration can be costly depending on the quantity of cloud computing applications or services. There is also the possibility to train employees in suitable time for new systems and practices. Savings are due to the lasting reduction of operating costs, and managers must be prepared for it.

Purpose of Cloud Computing Applications in Academics

The following benefits could be seen in teaching and learning, by opting to use cloud computing.

The students

1. can virtually attend their classes.
2. can check research projects and related activities worldwide to equip them.
3. can perform data collection using cloud computing applications for their research works.
4. can download the software freely through cloud computing.
5. can use web tools for research explorations and academics.
6. can access unlimited research papers while selecting their area of research.
7. can enjoy free storage offered by web applications.
8. can do money transactions through the online mode for education.
9. can enjoy enormous facilities while using cloud computing.
   Apart from this, both teachers and students
10. can upload and download videos for academic purposes.
11. can access the online resources at any time.
12. can visit online websites and update themselves.
13. can download statistical tools for analysing data.
14. In addition, teachers can use web-based materials for their teaching.

Conclusion

Administrators need to evaluate the benefits alongside the needs and regulate which would be the best solution for an educational environment. When cloud computing encounters education, both students and teachers open up new opportunities. Cloud computing applications help to create low-cost, affordable, scalable, and sustainable academic products and packages. Cloud computing, like other technologies, has both advantages and disadvantages, but in the education sector, it may be an essential source of scoring and an important source of e-learning, particularly collaborative learning, mobile-based learning, distance learning, and online learning via the World Wide Web. Perhaps the big challenge is the full coverage of the high-speed internet access service.

References

A Defenx Company. (2017). *Protect Your Files.* Https://Www.Memopal.Com/. https://www.memopal.com/

Adeoye, Blessing F. (2015). Utilization of Cloud Computing in Education. *Journal of Global Research in Computer Science, 6*(4), 10–11.

Amazon. (2021, August 2). *Amazon Drive*. Https://En.Wikipedia.Org/. https://en.wikipedia.org/wiki/Amazon_Drive

Apple Inc. (2021). *Pages*. Https://Www.Apple.Com/. https://www.apple.com/in/pages/

Apple Inc. (2021a). *Keynote*. Https://Www.Apple.Com/. https://www.apple.com/in/keynote/

Apple Inc. (2021a). *iCloud*. Https://Www.Apple.Com/. https://www.apple.com/in/icloud/

Buchanan Technologies. (2021). *The Main Benefits & Challenges of Cloud Computing in Education*. Https://Www.Buchanan.Com/. https://www.buchanan.com/benefits-cloud-computing-education/

Dropbox. (2021). *Dropbox*. Https://Www.Dropbox.Com/. https://www.dropbox.com/features/cloud-storage

Google. (2021, September 10). *Google Docs*. Https://En.Wikipedia.Org/. https://en.wikipedia.org/wiki/Google_Docs

Google LLC. (2021, August 30). *Google Slides*. Https://En.Wikipedia.Org/. https://en.wikipedia.org/wiki/Google_Slides

J2 Global. (2021, May 6). *SugarSync*. Https://En.Wikipedia.Org/. https://en.wikipedia.org/wiki/SugarSync

Microsoft. (2021, September 21). *Microsoft OneDrive*. Https://En.Wikipedia.Org/. https://en.wikipedia.org/wiki/Microsoft_OneDrive

Microsoft Corporation. (2021). *Word Cloud*. Https://Appsource.Microsoft.Com/. https://appsource.microsoft.com/en-us/product/office/wa104380752?tab=overview

Micu, D., Orza, B., Porumb, S., & Porumb, C. (2012). Cloud Computing and its Application to Blended Learning in Engineering.

Sai Vennam. (2018, August 18). Cloud Computing. Https://Www.Ibm.Com/. https://www.ibm.com/in-en/cloud/learn/cloud-computing.

Sivakumar, A., & Singaravelu, G. (2016).Utilization of Cloud Computing Application. *American Journal of Educational Research*, *4*(11), 792–797.

SonicWall. (2021). *Capture Cloud Platform*. Https://Www.Sonicwall.Com/. https://www.sonicwall.com/capture-cloud-platform/

The Scientific World. (2020, February 12). What are the Applications of Cloud Computing in Education Sector? Https://Www.Scientificworldinfo.Com/. https://www.scientificworldinfo.com/2020/02/applications-of-cloud-computing-in-education-sector.html

Walter Stone. (2019, October 10). 8 Surprising Ways Cloud Computing Is Changing Education. Https://Cloudacademy.Com/. https://cloudacademy.com/blog/surprising-ways-cloud-computing-is-changing-education/

Wikimedia Foundation, Inc. (2021, July 5). *Cloud Printing*. Https://En.Wikipedia.Org/. https://en.wikipedia.org/wiki/Cloud_printing

ZipCloud. (2021). *ZipCloud*. Https://Www.Zipcloud.Com/. https://www.zipcloud.com/features

Chapter 19

Mobile Learning in Higher Education

P. Subramanian

Department of Educational Planning and Administration, Tamil Nadu Teachers Education University, Karapakkam, Chennai, Tamilnadu, India

Objectives

This chapter provides a simple introduction to the concept of mobile learning. It gives the reader an understanding of the importance of mobile learning and the different types of mobile apps available in various subjects. This chapter also provides an overview of mobile learning in higher education. It also deals with the advantages of mobile learning, the challenges of mobile learning in education, and the impact of mobile learning in education. The chapter ends with an explanation of creating online mobile courses.

Introduction

We live in a digital world, and it is easy for us to access any information at lightning speed. We encounter technology in all spheres of life in one way or another. If we want an answer any kind of question or want to know how something works, we can surf the internet and get access to tons of information and videos in a second. There have been many changes in how we work, how we play, and mainly how we learn. The world is overwhelmed with the use of technology. People are engaged all the time with their electronic gadgets like

DOI: 10.1201/9781032675176-19

mobile phones, laptops, etc. Anybody can learn anything, anywhere on the go, and at their convenience.

Nowadays almost every student is a digital native and is proficient in the use of the latest technologies. They don't solely rely on their teachers for information. Everybody can get instant access to information anytime and anywhere. It has made the students independent and has inculcated self-learning. Smartphones and human beings are inseparable in today's social milieu. These technologies must be used for constructive purposes alone. There are umpteen numbers of online platforms to learn and explore new things. Learning is filled with fun and enjoyment. Students could learn many things apart from their curriculum and attain knowledge at an advanced level.

There are massive open online courses, digital libraries, e-resources, and digital content available online to quench the thirst of knowledge seekers. Lifelong learning and distance learning is made easy. Over the last couple of years, the popularity of PCs and laptops has been challenged by the arrival of tablets.

The application of mobile technology for educational activities has metamorphosed from being just pilot studies to their formal implementation in institutes. Mobile technologies enable seamless connectivity with peers and experts, which aids in meaningful interaction and knowledge sharing with the outside world. At all times, internet connectivity facilitates access to various educational resources.

Mobile Learning – The Vogue

People use mobile devices differently in different environments. Mobile learning is in vogue among students, especially in higher education, these days. It has been a top learning trend over the last couple of years. Nowadays mobile learning is not an option but an inevitable one forming an important part of informal learning. Mobile technology in learning may also clear the boundaries between colleges and leisure time, promoting self-directed and informal learning. Technology can transform and advance learning.

There is a difference between electronic learning and mobile learning, though they sound synonymous. Mobile learning technologies are handheld devices such as mobile phones, tablets, iPods, etc. that are portable, whereas electronic learning refers to learning carried out through electronic devices that are connected to the internet. It not only refers to learning with computers but also through CD Roms, watching an educational program through television, radio, and all that which keeps the learners tethered to their desks, but this is not so in the case of mobile learning. Mobile learning is a part of e-learning, and they both depend on digital communication to provide services.

Aims and Scope of Mobile Learning

As we are in the 21st century, we have experienced a drastic change in the environment, and in society – it's not the same as 10 years back. There has been all-around development in all sectors. Therefore, most higher education institutions are looking for a new method of teaching so that the students will show attention and interest in the learning process. Mobile learning is a very new and effective concept that can reach everyone easily, and there will be a learner-centred learning process. It is very easy to share the study materials with the students, and there are many easy ways of communication through a mobile device. We can share and create many images and videos related to the topic so that the learner can understand the concept easily.

Many universities are now trying to adopt new methods of teaching effectively using mobile devices to promote student-centred learning. M-learning created a strong base in higher educational institutions and promotes educational practices. It supports many flexible learning methods, and with the use of ICT, students can get any information related to their learning process. M-learning encourages learners to have a conversation with their teachers anytime if they have doubts, without hesitation. Mobile learning encourages the students to explore their world. They can easily share their ideas and views instantly with the world, and they can learn through interactions with many people's expertise rather than depending on one teacher or peer groups to explain things to them. Mobile learning allows students to have instant communication with the international information network.

Role of Mobile Learning in Higher Education

When a student moves on to higher education, technology becomes a crucial part of their life. To enhance their career, the student has to depend on technology. In higher education, mobile learning plays a vital role and also is gaining popularity in the education sector. Mobile devices such as notebooks, tablets, and smartphones have become unavoidable in institutions of higher education. Nowadays, all students own a mobile device of their own, and that supports them to learn beyond their classroom. Mobile devices are flexible and can be carried everywhere, wherever students feel they can be accessible. This is the most important reason why students use their mobile device in their higher education.

Lectures are being given online by lecturers, which helps students to learn from their homes. Students who pursue their higher education mostly rely upon mobile learning because they find more information beyond their book in mobile learning and it helps them stay updated. So, the role of mobile learning has become vital in the present era.

Wealth in Mobile Learning

The biggest wealth in mobile learning is its 'flexibility'. Mobile learning is flexible and could be used anyplace, anytime, and in any situation. Mobile learning is not like classroom learning, where a student needs to be in a particular place at a particular time. It is just the opposite; students feel flexible in learning their topics when they have time.

Another important key factor in mobile learning is students get easily engaged and collaborate among themselves. Students have a learning community that can help them to share their knowledge among themselves. This particular concept is lacking in classroom learning. Mobile learning can make students search more and update more. The features of mobile learning are the important wealth of mobile learning. Mobile learning provides various features such as interactive videos, animated videos, and video conferencing. These features make the students feel enthusiastic and also create a passion for learning.

The significant and rapid growth of mobile learning has made educational institutions provide many online classes and courses to enhance the innovative strategies of students in this digital era. In recent days, educational institutions have been giving video classes and conferences to students. In the present situation, since people are being locked down for their safety, mobile learning helps students to be actively engaged with their subjects. Teachers or lecturers are providing their guidance and are also teaching through mobile learning. Mobile learning is far-reaching in the current situation.

The popularity of mobile learning is due to the personalised and continuous learning path that it provides. Various platforms are learner friendly and offer learners the courses they need, and the learners are given reminders to attend their courses. This helps a lot with learning. Mobile learning has gone a step ahead to provide online courses that can also provide a certificate. Many certification courses are being conducted online that are related to the core subjects of the learners. The certificates that are provided are approved by the government and are even useful for the students to get a good job. Mobile learning serves as a great platform for learners to keep themselves updated.

Deprivation in Mobile Learning

Though we feel that mobile learning is a great wealth, it also has some drawbacks. Every coin has two sides, and here are the drawbacks of mobile learning. The smooth mobile learning experience can sometimes be interrupted by software issues. Software issues do not occur often, but once they happen, it becomes a hindrance to the smooth learning experience. Learners also experience software crashes and many such issues in mobile learning. That type of issue could be experienced all of a sudden by anyone, and it could cause the end of learning at that moment.

As with software, another issue that learners face is hardware issues. The hardware is the mobile phone that the learner is using, which may wear out after some time. When a device is being used for a long time, it may run out of battery or become overheated, which could interrupt mobile learning. Another major drawback is not because of the device; it is because of the user of the device. Distraction of the user is another major problem. When a student has a mobile device in their hand, they tend to get distracted because of social media. If a notification pops up, the student would automatically be curious to find out what it says, and the student would end up looking at social media. The student would waste their time, and their task would not be meaningful anymore.

The most notable problem is misuse of the device. Students in higher education are typically people in their adolescent period. They have a mindset to quit whatever becomes challenging for them. So, the mobile devices used for learning could be used in the wrong way or for fun, etc., which would not help them to continue their mobile learning. They may end up quitting. Another major problem in mobile learning is the problem faced by people in rural areas. They face the problem of poor internet connection. The main source of mobile learning is an internet connection, and this becomes a great hindrance for people in rural areas.

Mobile Devices – The Tool for Learning

Search Engines

Using widely popular search engines like Google, students can look on the internet and find answers to questions that they cannot locate on their own. Also, not just a local, but a global overview of things is possible because of mobile learning. Inside a classroom, students can approach only one teacher, but mobile devices let students choose from a wide variety of options.

Video Lessons

In addition to textbooks, there are a lot of teachers/lecturers/professors who upload their videos on YouTube and other video hosting websites, which are free to access. Except for the cost of the internet provider and the electricity to charge the mobile battery, there's no cost involved in accessing these videos, which are highly resourceful for learners.

Online Classes

Apart from videos, online classes provide students with the option of interactive sessions instead of being passive listeners. While listening to the lectures, students can raise their hands and ask questions to get clarification immediately. The teacher too can choose to mute and unmute the students' mics, ensuring an undisturbed session. Such classes also come with the option of recording, so that even if a student misses a class, they can access the recorded video and learn the topic covered.

Online Tests and Exams

No learning is complete without getting tested. And there's no proof that something has been learned without being tested. So, tests and exams are the only way to qualify and testify that the students have learned/acquired a particular skill. In addition to the ease of just typing (even voice typing), and choosing from multiple choices that avoid strenuous and lengthy writing tasks, online tests also are a way of going paperless, which helps the environment. During the pandemic period, graduates would remain without their degrees even after the end of the academic year. To avoid such lacunas, standardised online testing methodologies can be easily adopted and supplemented to let education go on without a break. Even computerised review can make corrections more valid and avoid any malpractice, too.

Group Discussions

Apart from the online classes/video access, etc., mobile phones can provide the opportunity for students to form a group among themselves and support peer learning. Those questions that might be hard to be clarified by the lecturer can still be clarified by peers who are like-minded, in a free and easy manner. Group discussions improve collaborative work among students.

Hands-on Demonstrations

Not just theoretical classes, but hands-on demonstrations are also available in a wide range. During the lockdown, many organisations asked for innovative solutions from young minds, which triggered their creativity. Online hands-on demonstrations are a great way to learn because, at any step, students may pause, revisit, and get clarity on a particular step to master the art of doing things. Also, there are many forums that invite discussions and comments on such demonstrations that help people come out with even simpler solutions for complex problems. This enables students to experience multiple perceptions and multi-dimensional aspects of many similar innovators around the world.

Advantages of Mobile Learning

Students may not be alert and attentive during the entire class when the teacher talks the entire time. Students' span of attention is very short, and though they are physically present, their minds might be wandering somewhere else. They might be hungry or in need of a break, etc. Since there is a lack of concentration, they may not be able to understand what the teacher is explaining. Learners can grasp the content only if they are fully focused. Mobile learning paves the way for learning when the students are alert. They might learn anytime when they are alert and attentive.

Education does not end after obtaining a master's degree or after obtaining a doctorate. Learning is a continuous process. Learning is lifelong, and there is no end to learning. Learning is considered a human right that must be utilised by people. There is no age limit for learning. What we know is only a handful of information, and what we do not know is as vast as our awesome universe. There are many things to be learned, and it serves a variety of purposes. People might learn how to make a good living, how to fulfil their passion, or how to have good status, to self-actualise, to serve society, etc. With the help of mobile devices, lifelong learning is made possible.

Learning is not confined to the four walls of the classroom. Gone are the days when schools and colleges were the only places where education was imparted. Even outside educational institutions, learners can learn. When waiting for a bus or train, during their daily commute, and whenever students find time, they can learn anywhere and at any time. A fair amount of time could be used to learn. This is all because of the technology that lives inside students' pockets.

Nowadays geographical conditions are not a hindrance for those who wish to learn. Everybody has a wonderful opportunity to access the best educational resources from around the world. Due to economic, health, and other conditions, a learner might not end up at a top educational institution. Yet, with the help of technology, the learner could access those institutions' materials. Thanks to technology, there has been a great breakthrough in learning. Steps have been taken for native people and people in remote areas to access learning with the help of these mobile devices. At this moment, when the world is suffering under the clutches of the pandemic, learning continues. Students and teachers are still connected.

Every learner possesses a different learning style. When it comes to understanding things, people are different. How one student understands and perceives things is significantly different from another learner. Mobile learning allows learners to have a personalised learning experience. Different learning preferences are met. Some students might understand better and retain what they have learned through audio lectures; some might learn better if they see graphical representations, images, animations, and so on. A deeper understanding can be gained by hands-on practice, for which videos help to a greater extent. Learners can rewind and learn a particular topic again and again, which would be exhausting for a teacher.

Learning should always be student centred, which yields the optimum results. This makes students independent. They can easily find ways to overcome their weaknesses. Mobile learning is learner centred, and this gives students autonomy.

Self-learning is highly enhanced. This gives the learners ample opportunities to explore. The students become active participants, which is essential for their education. Only if they are willing participants will the concepts sink into their minds for fun and enjoyment. Gamified quizzes and gamified learning kindles the interests of the learners.

The needs of special children are catered to, too. They can be independent and need not rely on other people always. They can avail the resources at their seats. Google assistants are at their disposal to get access to any information or even guidance. Online tutoring is done for those who are homeschooled. No society could stop a woman or a girl from learning through a few swipes. Due to many reasons, most women are denied higher education, but distance education in higher education is seamless with the help of mobile devices. Mobile devices play a great role in removing all kinds of barriers to learning.

The prime advantage of mobile learning is accessibility. The tip of the finger is sufficient to do this. Learning can be accessed at one's convenience. Mobile learning provides personalised learning experiences along with individualised tutoring. It keeps the learners engaged in their learning. The use of video will lead the students to obtain the necessary skills and training. The support provided to learners is continuous, and it is a rewarding experience to learn through mobile devices. Learners get the flexibility to learn on the device of their choice.

Disadvantages of Mobile Learning

Distraction is the foremost disadvantage. These distractions may be in the form of a simple text message, notifications, etc., while one accesses online content. It spoils the attention and focus of the learners. They are not able to learn at a stretch without any disturbances. Messages from social media make their mind wander somewhere else. Entertainment makes the learners fidget with the mobile device often and not learn. They get into the shackles of the false illusions of the media, which might derail the students from the right path. Young girls are vulnerable, and their lives are at stake if they are ignorant.

The next disadvantage is regarding the devices. Almost everybody or at least one per house owns a mobile phone. But everybody may not be able to afford a mobile device of good quality with many features. A mobile device with limited functional capacities may not be suitable for mobile learning. Be it a laptop, phone, or any other device, the student has no other option but to get one with the required level. Most of the devices discharge quickly, especially when there are several apps active on the device. The short battery life could be a major problem for learning over a lengthy period.

The mobile device normally has a small screen. The students might end up straining their eyes. Heads always down with eyes never winking will cause dryness in the eyes and other eye problems. The exposure to radiation emitted through phones will also cause serious effects like headaches, damage to the brain, etc. Though the health-related issues may not be evident at the beginning, they will have a toll on the users later. It makes the students lazy, consuming a great deal of time and denying them the pleasure of physical activities and games.

Mobile Learning in Higher Education

Mobile learning can support education at all levels. It is especially an important area where its potential can be leveraged because of its importance on college campuses. The pedagogical advantages of mobile devices have altered students' way of understanding, specifically in higher education. Mobile phones are now the most common device used to access the internet worldwide, and increasingly students use smartphones, which have touch screen control. Consequently, a lot of what students can do with a tablet, they can also do with a smartphone. These smartphones, along with tablets, allow learners and teachers to access a wide number of collaborative tools, websites, e-books, and – importantly for tablets and smartphones – apps, which can be of great help to the learning process.

Impact of Mobile Technology on Education

Mobile learning in the education field is transforming learning for digital natives. Mobile learning or the delivery of educational content, specifically using mobile technology, is gaining rapid popularity in the education sector. Mobile learning in education can be an excellent solution for students demanding increased flexibility in study options. Further, mobile learning in education is an extremely friendly way to adopt modern teaching methodologies. Not only does it support visual learning (via audio, video, and images), but it also makes learning dynamic and fast paced, thereby keeping students more engaged in a classroom as it conveys course material in a much more effective fashion.

In this digital era, technology, to a maximum extent, quenches the thirst of techno-savvy students who are digital natives. Since these technologies play a significant role in day-to-day life, students must try to get the utmost benefit out of these technologies instead of using them solely for entertainment purposes. Educational institutions are embracing technologies to provide better learning so that learners become competent to reach great heights. Though there are pros and cons, students should bend technology and use it wisely for their betterment and hone their skills to thrive well in this competitive world. MOOCs and other platforms serve these purposes in higher education. Mobile learning is a great boon; even if the entire world is severely hit by the pandemic, nothing could stop a person from learning, which is made possible through mobile technology.

Changing Role of Teachers

Teachers are overwhelmed with responsibility after the advent of technology. Most students possess electronic gadgets, and learning does not happen only inside the classroom. It also happens outside the classroom, anywhere and at any time. The role of the teacher is transformed into that of a coach or a guide. Teachers are challenged to create a better learning experience using these resources.

The teachers need not be the only experts in the classroom. They can teach the students how to access information and evaluate whether it is reliable or not. And the students are no longer the consumers of information; rather, they create and learn in many ways because the information is easily accessible to everyone. The teachers must teach the students how to use these resources to reach their full potential.

Today, most jobs to some extent, including teaching, require technical skills. Most teachers are not born as digital natives. So, the teachers must equip themselves with adequate knowledge of the technology. They have to be digitally literate to teach effectively in a smart classroom environment. They have to get adequate training for the future fully surrounded by technology.

The teachers have to prepare themselves to be professionally competent so that they perform their roles effectively. They should be ever ready to meet the demands of the students and must be able to teach the students experimentally. There is a need for realistic and sensible teachers.

Students can acquire every kind of information and knowledge from the internet at any time, and transferring of knowledge and information is not only from teacher to student but also from student to student. The teachers play the role of an advisor, supervisor, and one who supports the learning of their students.

In the future, there will be a demand for teachers who can use ICT effectively so that they may help the students to learn better and make way for self-learning. As a first step, the teacher trainees must be provided with adequate training so that they are made ready to face the challenges of technology and make learning and teaching effective and simple.

The teachers must know how to use the utmost technology of any form so that it benefits the teacher as well as the students. Poor computer skills may lead teachers to lose their self-confidence and have a negative attitude towards technology. Teachers who are not confident in using the technology may be afraid that they might be embarrassed in front of the students.

The teacher training programs need to be mainstreamed with multimedia and added technology. This will help the teachers to address the requirements of the students, and it will be easier for teachers to handle techno-savvy students in the future. The teachers should not be technophobic. They must make their students feel enriched and engaged in their subjects using mobile devices.

Technology should not be a substitute for the instruction given by a skilled teacher nor should it replace the interaction between the student and the teacher. On the contrary, well-designed content on mobile devices can help students to carry out learning at their own pace in a way that is suitable for the students, and the teacher can devote more time in the classroom to help students individually.

Reasons to Use Mobile Apps for Teaching and Learning Processes

Remote Learning

Teaching away from the classroom will give a lot of experiences to the students for their development. It will help the students to improve their technical skills, which is very important for their skill development.

Utilisation of Free Time

It is highly useful for students to use their leisure time purposefully. To avoid unhealthy habits, this type of learning is highly needed for every student. It will also increase the student's creativity. It will develop their self-confidence and self-esteem.

Enjoyable and Informal Learning

Students never get bored when they are engaged with mobile phones. Sometimes the classroom lecture is ineffective. In that case, teaching through mobile phones has a prominent effect.

Changes in the Educational Standards

Mobile technology in education brought a lot of changes in the field of teaching–learning, and evaluation. In the olden days, teachers used palm leaves to provide written information to students. Later, it was replaced by the chalk-and-talk method. Now, it has been replaced by virtual teaching. Technology started to find its place in the classroom. Technology is playing a very important role in the curriculum transaction process.

Mobile Apps for Education

In the education context, mobile apps can be used in the following categorical ways in classroom curriculum transactions.

Mobile Apps for Managing the Classroom
Mobile Apps for Communication
Mobile Apps for Collaboration
Mobile Apps for Creativity
Mobile Apps for Teachers' Professional Growth
Mobile Apps for Assessment

Mobile Apps for Managing the Classroom

Class Dojo

It is a virtual classroom environment for all types of users. It allows teachers, students, and other stakeholders to interact with one another. Teachers can use this platform to send feedback to their students and send messages to parents about their children's grades. The best part of the platform is that it is free to everybody. It's a way to help keep everybody in communication with one another.

Edmodo

Edmodo is another virtual classroom app that is highly useful for the learning process, but this one goes the whole nine yards. Using this app, everyone will create a virtual classroom for the students.

Google Classroom

This app is frequently used in higher education. It has a lot of advantages for students as well teachers. With this app, the teacher can create an assignment for the students, and this app is highly useful for the teachers to evaluate students' performance.

Mobile Apps for Communication

Remind

This app is frequently used by educators to communicate with parents and learners outside of the classroom.

WhatsApp

WhatsApp has a lot of advantages like Facebook and Twitter. Educators can use the WhatsApp group or broadcasting features to communicate with their students. Nowadays, teachers can interact with their students through WhatsApp video calls and chatting via text. Educators can circulate learning materials and important instructions through this app. It is an easy medium to communicate with the group members and get their feedback immediately. It is highly useful for the teachers to monitor the students' activities and supervise students' progress. Today, the younger generation is using this app to establish a good relationship with their friends and their learning process. In universities and colleges, this app is highly useful for the circulation of important events and circulars to employees.

Mobile Apps for Collaboration

Collaboration in the classroom is helpful for the students to deepen their knowledge. The following are mobile apps for collaboration: Dropbox and Padlet.

Mobile Apps for Creativity

Evernote and Mindmeister are mobile apps for creativity.

Mobile Apps to Enhance Teachers' Professional Growth

EdX – Online Courses

EdX offers courses from world-leading universities and colleges. Students can learn from the experts at Harvard University, MIT, UC Berkeley, Microsoft, Linux, and more.

Coursera

Learn on the go with the free Coursera App for Android. This platform organises a lot of courses in different branches of study.

Udacity – Learn Programming

Like SWAYAM – MOOC Courses, Udacity is another learning platform that is highly useful for learners to improve their knowledge. Udacity courses are taught by industry experts from Facebook, and Google. These classes range from the very basics of programming to more advanced courses that help users make sense of data.

Mobile Apps for Formative Assessment Apps

Kahoot, Socrative, Zoho Forms, and Nearpod are mobile apps for formative assessment.

Subject-Specific Mobile Applications

English Subject

Duolingo,
Study flash,
Fluent,
Memrise,
Culips.

Mathematics Subject

MyScript Calculator,
Desmos,
Geometry Pad,
Grapher,
Photomath,
Math & Science,
Tutor,
All Math Formula,
Quick Brain Mathematics and Pocket Mathematics.

Science Subject

NASA,
Anatomy 4D,
Touch Surgery,
Sky View,
BrainPOP,
Science Bank,
3D Brain,
Extramarks,
Science Experiments,
VIDEOs,
Books of Science,
Math & Science Tutor.

Social Science Subject

SSC Social Science,
Today in History,
Indian History in English.

Physical Education Subject

Yoga Daily Fitness,
Yoga for Weight Loss,
Track & Field,
PET: Sports App,
PE Games,
Edu Sports.

Computer Science Subject

Computer Science Dictionary,
NPTEL: Computer Science,
Learn Computer Course.

Users of Mobile Learning

Educators

Generally, teachers are using mobile education to a greater extent. They have to update their knowledge of their subject. Teachers should also have knowledge of applications of mobile technology in the field of education.

Parents

Nowadays, most parents have smartphones. They have a thorough knowledge about the various apps that are available in the field of education.

Students

Students have smartphones for their learning. They are more advanced in using mobile phones when compared to their teachers and parents. They are more interested in learning any subject through mobile learning. Nowadays, through mobile learning, students are learning many courses through MOOC – SWAYAM Courses and other online courses.

Apparent Reasons for Mobile Learning

Students these days are said to be digital natives as they grow in the digital era. They are techno-savvy, which makes them more proficient in the use of mobile devices than adults. It is because they are raised in a world that is rich in media. They smartly handle these devices compared to adults, who did not enjoy the privilege of being familiar with technology at a very young age. This is an obvious reason for mobile learning.

Digitisation of information and learning materials has also paved the way for mobile learning. There is an umpteen number of digital repositories of dissertations, theses, and articles, thus making learning more meaningful. The adoption of gamification has made learning easy with other learning materials. Digital libraries increase the availability of resources to all. Students could access libraries across the world around the clock, which cannot be done in physical libraries. So, it is handy to have mobile devices for learning.

Information and knowledge explosion have also led to mobile learning. There is a huge amount of published data. Lots of open online education resources are available to those who possess these gadgets. A single click will provide the necessary information one needs. It is a wonderful opportunity to enrich knowledge, where everyone can learn everything with ease. Only if the students are digitally competent will they thrive in life.

Improvement of Education through Mobile Learning

The education system has improved a lot compared to the traditional way of educating students. Mobile learning paved a new path in the improvement of education. Mobile learning has made the education system a different method of learning and teaching. Most foreign countries were popular in e-learning, mobile learning, online learning, etc., but India has also proved its stability in the form of mobile learning in educating students. Mobile learning has showcased its full talents in educating students through the internet. Students are able to take the necessary information from mobile learning. They also can save it for future use, and they can refer to it whenever they are in need. Mobile learning has provided many social apps for the improvement of education.

It's not only that the students can learn from mobile learning apps, but they can also use some of the learning apps that were created for the improvement of education. Learning through mobile devices and using a few search engines will save time for the students instead of searching for information and going to libraries in search of books. Mobile learning creates awareness among students about learning and teaching. It builds a relationship between the teacher and the learner; they get connected, chatting while learning. So, the relationship becomes stronger, then communication becomes easier, and learning is also made easier in this manner. Therefore, every learning app provides a benefit to the students in their education.

Creating Online Mobile Courses

Nowadays, most universities and colleges are creating online mobile courses for their learners. It becomes mandatory for all higher education institutions to create online courses on their institutions because of the advancement of e-learning technology. In most of the online mobile courses learners are very much interested in joining online mobile courses and updating their knowledge. Teachers are learning technological tools for the implementation of online mobile courses. E-learning is having a significant role in the curriculum transaction process. All the stakeholders realised the need for e-governance in all the fields of education. Mobile technology is highly useful for all stakeholders to easily execute their work.

Conclusion

The evolution of educational technology and the development of mobile applications in the last few years, especially for higher education, have been nothing short of spectacular. The flexibility, cost benefits, and effectiveness of mobile learning further hold more potential for the future. Mobile learning in education comes up with a specialised approach that addresses several common educational issues seen in other traditional modes of learning. The evolving technological landscape and tools have set the stage for learning that can harness the speed and ubiquity of digital capability. Integration of mobile devices in the teaching–learning process has generated a new era in education. It makes the teaching–learning process more interactive and effective. It can help to bring quality education to everyone from everywhere. The implementation of mobile apps and technologies as a whole can offer many benefits to evolving technological areas, and tools have set the stage for learning that can harness the speed and ubiquity of digital capability. Learning through mobile devices and other digital means also allows students to have a more individualised and accelerated learning experience that gives them the power to unlock their true potential. In this digital era, technology, to a maximum extent, quenches the thirst of techno-savvy students who are digital natives. Since these technologies play a significant role in day-to-day life, students must try to get the utmost benefit out of these technologies instead of using them for entertainment purposes. Educational institutions are embracing technologies to provide better learning so that learners become competent to reach great heights. Though there are pros and cons, the students should adjust technology, use it wisely for their betterment, and hone their skills. Many online platforms serve these purposes in higher education. Nothing could stop a person from learning, and it is evident at this time, when the whole world is hit by a pandemic preventing people from coming out of their homes. Such a boon is what mobile devices render to their beneficiaries.

References

Anderson, L.W., D.R. Krathwohl, et al. 2001. *A taxonomy for learning, teaching and assessing: A revision of Bloom's taxonomy of educational objectives*. New York: Longman.

Bransford, John D., Ann L. Brown, and Rodney R. Cocking, eds. 2000. *How people learn: Brain, mind, experience and school*. 1st ed. Washington, DC: National Academies Press.

Dean, B., M. Zanko, and J. Turbill. 2015. Mobilizing PD: Professional Development for Sessional Teachers Through Mobile Technologies. *Handbook of Mobile Teaching and Learning*, ed. Y. Hang, 165–182. Heidelberg: Springer.

Prensky, M. 2001. Digital natives, digital immigrants. *On the Horizon (MCB University Press)*, 9(5): 1–6.

Ramnath, R. and A. Kuriakose 2019. Mobile Technologies for Teaching and Learning. *Handbook of Mobile Teaching and Learning*, 2nd edn., Singapore: Springer Nature.

Zhang, F. J. 2019. A Novel Education Pattern Applied to Global Crowd of All Ages: Mobile Education. *Handbook of Mobile Teaching and Learning*, 2nd edn., Singapore: Springer Nature.

Zhang, Y. A. and J. Hu 2019. Development of Mobile Application for Higher Education: An Introduction. *Handbook of Mobile Teaching and Learning*, 2nd edn., Singapore: Springer Nature.

Zhang Yu (Aimee), Dean Cristol. 2019. *Handbook of Mobile Teaching and Learning*, 2nd edn., Singapore: Springer Nature, 1416 pp. https://onlinecourses.swayam2.ac.in/arp19_ap62/unit?unit=65&lesson=67

Index

Pages in *italics* refer to figures and pages in **bold** refer to tables.

Milton Keynes UK
Ingram Content Group UK Ltd.
UKHW020035240424
441592UK00002B/5

9 781032 467191